THE BOOK OF BULBS

THE MACMILLAN COMPANY
NEW YORK · BOSTON · CHICAGO · DALLAS
ATLANTA · SAN FRANCISCO

MACMILLAN AND CO., Limited
LONDON · BOMBAY · CALCUTTA · MADRAS
MELBOURNE

THE MACMILLAN COMPANY
OF CANADA, Limited
TORONTO

THE
BOOK OF BULBS

A GUIDE TO THE SELECTION, PLANTING, AND
CULTIVATING OF BULBS FOR SPRING, SUMMER,
AND AUTUMN FLOWERING—AND TO WINTER-
LONG BEAUTY FROM BULBS INDOORS

BY

F. F. ROCKWELL

AUTHOR OF "AROUND THE YEAR IN THE GARDEN,"
"GARDENING UNDER GLASS," "THE HOME GARDEN HANDBOOKS," ETC.

*Illustrated with Photographs by the Author and by
A. T. DeLaMare Company; and with Drawings
by the Author and George Hollrock.*

New York
THE MACMILLAN COMPANY
1946

Set up and electrotyped. Published May, 1927.
Reprinted with corrections, March, October, 1928;
November, 1929.
Reissued, July, 1931. Reprinted April, 1932;
March, 1935; November, 1937; January, 1942 ;
August, 1944; October, 1945 ; November, 1946.

PRINTED IN THE UNITED STATES OF AMERICA
BY BERWICK & SMITH CO.

ACKNOWLEDGMENT

IN the gathering of the material for this book, I have been assisted greatly by the generous coöperation of many individuals and firms. Among these are Henry A. Dreer, Inc.; W. Atlee Burpee & Co.; Henry F. Michell Co., all of Philadelphia; John Scheepers, Inc., Stumpp & Walter Co., Peter Henderson & Co., and Wm. E. Marshall & Co., of New York; Chester J. Hunt, Little Falls, N. J.; Bobbink & Atkins, Rutherford, N. J.; The Wayside Gardens, Mentor, Ohio; and Vaughan's Seed Store, Chicago. Mr. A. E. Kunderd, Goshen, Ind., of gladiolus fame, and Mr. L. K. Peacock, of Dahlia-land, N. J., are old friends who have always been ready to help. I am indebted, also, to Mr. Chas. F. Seabrook, who developed the bulb industry at the famous Seabrook Farms, Bridgeton, N. J., and Mr. David Griffiths, in charge of bulb work for the U. S. Department of Agriculture, who has done so much to forward commercial bulb culture in this country.

From Mr. George Hollrock, himself a keen gardener as well as an artist, I have had painstaking and patient work in the preparation of the many drawings which illustrate the pages of this book. His part of the task was no easy one, and has been well executed. And, finally, most of all I owe to the ever-ready and never-tiring assistance of the little lady who for many years of my life has made vital the meaning of that good old English word, "helpmeet."

FOREWORD

The purpose of this book is threefold.

First: to go with the reader out into the garden and to endeavor to show, by pictures and by text, what enchanting effects may be obtained with bulbs as subjects for general use, and not as they are too often considered—as a race apart from other garden plants.

Second: to help introduce to the beginner some of the bulbs whose friendship he or she has not yet been fortunate enough to claim, and thus stimulate a greater interest in this wonderful class of plants as a whole.

Third: to give brief but definite and comprehensive suggestions as to cultural requirements, so that the reader should be able to achieve success with whatever bulbs he grows.

The writing of this book I have had in mind for several years. Through the past decade, the interest in bulb gardening in this country has developed astonishingly: and yet we have had no American book on bulbs for a generation—long before there was any commercial bulb production, or any real bulb gardening in this country. All that was written, even long ago, was modeled largely on the existing European works, being mostly in the nature of comprehensive compendiums on bulbs from the botanist's point of view. Splendid as these older works were in their way, none of them meets at all adequately the need of the present-day amateur bulb gardener; in fact, the "bulb garden," in the modern sense of the term, was a thing unknown in the days when these books were published.

A bed—round, square, or of complicated geometrical

design—with stripes or segments in horribly contrasting colors, done in hyacinths or early tulips, constituted the "bulb garden" of that era.

The more modern bulb books of the "other side" are, of course, written for English or continental conditions which are quite different from ours; and they still stick rather closely to the alphabetical-botanical arrangement, which the American gardener has never seemed to cherish.

All my life I have been a bulb enthusiast. If there is anything gleaned from many years of experience in both amateur and commercial growing that I can pass on to the new proselyte, I count it a reward in itself to be able to do so. At any rate, I have derived a good deal of pleasure from making the attempt.

With one request to the reader, I close this foreword. That request is that he—or she, for I know that the fair sex is by far the worse offender in this respect—does not begin reading this book at the end, or even in the middle, but start in at the beginning and follow through. Remember, impatient sisters, that the most entrancing flower from any bulb has its beginning in *the soil!*

CONTENTS

xi

ILLUSTRATIONS

IN A SPRING GARDEN

APRIL DAWN

After incessant rain,
Sun—and a robin's note!
Who dreamed this lyric strain
Lurked in his rusty throat?
Silvered with pearls of dew
Hung from a branch of yew,
The spider's silken chain
Curves to the hawthorn hedge.
On bending daffodil,
Clutching its fluted edge,
A velvet-vested bee
Plunders his honeyed fill;
Then buzzing drunkenly
The pilfered pollen-gold
Wastes in a hyacinth bell.
Rising from hill and wold
Slowly the mists dispel . . . . .
    This air is like old wine to drink:
    Let one quaff deep of it, I think
    He could go forth and gather up
    The carping world in a crocus cup!

MAY DUSK

Athwart the level length of lawn there lies
A cypress' spire-slim shadow.   Elfin light,
Like golden dust from jewel-eyed butterflies
Beating their wings in ineffectual flight
Against the purple windows of the night,
Sifts down through those last javelin rays the sun
Hurls backward in departing—shafts so spent
They do but glance the bronze and copper cups
Of towering tulips, without marring one!
The shadows merge, and silence closes up
Even the humming portals of the cherry's tent.
    Here, as the light fades and the twilight falls,
    From the dark cedar-grove Pan's faint flute calls
    To gardens long since passed, in lore and rhyme,
    Into the hands of the gray gardener, Time,
    Who keeps them fresh forever . . . . .
                Through endless spring
    I tread these far dim gardens, walking in this,
    Grape-scented dusks where Omar's songs still ring,
    And hanging spice-groves of Semiramis.

                                 F. F. R

THE BOOK OF BULBS

THE BOOK OF BULBS

CHAPTER I

BULBS FOR GREATER BEAUTY IN EVERY GARDEN

No other class of flowering plants has grown so rapidly in popular favor, during recent years, as bulbs.

The quantity used annually has increased by leaps and bounds. Home production and importations from abroad have both grown at a tremendous rate, and yet they have hardly sufficed to satisfy the ever-increasing army of bulb users.

American gardeners have thus far been content, for the most part, with the more ordinary kinds and varieties; but already there has begun to develop an advance guard of real bulb enthusiasts, and the day is not far distant when this wonderful race of flowers will really begin to come into its own in American gardens.

What has been the cause of the remarkable growing popularity of bulbs?

Nothing but the intrinsic advantage of bulbs as a class compared to any other flower. There is no other group of plants from which so much beauty is to be got so surely, for so little expense and effort. That is the brief but very sufficient answer. And as this advantage will continue to exist, the popularity of bulbs is bound to continue to grow.

In the popular favor which bulbs have so far won in this country, there are two which have rather outstripped all others—the gladiolus and the dahlia. In England and Europe, however, these two occupy only a modest, not to say secondary, place in the bulb grower's esteem.

What is the reason? It would be interesting, even though it may not be highly important, to know. Both of these flowers are, perhaps, in their vigorous growth, brilliant and somewhat crude colors, and bountiful production, typically American. They are suited to a somewhat rough-and-ready type of gardening; you might term them good "go-getter" flowers for the Main Street gardens of new and energetic towns, whose owners have but recently won the leisure to turn any attention to the development of the outdoor part of their homes.

The statement above, I realize, will give ground to some American critics, who are enthusiastic supporters of the gladiolus and the dahlia, to make the assertion that I am prejudiced in favor of foreign bulbs, and do not have the proper appreciation for the kind that have proved most popular in America. Therefore I make my answer to any such criticism now, in advance, with both a denial and a challenge. The denial is that I do fully appreciate both the gladiolus and the dahlia—as I think will be evident to any one reading the pages of this book devoted to these two splendid flowers. Nevertheless, I challenge any admirer of those flowers to stand before a dahlia "garden" with its stiff-stemmed, pruned, and bandaged-up plants and obtrusive stakes—or before the straight, rigid ranks of the "sword lily," and then say that they make as beautiful a *garden* as the winding border of tulips or narcissus, swaying or waving in the spring breeze, fitting perfectly into the landscape picture, and offering just as great a wealth of form and color for the living room indoors.

No, the gladiolus and the dahlia, *as developed so far* in this country, are primarily valuable for flowers for cutting. Their possibilities as garden material we have barely begun to realize.

As *garden* material, the "Dutch" and other spring-flowering bulbs are far superior to our two favorite bulbs; there is no getting away from it. And to deny it, on the ground that an un-American attitude is being displayed, is merely to shut the gates of common sense against the only things which no quarantines or embargoes can ever bar out—the exchange of ideas and the growth of æsthetic appreciations. It is surely commendable to appreciate that which we have; but where we can find better or different things overseas, we should be most shortsighted not to acquire them, especially when such acquisition does not rob the original possessor. The exchange of ideas, you know, is the only kind of barter in the world at which both parties may double their original capital.

THE ADVANTAGES OF BULBS

It was not my intention, however, to start any odious comparisons as between one class of bulbs and another. I hold no brief for any particular kind. My favorites, of course, I have—as who has not? But that is beside the point.

One of the things I have tried to do in this book, as already implied, is to lead the reader to realize more fully the advantages of bulbs, all bulbs, as compared to any other class of plants. We want the other things too, of course. But for the most part they have their advocates, and very able ones. So I have no fear of overstating the case for that class of plants which, without any question, is least known and appreciated in proportion to its real merits.

We have, so far as I know, no "judge's scale of points" by which to take the measure of the various classes of garden plants, as we have for rating the individual varieties within a class, such as "glads," peonies, or roses. But if such a scale did exist, based on the requirements of the amateur gardener, these four characteristics would undoubtedly score many "points" each:

1. Surety of success.
2. Quickness in results.
3. Length of season of bloom.
4. Economy—in money cost and in time required for care.

Let us see how bulbs, judged by such a scale, would compare with most other flowers.

On the first score, bulbs win. With no other flower can you be so certain of success, because the bulb grower has delivered to you a finished product, ready to bloom.

If you will cut open a tulip or a narcissus bulb from top to bottom, you will find within it a perfect miniature flower, complete in every detail—stem, petals, even stamens and pistil. In almost any soil, even in cinders or moss, and under almost any conditions, so long as moisture and warmth are present, the bulb, with the assistance of the food stored up within itself, will develop this flower. Even with bulbs of the "corm" type, such as the gladiolus, in which there is no embryo flower, satisfactory blooms are almost certain to be developed, as the corm itself supplies much of the nourishment for that purpose. Bulbs of the "tuber" type, such as the dahlia, are less certain, because the flowers are produced not from the bulb itself, but upon a new plant, just as with most other flowers. Taken all in all, however, there is no other large class of flowers with which the amateur gardener can so confidently look forward to success as he may with bulbs.

Consider, next, the second point in our scale—quickness in getting results.

With all the fall-planted bulbs, you do your planting in September or October, or possibly, even in November. In December, you put a light mulch over them, although this is not absolutely essential. Then they may be forgotten— no hoeing, no weeding, no spraying, no pruning; give them not a thought in the world. And then, some morning next March or early April—before you are aware even that spring has come back to the sunniest nooks and slopes; before the swallows have dared to return—there on your lawn, or in your hardy border, gay crocuses, cheeriest of all flowers, and golden daffodils will "take the winds of March with beauty" and hail you to say that winter is routed, and that even now Proserpina, goddess of spring flowers,

Tulips and daffodils in a corner of the author's garden—and the assistant gardener whose ever-ready coöperation has made possible the writing of this book.

Bulbs are equally fitting for the small and the large place. (*Left*) Poet's Narcissus and ferns against the house foundation. (*Right*) Tulips for gayety and color in the early flower border.

comes tiptoeing over the next hill to fill your garden anew with gladness.

Bulbs you plant in the spring—gladiolus, cannas, dahlias, and others—will not be quite so quick in the return they give, but what other flowers of anywhere near equal character and substance will do better? And if you consider bulbs for forcing indoors—and every lover of flowers will—then surely there is no other class of plants that can be placed ahead of bulbs in *quickness of results*.

And now, as to the third consideration, length of the season of bloom.

To me this has always seemed a most important factor in the pleasure which any flower can give us. Many fine things have the serious drawback that they are "here to-day and gone to-morrow." It is by no means necessary to go to such an extreme example as the "Night-blooming Cactus" to illustrate this. You know that many of your garden favorites, not excepting that queen of all flowers, the rose, pass so quickly that they are gone just as you are beginning fully to enjoy them. Possibly we think all the more of them for their brief stay, leaving us, like Oliver Twist, hungry for more; but I doubt it. I know that there are flowers, such as the tuberous begonias, and "glads" planted in succession—which yield their beauty not only week by week, but month upon month—and I am always as filled with regret to see the last precious blooms of these constant friends finally succumb to Jack Frost, as I am glad to see the first buds which open.

You can have bulbs in bloom throughout the entire year. Starting with the snowdrops, scillas, grape-hyacinths, in early spring, they follow through a constant succession: daffodils, tulips, bulbous irises, hardy lilies, tuberous begonias, cannas, dahlias—until killing frost in September or October. And in November, with very little trouble, and in any ordinary sunny living room, you can have the first of your winter-bulb blooms, with a succession of them until the following Easter! With what other class or family of

plants can you duplicate that record of a constant, uninter-
rupted succession of bloom around the entire circle of the
year?

And so we come to the fourth item in our scale of points
—economy, in cost and in time.

The comparison of first or original costs is a rather difficult matter, because prices may vary from year to year.
But we can get some sort of an idea of it from the following: a good rose of standard variety costs from $1.00 to
$1.50; a shrub, 60 cents to $1.00; a hardy perennial, 35 cents
to $1.00; a dozen bulbs of tulips, narcissus, or gladiolus,
50 cents to $1.50; a standard dahlia, 50 cents to $1.00;
tuberous begonias, $2.00 to $3.00 a dozen.

Certainly the rose or the shrub will require more time for
planting and care than will most bulbs. Even the dahlia,
which demands more attention than almost any other bulb
in the way of tying up and pinching out, if you want big
flowers, is comparatively free from insect and disease
troubles, compared to many of the popular garden flowers.
Moreover, your rosebush or shrub, and many perennials,
will remain one plant, while most of your bulbs will go on
increasing, year after year, until you have a surplus to
replant for yourself or to "trade" for other varieties. I am
not talking against the rose or any other flower. I want
just as many flowers as I can get, and have room for. But,
personally, I always feel that a dollar invested in bulbs
is going to bring me greater returns than it would in any
other kind of flower—in so far, of course, as one can
measure so intangible a thing as beauty with a tape measure
made of greenbacks.

Such, then, is the case for bulbs, as a class or family
compared to other garden material—as it looks to me. And
on the basis of that comparison, I believe that bulbs are
less appreciated in America than any other class of plants.
Possibly I should write "have been" instead of "are" in
that last sentence, but I fear the time is not yet quite ripe

for that change in tense! If this book can help effect that change, I shall feel richly rewarded for the effort put into its making.

Bulbs fit the smallest as well as the largest garden.

I am not yet quite through with my argument for bulbs. I have endeavored to make a fair comparison between them and other garden flowers on various definite points. But there is another important thing to be said in favor of bulbs, and that is this: *they bring joy in equal measure to the smallest nook of a garden, tucked in somewhere against a house wall, and to the most elaborately planned beds of the big country estate.*

Very few other plants can be used through such a wide range of circumstances, and still so absolutely "fit into the picture" under all conditions. Some of the illustrations in this book give a very definite idea of what is meant.

The fact that bulbs, or most of them, will grow in such a wide variety of soils also helps to make them exceptionally suitable subjects for the very little garden, where there is no choice as to soil conditions. I have grown a great variety of bulbs successfully in both sandy and, what is still worse, even gravelly soil; and in very heavy loam, almost clay.

Moreover, the range in price for different varieties is such that every purse can be suited. In tulips, for instance, you can get such beautiful varieties as Clara Butt or Rev. H. Ewbank for around sixty cents a dozen; or you can buy some of the new introductions at from several dollars a dozen to a hundred dollars a bulb. The same holds true with narcissus and "glads." Then, in dahlias, you can run the range from a quarter to fifty dollars a tuber.

And so, for all these reasons, if you are a lover of flowers but have never become a bulb enthusiast, I recommend to you this great family, which will bring into your garden endless variety of form, a range of colors which rivals the rainbow, certainty of success, if you possess the gardener's "touch" to any degree at all, and some new joy for every month around the calendar.

Having thus taken a glance at some of the treasures which bulbs have to offer, let us look now at the several uses to which they lend themselves.

CHAPTER II

BULB GARDENS, LARGE AND SMALL: NATURALIZING BULBS

THE gardener, of course, is interested in the garden pictures which he can create with bulbs fully as much as in the individual bulbs themselves. It is with the use of bulbs, as one of the most important of all mediums for the making of beautiful gardens, that this chapter deals.

First of all, it cannot be too strongly emphasized that every one and any one can grow bulbs. A word already has been said concerning the certainty of the results which may be expected in the growing of bulbs of practically all types. I would like to make plain in terms just as strong the fact that bulbs may be used to advantage on any place, no matter what its location, its soil, or its size.

Bulbs for Small Spaces. Because of the little space which they occupy in proportion to their display of flowers, bulbs are quite ideal for the planting of very limited areas. The illustration facing page 5 gives an excellent idea of the way in which they fit such conditions.

One of the great advantages of bulbs for planting in limited quarters lies in the fact that one can figure quite precisely how much space they will occupy; how high they will grow, and when and how long they will be in bloom. In small-plot gardening, where every square foot counts and must be made to do its part, it is extremely helpful to be able to calculate things to a nicety, rather than to guess approximately, as has to be done with most plants other than bulbs.

In small-space gardening, if artistic results are desired, it is highly important that the matter of scale or proportions be kept in mind. Under such conditions it is often much better to restrict one's planting to the smaller growing things rather than to attempt to plant the tall growing and more imposing ones. A giant flowered Darwin tulip, three feet high, for instance, that would be perfectly stunning in a suitable environment, may be much less attractive, in a very limited space, than a small-growing tulip, or even one of the "minor" bulbs, such as grape-hyacinth, scillas, or snowdrops. No matter how beautiful a flower may be in itself, if it is out of proportion to the garden picture as a whole, it may be undesirable because out of place. Hyacinths, and the smaller varieties of narcissus, are quite ideal for the very small bulb garden.

Another thing to be scrupulously guarded against, in planning the miniature garden, is the selection of too many varieties. There will always be the strong temptation to get at least a sample of each of the many fine things one would like to have, and thus to purchase a considerable variety. It is much better, however, to curb this natural desire and to restrict the list to a few things, so that the little garden, even though it be small, will still have character and be a thing of beauty.

Bulbs for Foundation Plantings. Another way in which bulbs may be used most effectively within quite a limited area is to plant them either in a continuous bed, or in a number of small groups, around the base of the house next to the foundation. This also means planting in a very limited space, but the conditions are decidedly different from those referred to in the preceding paragraph, because the wall of the house itself gives both a background and a protection which does not exist in the small open garden. This makes it not only possible but also desirable to use a number of the taller-growing things, such as the largest of the lilies, gladiolus, the summer-hyacinth, tuberoses, and many others, which give very striking and very charming effects. In front of these may be planted a number of the lower-growing bulbs, such as narcissi, early tulips, hyacinths, crocuses, and so forth, for spring flowering; and tuberous begonias, fancy-leaved caladium, and other medium-sized summer bulbs for later on.

In planting next to the house, unless the soil has already been well prepared for other plants, it is best to dig out a strip from a foot to three feet wide, according to the space available, removing the soil entirely if it is gravel or sub-soil left by the builder, and filling in with garden loam to which a generous quantity of sand and well-rotted manure have been added. It is not a great deal of work to do this, and it will help make sure of your success for years to come with whatever you may plant.

The arrangement of the bulbs which are to go around the base of the house is a matter which will go far toward making or marring the results obtained, regardless of what bulbs are planted. If bulbs alone are to be used for the foundation planting, and if a rather formal effect will best suit the arrangement of the walks and other architectural details, then the bulbs should be planted in straight lines in a solid bed, in the formal manner. If, however, ever-greens, shrubs, or hardy perennials have already been planted around the house, and the bulbs are to be associated with these, then have the courage to break away from the ordinary method and plant your bulbs in small groups or clumps, from half a dozen to a dozen each, and spaced with sufficient irregularity to give a naturalistic effect. The results will be, when the bulbs begin to come into flower, not only out of the ordinary run but decidedly charming. You will never regret having made this experiment.

Bulbs for the Hardy Border. Not so very long ago, when it was generally considered that most bulbs, with the possible exception of the hardy lilies, should be planted by themselves, usually they were placed in strictly formal beds or borders, rather than in connection with other flowers.

Fortunately the fashion in this respect has changed, for certainly there is no more pleasing and effective way of using the spring bulbs, such as tulips, daffodils, and hya-

cinths, and most of the summer-flowering bulbs, including
the lilies, tuberoses, tuberous begonias, and the summer- or
cape-hyacinths (*hyacinthus candicans*), than by planting
them in the mixed hardy border. Even gladiolus and
cannas may be used in this way, although generally they
are not.

The advantages of thus planting bulbs in association
with other flowers are several. In the first place, a much
wider range of types and varieties may be used than would
be desirable when planting in the ordinary bulb bed. Then,
also, the perennial borders are made glorious in early spring
when otherwise there would be little showing during the
bleak weeks of March and April. And furthermore this
method of culture well suits the bulbs themselves, because,
when they are through flowering, they may be left to ripen
their foliage naturally, as it will be largely hidden by the
growth of the neighboring perennials as it matures and
turns yellow. Thus the bulbs may be allowed to remain
undisturbed for several seasons, becoming, if conditions are
suitable, more beautiful every year.

In planting bulbs in the mixed hardy border, the same
principles of arrangement may be followed as apply to the
hardy perennials themselves; that is, some regard should
be had for the association of colors, both among the bulbs
and in connection with any of the perennials which may
be in bloom at the same time. The tall-growing sorts,
such as the hardy lilies, the tall-growing tulips, such as the
Darwins and Breeders, and gladiolus and cannas, if they
are used, should be kept to the back. In the middle ground
may go the tulips of medium height; the taller narcissi and
hyacinths; the bulbous irises; the tallest bluebell or scilla
(*scilla hispanica or campanulata*); and others of medium
growth. And at the front the lowest-growing things, such
as the "dwarf" narcissi and tulips, and the general assortment of minor bulbs—bluebells, snowdrops, snowflakes,
grape-hyacinths, and so on.

Once you have tried planting your bulbs in this way, you

will never go back to the old style of formal solid beds, or the hideous "design" beds. Another very practical advantage of planting in groups in the mixed border, is that you can buy a dozen or two of a kind at a time—or even two or three bulbs, of new and expensive varieties—and thus gradually build up your collection, whereas much larger quantities are required for solid beds.

Such special conditions as to soil and care as some of the individual bulbs may require, may easily be given in the hardy border by selecting locations in full sun or in partial shade; and in the soil by providing extra sand, leaf-mold, or whatever else may be necessary for the idiosyncrasies of some particular bulb.

To continue at their best, many bulbs will require taking up and replanting, as they become crowded, every two to five years. Some of the more tender ones, of course, will have to be taken up each fall for replanting again in the spring. These matters may readily be attended to in the hardy border; and the different sorts can be shifted to new locations and fresh soil, which is always desirable. Incidentally, also, this gives the gardener a chance to change and improve the picture from season to season.

For all the reasons given above, it is evident that the hardy border constitutes the ideal place for the growing of the great majority of the spring- and summer-flowering bulbs.

Bulbs with Evergreens, and Shrubs. Another special use for bulbs is found by utilizing as a background the foliage of evergreen plantings, which will set off to most striking advantage the beauty of the bulbs. By selecting suitable colors, particularly light shades, and whites and yellows which will stand out effectively against the dark-green foliage, strikingly beautiful effects may easily be obtained. Needless to say, the taller-growing bulbs are particularly well adapted for this purpose, the Darwin tulips and other strong-growing tulips in spring, and the Madonna and other hardy lilies for later on, being ideal. Gladiolus, cannas, and even the obstreperous dahlia, the most difficult of all popular bulbs to utilize in the general garden picture, may, in this way, be made use of.

This particular method of planting bulbs can, of course, be easily overdone, and the effect, if the scheme is not handled with restraint, is entirely lost. Plantings of this character should be points of accent in the landscape scheme, but applied in moderation; otherwise, the place may attain the appearance of a cheap advertisement, so full of exclamation points that they cease to mean anything, and indicate only a lack of good taste on the part of the gardener.

In planting against evergreens, it is best to use only one variety in a place, and not to associate any other flowers with the bulbs. As these plantings are usually made some distance from the house, the ripening foliage of the bulbs after the flowers have passed will not be conspicuous.

Shrubs may be utilized as a background for bulbs in much the same way as suggested for evergreens. If the foliage alone is to be counted on for the contrast desired, then the same plan may be followed, only keeping in mind that the background will not be so dark, and will not show up so effectively the white and very light colors, although better for dark reds and blues.

If, however, we take the opportunity of planting bulbs which will be in bloom at the same time as the shrubs, then some of the most charming color effects imaginable are possible. Blue grape-hyacinths, for instance, beneath the golden-laden branches of a forsythia, yellow daffodils against the white of a shadbush, or white and yellow ones near a pink-flowering cherry, make garden pictures never to be forgotten. And yet their making is within the reach of almost any one!

Bulbs for the Rock Garden. For a number of years, rock gardening has been rapidly growing in popularity in this country. The rock garden, as the reader is probably aware, may be greatly varied, in form, from extensive natural

Daffodils in natural-looking groups are much more beautiful than stiff rows in a "bed." (*Right*) A bulb and iris garden in the "naturalistic" style—not many plants, but what a pleasing effect has been created!

Tulips, daffodils, and hyacinths in small rockery.

ledges or groups of rock, to the small artificial mound of stones, with "pockets" of soil in between.

Bulbs as material for the rock garden have come to be appreciated but slowly. And yet there are many of the smaller-growing sorts which are unsurpassed for this purpose. On the other side of the water, they have long been recognized as supplying some of the most fascinating subjects for rock-garden work, and there is no reason why they should not be more generally used for this purpose here.

The rockery supplies conditions which are in many ways well suited to the growth of bulbs. The soil is thoroughly well drained; there is shelter and shade for the roots and foliage of small-growing bulbs, and the foliage may remain undisturbed after the plants have flowered. The many mossy and creeping plants ordinarily used in the rock garden, as well as the formation of the garden itself, help keep the little bulb blooms from getting rain-beaten and spattered with mud; and being somewhat elevated, they may be seen to the best advantage. Where any special requirements in the way of soil may exist, they can readily be provided for in the "pockets" of the rock garden.

Practically all of the dwarf-growing bulbs may be used for rock-garden planting, and many of them will be particularly well "set off" by the rock-garden background. Among those adapted to rock-garden planting are the various scillas or bluebells, the snowdrops, grape-hyacinths (*muscari*), chionodoxas, the checkered-lily (*fritillaria meleagris*). (Others are described in Chapter IX.)

It is not among these "minor" bulbs alone, however, that good material for the rock garden is to be found. Many of the tulips, narcissi, and crocuses are happily used for this purpose, especially the natural species or wild sorts. Among the tulips, for instance, is that little gem, *T. clusiana*, the "Lady Tulip"; and also the Persian tulip (*T. persica*) or *breyniana*, and *sylvestris* (*florentina odorata*)— the British wild tulip. Another very attractive dwarf form, an old species but only recently introduced in America, is *linifolia*. Other species are described in Chapter VI. Most of the species do not require annual or biennial "lifting," and may be left undisturbed for years. Narcissus species well suited to rock-garden planting include the "musk" daffodil (*N. moschatus*); the "cyclamen-flowered" type (*triandrus* and its hybrids) and *cyclamineus;* also *N. minimus, N. bulbocodium,* and *N. minor*. The small but early-flowering trumpet daffodil, Cervantes, and the little white W. P. Milner, are also excellent.

With crocuses, as with tulips and narcissi, the species are better adapted to rock gardening than the cultivated sorts. The Scotch crocus (*biflorus*), sieberi, susianus, tommasinianus, and imperati, are some of the sorts which may well be used. The dwarf irises, such as christata, tectorum, pumila, and chamaeiris, and similar sorts mentioned in Chapter XII, are quite ideal for rock-garden planting.

For summer and fall, there are such bulbs of moderate growth as the trailing tuberous begonias, zephyranthes, tigridias, oxalis, and the autumn-flowering crocuses; while all of these except the last will have to be taken up on the approach of frost, they may be easily stored over winter, and are well worth the slight trouble required.

Bulbs in Beds. Under some conditions, bulbs may be most effectively handled in solid beds.

It does not follow, however, that the geometrical or design bed need be employed. Never, I believe, is the use of such a bed justified, unless, perhaps, in a strictly formal planting around a hotel, or some other public or semi-public building; and even here, I do not doubt that a different treatment would be preferable from the public's point of view, if any one in charge of such matters had the courage to make a change, and get out of the usual rut.

In parks and on large estates, where there is plenty of space available, a series of solid beds of bulbs may be really artistic as well as strikingly impressive.

The tall-growing Cottage, Darwin, and Breeder tulips are

especially fine for this type of planting, particularly if some lower-growing plant of somewhat light and airy form is used between them. For this purpose, such early flowering, low-growing things as the perennial forget-me-not, dwarf phlox, rockcress (*arabis*), violas, or "tufted pansies" and wallflowers may be used. (For others see list of plants on page 48.)

If it is desired to leave the bulbs where they grow, instead of taking them out when through blooming as is usually done (see Chapter VI) the beds may be made beautiful with annuals, sown or planted between the bulbs. Shirley poppies, Eschscholtzia or California poppies, candytuft, annual pinks, calliopsis, phlox drummondi, snapdragons, and verbenas are among the flowers well adapted for this purpose.

Hyacinths are, from their natural habit of growth, quite the most desirable of all bulbs for "formal" bedding purposes. In Chapter VIII the various types are described. The early tulips, both single and double, are also excellent for low, formal beds, where uniformity of color, height, and time of bloom are the essential qualities required. A number of other bulbs may be used for bedding purposes; but these are the most satisfactory.

Most of the summer- and autumn-flowering bulbs are not much used, and are not very well adapted to planting in solid beds. Tuberous begonias are an exception; they are quite unsurpassed for the planting of a solid bed, or a long, solid border, in a shaded or semi-shaded location, especially at close range. They are equally to be recommended, however, for other methods of planting. Cannas, often planted in solid beds, are best employed to create a mass color effect at some distance; viewed too closely, they are somewhat disappointing. They are excellent for combination with other flowers, particularly the ornamental grasses which somewhat offset their stiffness in beds of mixed planting.

The Real Bulb Garden. For the gardener who becomes

a real bulb enthusiast, the garden of bulbs alone, in their many genera, species, and varieties, offers an endless opportunity for new thrills. They may be had in constant succession, blooming out of doors from February or March to November or December.

The garden of bulbs may be either the formal or the naturalistic type. The latter, of course, gives opportunity for using a much wider range of material in smaller quantities. In such a garden, a wide variety of conditions may easily be provided—sheltered, sunshine-filled corners, for the earliest little blooms of springs; shady nooks for the shade lovers; moderately heavy or light soil; a bit of rockery, even if it has to be of the very simplest form, for the species best adapted to rockery planting; and spots of peat and cinder-filled soil for the acid-loving, hardy lilies. Ferns and other plants which make the most charming "companions" for the bulbs, showing them off to the best advantage, will, of course, be included, but the garden may be primarily devoted to bulbs.

Do not think, because the allurement which such a garden holds out is great, that either the amount of space or the amount of money needed to make a start is considerable. You can have at least a little garden, to start with, for a very modest sum, and increase your planting from year to year. The majority of the hardy bulbs required will go on multiplying from year to year, so that the natural increase itself will enable you to expand your garden. It will grow at compound interest!—in both senses of the word. Such a garden is illustrated on page 10.

THE NATURALIZING OF BULBS

In grounds of considerable extent, one of the most charming methods of using many of the hardy bulbs is to "naturalize" them; that is, to so plant them that they will look as though they had grown naturally, and then leave them to "run wild."

Wherever a bit of woods, a stream, a meadow, or natural

slope is available, naturalizing may be done. Even on a place of quite limited dimensions, there may exist the opportunity to plant bulbs in this charming way. A few old apple or pear trees, a single tree, even, may afford the spot where a small quantity of bulbs, flung in a loosely spread group or groups, will give the *natural* effect which is all that is essential. Irregularly planted clumps, here and there along the edges of the shrubbery border, will answer the purpose and create a very pleasing picture, if no better position is available. The only real essentials are, first, planting conditions which will make it possible for the bulbs to continue to thrive, year after year, even when left to themselves; and, second, background or surroundings in which the flowers would look natural *if growing wild*.

As to the first of these essentials—growing conditions—*thorough drainage* is the primary thing to make sure of. The spot selected may be low—even marshy, in fact, for some things—but there must not be standing water around the bulbs during winter. The character of the soil itself is of less importance, but a heavy clay is least desirable. Either extreme, of clay or light sandy soil, may, however, be modified by the methods suggested in Chapter IV.

The principal object of "naturalizing" being to get a natural-looking effect, two things must be resolutely avoided. The first is the employment of too many varieties; the second, regularity in planting. As a rule—to which it is best not to attempt to make an exception—but one thing should be planted in a place. A very early and a very late sort may, however, be planted together, the one flowering after the other is through, thus extending the period of beauty. If two different sorts are to come together, there should be no sharp line of demarcation between them, but an overlapping and mingling along the mutual boundary line, as there would be in nature.

As in nature, too, the planting, no matter how many bulbs are being used, should be varied and shaded—here, dense; there, thinning out; and yet again trailing off into a thin fringe. Such a planting will produce a "drift" of blooms, and the name suggests the effort to be sought. The details of the methods of planting to secure these results are described in a later chapter, on making the bulb garden. (Chapter IV.)

As to the bulbs which are suitable for naturalizing, there are many. The narcissi, however, are by all means the most effective and the best adapted to this purpose. And the more natural-looking varieties, which have solid colors, such as Golden Spur or Emperor, deep yellow; Sir Watkin and Barri Conspicuus, softer yellow; and Poeticus, both Recurvus and Ornatus, pure white. The mixtures, often sold at tempting prices, are to be avoided, as the results will be much less satisfactory. If a mixture is used, it should, at least, be kept within the same "type."

Several of the "minor" bulbs, particularly the English Bluebell (*Scilla nonscripta* or *nutans*) and the Grape-Hyacinth (*muscari*), Heavenly Blue, are both easily grown and most charming when naturalized; as is also Lily-of-the-Valley which is quite perfect for shady places. The irises are another fine group for "wild plantings."

Of the summer- and autumn-flowering bulbs, the native and other extra hardy lilies are the best suited to naturalizing; but with these, especially in woodland, may well be used such wildlings as the trilliums, the ladyslippers or cypripediums, and the Dogtooth violets (*erythronium*).

While the above do not begin to exhaust the best of the good material for naturalizing, they will serve the beginner to make a start with. Others are suggested in the following chapters.

CHAPTER III

WHAT BULBS ARE

In order to get the most out of the chapters which follow, and the information presented relative to the growing of the different classes of bulbs, the beginner should have a fairly clear idea of just what a bulb is; how it functions; and the various types of bulbs.

The dictionary definition of a bulb is an "onion-shaped root." While this gives a fairly definite description of a large class of bulbs, it is nevertheless too general for our purpose. The botanical definition, "a modified underground stem," is more helpful in that it makes clear the fact that a bulb is entirely distinct from a seed. That is the first thing the amateur should realize.

The primary purpose of this underground, modified stem is to *store up* food for the future use of the plant. This food is not taken directly from the roots, but is returned to the growing bulb from the leaves and stem above ground. It is most important that this fact should be realized, because then the gardener will readily understand that *the bulb cannot develop normally to its full capacity unless the leaves of the plant are allowed to complete their growth*. In the great majority of bulbs this does not take place until after the flowering period.

With bulbous plants, as with others, Nature puts forth her maximum effort in maturing the seeds of the plant. For this reason, it has long been considered by the growers of bulbs that it is best with plants which are being grown primarily to produce bulbs, not to allow them to go through the process of forming and maturing seed, the theory being that a large part of the strength of the plant which would be required for maturing the seed is thus saved to be returned to the newly developing bulb under ground. For this reason, in the bulb fields in Holland, and in the gladiolus fields in the United States, where bulbs are being grown commercially, the flowers are almost always removed as soon as they have opened sufficiently for the grower to be sure that the plant is of the right variety. Some authorities dispute this theory, maintaining that the plant has naturally sufficient strength to develop both seeds and bulbs, and that the bulbs are fully as good where the seeds are allowed to develop. So far as I know there have never been any comprehensive scientific experiments carried out to prove this matter one way or the other. The weight of general practice, however, is in favor of removing the flowers.

So far as the amateur is concerned in the growing of bulbs for his own use, and in the increasing of his own stock of bulbs of new or rare varieties, he can allow the plants to grow through the flowering stage, and even to form seed, without any fear that his bulbs will be injured. There is, however, no sense in allowing the plants to fully develop the seeds unless one is attempting to raise new varieties (a subject which is treated in a later chapter). And as the plants look much better with the old flowers removed it is a matter of general practice to take them off as soon as they begin to fade.

In addition to their capacity for storing food for future use, all bulbs likewise possess the faculty of producing flower stalks; in other words, the bulb is, in a sense, a complete, compact, *dormant plant*, entirely different from a seed. In fact, in many bulbs, as already mentioned, the complete flower, perfect in every detail—petals, pistil, stamens, etc.—is already well developed in the bulb in embryo form before it is planted. All bulbs enjoy in nature, and require when grown under artificial conditions, a period of "rest" or dormancy between the time they complete their growth and the time the new growth begins.

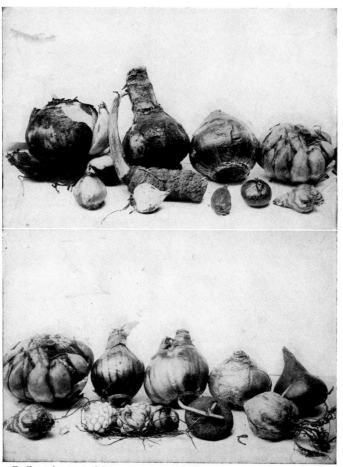

Bulbs of many different types including: hardy lilies, hyacinth, daffodil, snowdrop, feather hyacinth, narcissus (paper white), cyclamen, richardia (white calla), tulip, narcissus (Chinese sacred), Spanish iris, spring snowflake, amaryllis, crocus.

See if you can pick them out!

(*Left*) Preparing the soil for planting bulbs; this is the same garden as shown facing Page 4. The spaded ground is covered with raw, ground bone, ready to be dug in. (*Right*) Narcissus bulbs in place, ready to be planted.

During this period, important changes take place within the bulb itself. If, for instance, you cut a tulip bulb in two when it has completed its growth, there will be no sign of a new flower. Some weeks later, however, if the bulb is cut, provided it has been kept under proper storage conditions, the new flower will be found completely formed. In bulbs which do not form the new flower before growth begins, just as important changes are taking place, during

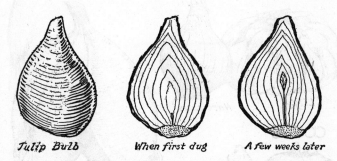

Tulip Bulb　　　　When first dug　　　　A few weeks later

the rest period, in the chemical composition of the flesh of the bulb.

So far, we have been using the word "bulb" in the general sense of the term as it is used by seedsman and gardener. Speaking more accurately, there are three general and distinctly different types or classes of bulbs. These are "true bulbs," "corms," and "tubers."

To make the distinction apparent at once to the beginner, we may say that the ordinary onion and the narcissus or daffodil are types of the "true bulbs"; the gladiolus and the crocus are types of the "corm"; and the potato and the dahlia are examples of the "tuber."

A true bulb is composed of scales or separate layers of flesh; it does not develop to its full size in a single season; and it increases by a process of splitting up or of "division," in which the "new" bulbs (or "splits") are actually parts of the original bulb.

There are several very distinct types of the true bulb: for instance, the lily, which is composed of separate fleshy scales which readily fall apart; the narcissus, whose thin layers of flesh, while separate, still form a fairly solid mass, just as in the case of the onion; the tulip, in which the layers of flesh are much thicker, but may be sepa-

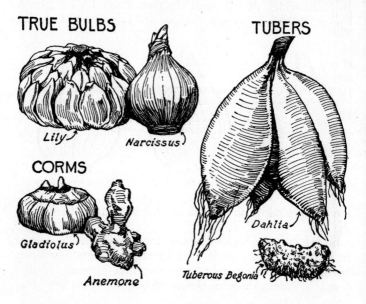

TRUE BULBS

Lily

Narcissus

TUBERS

CORMS

Gladiolus

Anemone

Dahlia

Tuberous Begonia

rated by small air spaces; and the squill or "scilla," in which the fleshy layers are rolled around each other.

A "corm" is made up of solid flesh; it lasts but a single season, an entirely new corm forming to take the place of the old, which shrivels up and falls off; and its principal method of propagation or increase is by the formation of "cormels" or "bulblets" (although large corms may form two or more smaller ones, which are not, however, parts of the old, original corm, but entirely new growths).

The "tuber" has solid flesh or substance, like the corm,

with rudimentary, inconspicuous leaf scales upon its outer surface; its growth may be confined to a single season, giving place to the development of new tubers, as in the case of the potato, or dahlia; or it may be a cormlike root passing from season to season, as in the case of the tuberous-rooted begonia and the gloxinia; it may propagate in the form of new tubers, usually in a clump or cluster, or have no natural means of increasing other than new tubers grown from seed. Most tubers are distinct from true bulbs and from corms, in that they have one or more "eyes" which put out buds, which in turn develop a root system, forming a new plant; whereas a true bulb or corm is formed with a "base" from which the roots are pushed out directly.

This brief and nontechnical description should enable the beginner to readily distinguish between the three classes of bulbs—that is, true bulbs, corms, and tubers—when these terms are used throughout the following chapters.

CHAPTER IV

MAKING THE BULB GARDEN

SOMEWHERE recently I read in an article about bulb growing that the gardener would be well repaid for taking the "trouble" to prepare the beds thoroughly. No explanation was given as to just what this thorough preparation should consist in; but whatever preparation might have been recommended would hardly have justified the use of the word "trouble" in this connection.

The real gardener does not consider as "trouble" the preparatory work which may be necessary to assure success with his favorites. As a matter of fact, I hold that such preliminary work is one of the keenest kinds of pleasure the gardener gets from his hobby, and, like Bret Harte's heathen Chinee, "the same I arise to maintain." I always have a great pity for the unfortunate silk-glove amateur whose only physical labor in connection with gardening is to carry a dainty basket in which to gather cut blossoms from professionally tended beds. You cannot properly appreciate the fragrance of the rose unless you have sweated over the compost dug into the subsoil down beneath its roots; nor fully appraise the treasure held within "the silken tassel of her purse" if your hands are innocent of scars and calluses from the spring pruning!

And so it is that to the real gardener in possession of this secret, the work of preparation is never "trouble." In his bright lexicon, the word does not exist!

Least of all with the bulb enthusiast should the details of providing the best possible conditions for growth take on any aspect of labor; for when the bulb bed is made, his work is practically over. Results are almost certain. His brother hobbyist, pursuing the rose or the sweet pea, may be in doubt up to the last minute whether the worldly hope he sets his heart upon will prosper—or turn to ashes! But given a properly made bulb bed and good bulbs, the bulb fancier can look forward with certainty to a harvest of beauty. With many bulbs, in fact, he can look forward to several years' such harvest, with little or no more attention on his part.

While it is true that a great many bulbs, both hardy and tender, will give very satisfactory flowers if merely "stuck in the ground and left," it is equally true that careful preparation will give better results. And, therefore, the gardener who would get the fullest pleasure from his or her bulbs, who wishes to see each species or variety develop to perfection, or as near it as conditions will allow, will gladly provide for them a bed as perfect as it is possible to make.

What, then, are some of the steps which should be taken to provide for bulbs in such a way that they will be sure to be happy in their environment, and in return make glad the garden where they bloom?

The different species, even individual varieties, have idosyncratic preferences in the way of soil, moisture, nourishment, shade, and so forth; but, for the most part, there are general methods to be followed which suit all. It is these general lines of procedure which we will endeavor to present first, taking up later, so far as possible, individual variations from them.

In making a bulb garden, as in making any other kind, the first step should be to lay out the garden.

If it is large or elaborate, this will be necessary; but even if it is a comparatively small and simple garden, this preliminary step is desirable even though not absolutely essential. It is so easy to make a change or to correct a mistake with an eraser on a piece of paper, and so difficult to do it when you are working with the soil, sod, fertilizers, and bulbs themselves!

The size of the garden; whether it will be of the formal, informal, or naturalistic type; whether it will be a garden of bulbs alone, or of bulbs used in connection with other flowers;—all these, of course, are questions which have or should have been settled before the actual making of the garden is undertaken. If, however, your ideas as to just what sort of bulb garden you wish are still somewhat indefinite and hazy, you will find that nothing will clarify them like putting down on paper a plan which shows dimensions, and indicates the varieties and their relative positions. Before you actually start work, make a plan, no matter how small the garden, nor how rough the plan. With your starting point thus established, the first thing to consider "on the ground" is the matter of drainage.

GOOD DRAINAGE IS ESSENTIAL

With exceptions so few that they are negligible, all bulbs require *thorough drainage*. And even the moisture-loving species of lilies and irises, which the beginner is likely to think of as almost amphibious, will not survive where water stands in the soil about the bulbs.

There are several ways of providing drainage. If the soil is naturally heavy and wet, it is best to plant on a slope if one is available, saving the driest spots for such bulbs as particularly prefer a dry soil. If the natural drainage is *not* sufficient, it can usually be rendered so by thoroughly breaking up the subsoil. This can be done by digging out the surface soil over the area of the bed to be planted, placing it on one side, and then thoroughly breaking up the subsoil with a pickax. Over wider areas, for instance where bulbs are to be naturalized, agricultural dynamite may often be used effectively without the necessity of removing the top soil.

Where, however, the land lies so low that it is not practicable to get rid of the surplus water by making it possible for it to work down through the subsoil, then artificial

Daffodils, tulips, hyacinths, and other early spring-flowering plants have been used to turn this formerly unattractive corner into a bower of beauty. A bank or slope gives an unusual opportunity for a striking arrangement.

A "close-up" of Darwin tulips. In this composition color contrast
has been skillfully employed.

drainage must be provided. For beds of moderate size this can be done without great inconvenience or expense, either by having a layer of drainage material under the surface soil, or by raising the bed itself a few inches—in extreme cases, several inches—above the average land level. Raising the bed is extremely effective in providing good drainage, and with this method bulbs may be successfully grown in ground which might be considered impossible for their culture.

In providing additional drainage material, the soil should be dug out of the bed down to the subsoil; the latter thoroughly broken up and pulverized, and, if necessary, removed to a depth of several inches; and then a layer of the drainage material placed in the bottom of the bed. For this purpose, sifted coal cinders—neither "clinkers" nor soft ashes—is better than anything else which I have ever used. If your own supply of these is not sufficient, they are usually to be had for the hauling from some near-by mill or railroad yard. Coarse gravel is also excellent. Broken stone, old lime rubbish, or anything similar will answer. On the top of this layer of drainage material, either the original soil or specially prepared soil is put. The first few inches of this may well contain pieces of sod or some other rather coarse matter. The four or five inches on the surface should, of course, be thoroughly pulverized. Where the bed is to be raised above the general surface, the same method should be followed excepting that the subsoil should not be removed and the sides of the bed should be held in place either with boards or planks, stones or bricks, or sod, though the use of wood is objectionable as it needs replacing after a few years. Irregular pieces of stone, such as are used for rock-garden work, are both permanent and effective in appearance. Sod, which should be sloped at an angle of about 45 degrees, is in every way satisfactory. The accompanying design showing cross sections of a level bed and of a raised bed show clearly the details of construction.

PREPARATION OF BULB BEDS

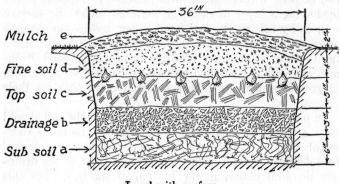

Mulch e →
Fine soil d →
Top soil c →
Drainage b →
Sub soil a →

Level with surface.

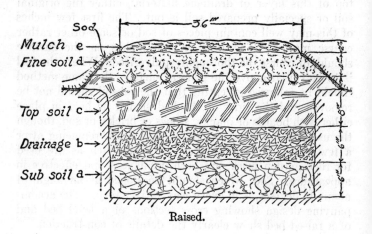

Sod
Mulch e →
Fine soil d →
Top soil c →
Drainage b →
Sub soil a →

Raised.

Where the entire garden is low and poorly drained, and there is a low point where it can be drained, it may pay to put in tiles for drainage. This is helpful not only for bulbs but for anything else which one may be aiming to grow in the garden. Putting in tile draining is not very expensive and is always a thoroughly well worth-while permanent improvement, which will add to the value of your place much more than it costs.

I have dwelt at some length upon this matter of drainage because it is the very keystone of the foundation arch of soil preparation. Also because in the many books and in the general literature on bulbs, it is given only a casual mention. It is one of those things which the successful grower, either professional or amateur, is likely to take for granted that the beginner knows all about!

PREPARING THE SOIL

And now comes the preparation of the soil itself.

Bulbs, like all other growing plants, must derive from the soil for their full development certain food elements. For absorption of this food, through their feeding roots, they are dependent upon an abundance of moisture and air in the soil.

With the general characteristics of a good garden soil the average amateur is familiar. It should, of course, be neither heavy clay nor very light, sandy soil, and it should contain an abundance of humus or decayed vegetable matter. If the soil is naturally heavy and lumpy, then sand, ashes, agricultural lime or land plaster should be added to lighten it and loosen it up. If it is light and sandy, adding a mixture of heavier soil, preferably from a pasture or meadow, and the addition of land plaster or agricultural lime, together with an abundance of the commercial humus, peat, or leafmold, will greatly benefit it.

All of these things, of course, have more to do with the *physical* condition of the soil than with its "richness," from the point of view of the actual plant food contained. Both the physical condition and the plant food are, of course, important. But in the growing of most bulbs in gardens, the former is, if anything, the more important. I have found that the great majority of bulbs take very kindly to the soil in which a generous amount of commercial humus or peat has been mixed. Whether or not peat and humus have some plant food value which the chemical analysis does not indicate, I do not know. But I do know that I would not think of attempting to make a bulb garden on new soil without one of these materials. Two years ago, I had occasion to make a bulb garden on raw, light, gravelly soil along the edge of a steep bank, about as unpromising a situation as one could well find. With the use of peat and humus and bone meal, and no other materials whatsoever, the result was a complete success.

MANURES AND FERTILIZERS

Having gotten the soil in the proper physical condition, the next thing to consider is what plant foods to use.

So far in our discussion of the preparation of the soil for the bulb garden, it has not differed materially from the preparation of the soil for any other garden. But right here we come to one distinct and most important difference, and that is in the use of animal manure as a fertilizer. A "dose" of fairly fresh or even of half-rotted manure, upon which most shrubs, perennials, or annuals would thrive, may prove quite disastrous to a planting of bulbs. Rotted manure, particularly cow manure, makes splendid plant food for bulbs, but it must be used with discretion and *never* until it is thoroughly well decayed. I have a quantity which I am planning to use in making a bulb garden next fall. It is already a year old, but even so I am making a compost heap of it with sods and leafmold which will be forked over two or three times during the summer, and then put through a coarse screen, before it is put on the bulb bed. With such treatment, I know from experience it will be perfectly safe to use it. If only fresh manure is to be had, and there is not time to rot it thoroughly in a compost heap, it had better be omitted altogether, and the beds made with other materials.

Among fertilizers, my preference for making a bulb bed is bone meal. There is a great deal of difference in the various grades of bone meal which you can buy. It is best to get genuine raw ground bone, not the "acidulated" which has been treated with acid in manufacturing processes, but, if possible, the raw bone shavings, known as "button" bone or "knuckle" bone. Mix this and finely ground bone flour in equal parts. The bone flour will give the roots a strong, quick start in the fall, while the coarse bone, which becomes available more gradually, will enable the plants to continue vigorous growth after they have bloomed in the spring, thus building up good strong bulbs to produce flowers the following year. For spring-planted bulbs such as gladioli or dahlias the same advantages hold. A quantity of tankage or dried blood, one to five or six of the bone, may be employed for hastening an early growth; or the tankage may be applied and worked into the soil before growth has started in the spring or early summer. The bone meal contains phosphoric acid and a reasonable amount of ammonia, or nitrogen. The blood or tankage contains additional nitrogen. Nitrate of soda, which is an excellent stimulant for many flowers, is not desirable for most bulbs. As a source of potash I much prefer wood ashes or tobacco fertilizer to any of the chemical fertilizers. The ashes also improve the texture of the soil.

Whether or not lime should be added will depend both upon the natural character of the soil from which the bulb bed is being made, and upon what is to be grown in the bed. Many bulbs, and particularly the majority of the hardy lilies, prefer a rather acid soil. But the general run of bulbs, both early spring flowering and summer flowering, if the soil is naturally very acid, will do better with the addition of a reasonable amount of lime—say ten pounds to each one hundred square feet of surface when the bed is being prepared.

With bulbs, as with other forms of plant life, no amount of plant food in the soil will be of any avail unless there is also sufficient moisture so that the growing roots can take up or absorb this plant food. This they can do only when it is in the form of a liquid solution in the soil. Although it is important that all surplus moisture be gotten rid of by thorough drainage, it is equally important that there should be sufficient moisture to make continuous and vigorous growth possible. With bulbs, there is not the same opportunity to conserve the moisture in the soil by surface cultivation and the maintenance of a "dust mulch," as there is in growing vegetables or flowers. Mulching the bulb beds will to a great extent help to conserve this moisture; but if one wishes to be absolutely sure of results, a means of supplying water to the bulb bed during very dry weather should be provided. It very often happens that the soil is quite dry when the bulbs should be planted in the fall; and often in early spring when the summer-flowering bulbs are being planted the same condition exists.

If means can be provided for making the soil thoroughly moist immediately after planting, a vigorous, quick growth can be started. If the bed is not so situated as to be within easy reach of the hose, it is not a difficult or an expensive matter to lay a few lengths of three-quarter-inch pipe at the time the bulb bed is being made, so that water can be brought within reach. This pipe, as it will never be necessary to use it during freezing weather, need not be put down over a foot or so below the surface. For my own beds, I use a small portable irrigating system which consists of a pipe line about twenty feet long, with regular irrigating nozzles—not a circular "sprinkler," which does much less effective work. This portable outfit cost me but a few dollars; it can be set up anywhere in a few minutes, and used to water either a long, narrow bed or a border of any width, without wasting any water where it is not needed. As the water falls in a fine mistlike rain, the ground can be thoroughly saturated without in the least washing or packing it. With it I can be certain that my bulbs have actually started to grow within a few hours after being planted, instead of lying dormant in the soil for days, as they sometimes do, when they have to wait for rain.

Some bulbs prefer a particularly dry situation. These are, for the most part, the small-growing things which are suitable for planting in the rock garden. If a bulb garden is being made, it will be well to provide for these things by having one portion of it, particularly well drained and dry, set aside for them. A rockery corner in the bulb garden is not difficult to make and will add the charm of variety. Other bulbs which prefer a peaty or acid soil and some shelter or ground cover, such as many of the lilies, may well be provided for among rhododendrons, azaleas, laurels, and other ericaceous plants, or in the shrubbery border.

PLANTING THE BULBS

With the soil thoroughly prepared, our next step is the actual planting of the bulbs themselves, and this, after the preliminaries have been properly carried out, is quick and easy work.

Sometimes, for one of a number of reasons, it is not possible to plant the bulbs immediately upon their arrival. If they can be so planted, so much the better; but if not, we should see to it that they do not become injured, as easily may happen during the time which must intervene before we get them into the soil. In nature, bulbs have a dormant or curing period in the soil. It is not natural for them to remain out of it, and so, when for gardening purposes they must be taken from the soil, we should be careful to give them suitable conditions. The ideal way would be, of course, to keep them buried in dry sand or soil in boxes. As a matter of fact, this is the best way to keep many of the tender-flowering bulbs, such as tuberous begonias, tuberoses, etc.; also the hardy lilies, the scales of which dry out quickly, and fleshy roots such as irises or peonies. Where it is not convenient to use sand or soil, sphagnum moss, sawdust, or peat may be employed. Hyacinths, tulips, and other bulbs for fall planting should be opened and examined immediately upon receipt. If in perfect condition, they can be kept in their bags, provided these are well ventilated; but they should never be kept in a closed, air-tight receptacle. Plenty of ventilation and a cool temperature are the two essentials. These conditions are usually found in a cool cellar, with a window for ventilation. Moisture may produce premature sprouting. Bulbs which are slightly dried out or shriveled when received may be plumped up by covering them with moist sand, sawdust, moss, or peat for a week or so.

There are two methods of getting the bulbs into the ground. One may remove entirely several inches of soil, place the bulbs in position, and then replace the soil over them. This method has some advantages, but involves a considerable amount of work. The bulbs can be placed exactly as wanted, set firmly in the soil, which is important, and covered to an exact depth. The amount of labor involved, however, is often the objection.

The other method is to plant the bulbs in individual holes. In doing this, two things should be watched with extreme care: first, to get them in to the proper depth; and second, to have the hole broad enough at the bottom so that the base of the bulb will sit firmly on the soil and not be left suspended over an air pocket. A broad trowel, or, in very soft soil, a blunt stick should be employed rather than the narrow trowel or pointed dibble which is often used. With either of these, an inexperienced hand is very likely to leave an air space, or loose soil just under the base of the bulb, where the first roots will be put out. If

Naturalizing bulbs. (*Above*) They are thrown on the ground in handfuls and planted where they fall. (*Below*) A prepared bed is being marked off "both ways" to get the bulbs in uniformly. The planters stand on boards to avoid packing the mellow soil.

How bare this beautiful garden would have been in early spring without bulbs! When they have passed, the hardy perennials will carry on the pageant of summer's bloom.

the soil is at all heavy, it is an excellent plan to have a pail of sand available, and to drop a handful where each bulb is to be set. With the bulb bed itself, however, properly prepared, this will hardly be necessary.

The bulbs should be taken out, one variety at a time, and placed where they are to be planted, either in straight rows or in "designs," if that archaic method is to be fol-

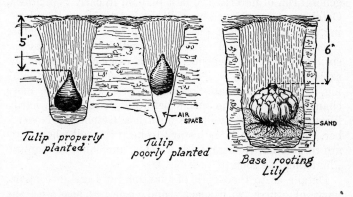

Tulip properly planted

Tulip poorly planted

Base rooting Lily

Tulip bulbs planted for bedding

lowed in planting, arranged in irregular groups in the border, broadcast, or put in "colonies" for naturalizing. To give a really natural effect, the bulbs should be thrown or dropped in handfuls and planted where they fall, some quite close together, and others strung out more thinly. It is next to impossible to get a naturalistic planting if one attempts to place each bulb by hand.

In planting in sod, either a cross-cut may be made with a sharp spade, or with an edger, so that the edge of the sods may be turned back; or a small piece of sod may be removed and then replaced after the bulb is planted. There are special bulb planters for use where large numbers of bulbs are to be set.

As to *when* to plant, a safe general rule is "the earlier the better." A few of the fall-planted bulbs, such as the Madonna lily, should be got in in August, if possible. The general run of narcissi are best planted in early September; October or even November will do, but the later the planting, the less the root growth which will be made before freezing weather, and upon this growth the quality of the spring flower show depends. Tulips can be planted at the same time, but will be less adversely affected by late planting, especially the late-flowering types, which have more chance to grow in the spring before flowering. The hardy lilies often are not available until late October or November. It may even be necessary to keep the soil where they are to go from freezing with a heavy mulching of manure. Plant them as soon as possible.

Details as to the depth of planting, and distance apart, vary, of course, with species and varieties; also with the type of planting. Most catalogues give fairly complete information upon this point; as a general rule, the bulb should be covered to three times its greatest diameter. This will give from four to six inches for tulips and narcissi, and six or even eight for hyacinths; hardy lilies require three to four inches for some species, and as much as ten or twelve for others. Tulips should be planted four to six inches apart; narcissi a bit more.

If at all possible, give the beds a thorough soaking immediately after planting. This settles the soil firmly about the bulbs and induces quick root action. Thereafter, nothing remains to be done but wait for the flowers to appear. A mulch of strawy manure or leaves may be put on *after* the soil is well frozen, but this is not essential if the bulbs are thoroughly well covered. This mulch should, of course, be removed as the plants appear in the spring.

CHAPTER V

SPRING-FLOWERING BULBS AND THEIR CULTURE

THE classification indicated by the title of this chapter is made not on the botanical or scientific basis, but rather from the point of view of the amateur gardener. In a general group under "spring-flowering bulbs" have been included those species and varieties which flower from early spring to early summer, or, in most sections of the United States, from late March until early June. The majority of these bulbs require the same general system of culture. In a later chapter, we will discuss the summer- and autumn-flowering bulbs, *i.e.*, those which generally bloom from late June until frost.

By far the most important of spring-flowering bulbs are the so-called "Dutch bulbs," narcissi, tulips, hyacinths, and crocuses; and, in addition to these, the less well known but equally beautiful "minor bulbs" such as chionodoxa (glory-of-the-snow), eranthis (winter-aconite), galanthus (snow-drop), leucojum (spring snowflake), muscari (grape-hyacinth), scilla (wood hyacinth), fritillarias; also the less hardy anemones, ranunculus, and bulbous irises, which, with a little care, may be easily grown out of doors.

Practically all of the spring-flowering bulbs should be planted in the autumn (the few exceptions are noted later in the remarks concerning the individual bulbs).

The steps to be followed in the preparation of the soil for planting have been covered in the preceding chapter. Planting, as has been already suggested, is usually best done as soon as the bulbs are received. If the bulbs are covered as deeply as they should be, there is little chance of any top growth being made, even though freezing weather may

not set in until later than is normally the case. The later
the planting, the more essential it is that the root growth
should be started quickly and, therefore, the more important is the thorough soaking of the soil with a modern
irrigating equipment if the weather is dry.

Winter Mulching. The winter mulch which is usually
applied should not be put on until *after* the ground is
frozen.   Tulips will not be injured even if no protective
mulching at all is given.   Narcissi and hyacinth are somewhat more susceptible to winter injury, and for them, therefore, mulching is more advisable.   The various hardy
"minor" bulbs will usually do all right without it, except
where the soil has a tendency to "heave" during the winter.
For the more tender things, however, such as the bulbous
irises, anemones, ranunculus, and the like, thorough mulching is not only advisable, but, excepting in quite mild climates, very essential.

The material for winter mulching may be marsh hay,
spent manure, leaves, peat, leafmold, or any light, dry
material which will not become water-soaked and pack
down hard on the one hand, or be so light as to blow away
on the other.   One of the chief reasons for not applying the
mulch until after the ground freezes is to prevent its becoming a harboring place for mice, which might injure the
bulbs either in the fall or early in the spring.   If necessary,
the mulch, which should be put on from two to four inches
thick, can be held in place with evergreen boughs or some
other suitable material.

The mulch, which is of course left on throughout the
winter, should be removed in the spring as the bulbs begin
to show signs of growth above ground.   One advantage of
mulching is that premature warm spells in the spring will
be less likely to bring the tops through the ground to be
injured by cold weather later.   Care should be taken, however, not to leave the mulch on long enough so that the
tops begin to come up through it, as this will have a tendency to make the tops abnormally tall and tender, and,

therefore, easily injured by late cold snaps and heavy winds If the bulb beds can be watched carefully, so that this mulching can be removed gradually, it is better. It is necessary to take off only the coarsest part of the mulching, as the smaller particles can easily be worked into the soil the first time it is gone over, to destroy any weeds which may be starting and to break up the winter crust.

Cultivation. Almost all plants make more vigorous growth if the soil is kept thoroughly cultivated and loosened about them. The average spring-blooming bulbs are no exception to this rule. Care should be taken, however, not to cut either the foliage or roots. For this spring cultivation, I much prefer a small pronged hoe to the usual type with a solid blade and a sharp edge. With the prong hoe, the surface of the soil between the bulbs can be broken up and thoroughly loosened with little danger of doing any injury to the plants.

Top-Dressing. Unless the soil in which the bulbs are growing is already well "stuffed with plant food," a light application of fertilizer just as the spring growth begins will result in better and stronger flowers. The number of the flowers cannot be increased—that is already determined by the size and condition of the bulbs themselves—but the development of the flowers can be influenced. For this early spring fertilizing I use a half-and-half mixture of bone flour, or very fine ground bone, and a high-grade tankage or dried blood. A handful of this mixture will be sufficient for six to a dozen plants. It should be thoroughly worked into the soil. Liquid manure may be used, giving one or two light applications just as the flower buds are developing, but this will usually not be necessary if the bulb bed has been well prepared, and a spring top-dressing of fertilizer similar to that just described has been applied.

The bulb gardener, fortunately, is not likely to be troubled with insects or diseases. It is well, however, to keep an eye open for anything which looks "off color." Several which may appear are described in some detail in

Chapter XX. A safe, general rule is to take up carefully
and bodily—top, roots, soil, and all—any bulb which seems
to be decidedly wrong, and *burn* it.

Flowers which may be wanted for cutting, for use
indoors, should be taken before they have fully developed.
Those which are left on the plant should be removed immediately they begin to seem passé. They are not then ornamental, and may interfere with the development of the
new bulb which is wanted to produce next year's flowers.

Care After Blooming. As most gardeners will wish to
keep their bulbs from year to year, the care of the plants
after they have flowered is fully as important, perhaps more
important, than that which is received previous to flowering. The failure of the average gardener to realize this
very vital point is responsible for most of the "petering out"
of some bulbs which one occasionally hears complaints of.

First of all, the beginner should get it thoroughly fixed
in mind that the foliage is by no means to be cut off, if
he wants good flowers the following season. The reason
for this has, I think, already been made sufficiently plain;
but whether or not the beginner comprehends the reason,
the rule must be followed. By far the most satisfactory
way is to let the bulbs remain where they are growing
until the foliage has thoroughly developed and "ripened,"
which is indicated by its turning yellow and beginning to
die down. It can then be cut back to, or very slightly
below, the surface, so that other plants may occupy for
the balance of the season the space before taken up by the
bulbs.

Sometimes the ground where the bulbs are growing is
needed for other flowers, and it is desirable to remove them
as soon as they are through blooming. Personally, I much
prefer to plant, or to set out plants of, quick-growing
annuals which will be developing just as the bulbs are
dying down, and will take their place for the balance of
the season. This method and the plants suitable for it are
described on page 48.

If for any reason this cannot be done, and the bulbs must be moved, prepare for them a trench of deep moist soil, in shade or partial shade, where they can be watered thoroughly in case of very dry weather. Then, immediately the bulbs are through flowering, take them up carefully with a spade or a digging fork and transfer them to the new bed, with as little disturbance of the roots as possible. If the soil is decidedly moist, so that a good ball of soil can be taken up with each bulb, they will suffer little by the transfer, and if they are well planted with the soil packed firmly down about them they will go on growing naturally in their new position.

Harvesting or "Lifting." Harvesting the bulbs is important. This should be done every season with practically all of the tulips, and with some of the other bulbs which will be mentioned later. Narcissi should be harvested or "lifted" every second or third year, and the clumps divided, if the size of the flowers is to be maintained; other bulbs, as they may require it, from becoming overcrowded in their original position. The best time to harvest is when the foliage has turned yellow and begun to shrivel or to dry up, but just *before* it will separate readily from the bulbs. If the bulbs are taken up while the tops still cling to them, they may be much more readily gathered and will have developed fully.

As the bulbs are taken up, each variety should be carefully placed in a shallow wooden box or flat *with the label.* Never trust to memory if you wish to know just what varieties you are putting in when it comes time to plant them back, no matter how few varieties you may have nor how soon you may expect to replant them. With experience, you will soon be able to distinguish many varieties by the appearance of the bulb, but the surest, quickest, and simplest way is to get the habit of using labels.

If the number of bulbs taken up is small and if the soil is dry, they may be placed, when harvested, in paper "bulb bags." These are made of very heavy paper and perforated for ventilation, and will be found extremely convenient for this purpose. They may be bought in various sizes from concerns which handle Dutch bulbs.

Curing. The way the bulbs are handled after harvesting is of vital importance. During this period, chemical changes take place in the internal structure of the bulb, and, in many varieties, the flower for the following season is developed in miniature in the bulb itself. The general object to be aimed at is to *keep the bulbs dry and cool.* A perfectly dry, well-ventilated cellar is perhaps the best place in which the amateur can keep his bulbs. Failing the possession of a cellar, a thoroughly well-ventilated shed or an attic, if it is not too hot, may be used. If the bulbs are stored in shallow wooden flats or trays, these should be either placed on shelves or separated by small blocks of wood, if placed one on top of the other, so that there will be abundant circulation around and between them.

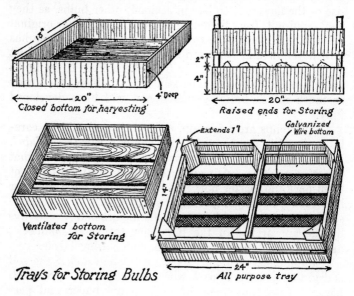

15"

4" Deep

20"
Closed bottom for harvesting

2"

4"

20"
Raised ends for Storing

Extends 1"

Galvanized Wire bottom

14"

Ventilated bottom for Storing

24"
All purpose tray

Trays for Storing Bulbs

As soon as the tops, soil, and bulbs have dried out sufficiently they should be gone over carefully, the tops pulled
or cut off, and the bulbs separated into two or three sizes.
They may then be left in the trays or flats, or carefully
labeled, in paper bags, to await the time of planting.

Replanting. The bulbs which one has harvested and
cured should be replanted in the same way and at the same
time as has been recommended for newly purchased bulbs.
(See page 39.)   They will, of course, be available for
replanting earlier if that seems desirable. Where a number
of bulbs are being handled, it will be well to get the home-
grown crop into the soil just before the newly purchased
bulbs will be received so that the work of planting need
not be crowded into too short a space of time. The larger
bulbs may be planted by themselves and the smaller ones
either set out in groups in the border, where they will flower
the second season, if not the first; or the small bulbs may
be kept separate and handled in a special propagating bed
or "nursery" as described in Chapter XX.   (See page 36.)

CHAPTER VI

TULIPS

THE tulip is at this time, in the United States, undoubtedly the most popular of all the spring-flowering bulbs. And, for some years to come, it will have a tremendous advantage over its nearest rival, the narcissus or daffodil, due to the fact that the free importation of the latter flower is no longer permitted. Just how long it will take American production to catch up with the normal demand for narcissus bulbs, it is impossible to say. But in the meantime, narcissi will be high in price and very limited in the number of varieties available, as compared to tulips.

The tulip is, in many respects, an ideal flower for spring gardening. Given good bulbs to start with, any one can succeed with tulips, and in the various types and varieties, almost every conceivable color is available excepting certain shades of blue. Not only in color, but also in size and habit of growth, the gardener may make selections to suit his object or requirements from a marvelous variety, ranging from dwarf-growing species but a few inches high to magnificent giant sorts which tower on stems three to three and one half feet above the garden bed. In the season of bloom also there is a very satisfactory range, the period of flowering extending from early April to early June. In most bulb catalogues, far too little attention is given to this very important point; consequently the average amateur orders his tulips with but little thought to maintaining a long and constant succession of bloom, and is disappointed at the brief season during which he is enabled to enjoy their wonderful flowers. To be forewarned in this particular is to be forearmed. Even the beginner, who will take the pains to order his bulbs with this consideration in mind, can enjoy his tulips for week after week during the spring.

Methods of Planting Tulips. Personally I believe that by far the most satisfactory method of using tulips is to plant them in groups in the hardy border, or in a border which is devoted mostly to various kinds of bulbs alone. Half a dozen to two dozen will make bold masses of color and also greatly enhance the beauty of the individual flowers. Where they are planted singly, or in long, narrow lines or "ribbons," they are always disappointing no matter how beautiful the individual flowers may be. Under exceptional circumstances, large, solid beds, preferably of one variety, or at the most not more than two, will produce beautiful effects; but this method of planting involves a very much greater expense for the bulbs, and usually looks very much out of place, unless on grounds of considerable area. The method of planting in groups in a mixed border does not exclude the use of the early-flowering varieties, particularly if the taller-growing sorts are selected.

Wherever tulips are planted in considerable quantities by themselves, they are almost always more beautiful when some other early-flowering "ground cover" plants are associated with them. In sections of the country where the winters are not extremely severe—that is, where the temperature will not often go down to zero or below—these plants may be sown or planted in the fall so that they will come into bloom along with the tulips. In colder sections, it has been my experience that it is far better to carry these "companion" plants through the winter in a low frame, where they can be mulched with leaves or evergreen boughs, and kept in proper condition, and then transplant them to the bulb bed early in the spring. Another method, which involves less work, is to rake over the surface of the tulip bed as early as possible in the spring, and sow seed of quick-growing, early-flowering annuals. Coming into bloom just as the latest tulips are over, they will keep the bulb bed beautiful while the foliage of the bulbs is ripening, without the slightest injury to the latter. The same method of using other plants along with the tulips can be employed just as well where they are grown in large groups in the mixed border as when they are grown in one solid bed. Of the various plants which may be used along with tulips in this way, some of which flower with the tulips and should be started the fall previous, either in the beds or for carrying through the winter in a cold frame, include the following:

PLANTS FOR USE WITH BULBS

Annuals for Early Spring Sowing on Surface Between Bulbs

Shirley poppies, pink, rose, various (blooms in six weeks).

California-poppies (*eschscholtzia*), yellow, gold, crimson.

Candytuft, white, lilac, crimson.

Clarkia, pink, white, rose (blooms in six weeks).

Annual larkspur, blue, pink, rose, white.

Lobelia, blue, white.

Phlox drummondi, various shades, pink, white, lilac, crimson.

Portulaca, most brilliant red and yellow shades.

Schizanthus, especially Garaway's Hybrids, various.

Asperula, bright azure blue.

Plants for Setting Out in Spring Between Bulbs

Sweet Alyssum, white.

Pansies, various shades, purple, blue, yellow, white, etc.

English daisies, pink or white.

Lobelia, especially Crystal Palace, blue.

Candytuft, white.

Wallflowers, shades of red, maroon, and orange.

Siberian Wallflowers (*cheiranthus allioni*), distinctive orange; (*C. mutabilis citrinus*), pale yellow.

Myosotis alpestris, blue.

(*Above*) Grape-hyacinths show well the detail of the rock-garden type of planting. (*Below*) Tulips, widely spaced, have been interplanted with pansies to create a charming effect.

Most of the tulip species are extremely hardy and well adapted to naturalizing. Those shown above are, from left to right, *sprengeri, clusiana, acuminata.*

Hardy Ground-Cover Plants for Surface of Bulb Bed

Arabis (Rockcress), white, pink, or rose.

Alyssum (*A. saxatile compactum*), bright yellow.

Alyssum (*A. saxatile citrinum*), pale yellow.

Aubrietia (Rockcress), pink, violet, crimson, lavender, blue.

Cerastium tomentosum (Mouse-ear Chickweed), white, June.

Gypsophila, dwarf or creeping varieties, white, rose.

Mentha (mint), blue.

Mossy Saxifragas, white, yellow, rose (sun or shade).

PLANTS TO USE AFTER REMOVING BULBS

Asters.	Heliotrope.
Begonias, fibrous rooted.	Lupines.
Begonias, tuberous rooted (in partial shade).	Marigolds.
	Snapdragons (*antirrhinum*).
Cannas.	Verbenas.
Clarkia.	Zinnias.
Geraniums.	Violas.

Tulips for Naturalizing. Many as the uses and advantages of tulips are, they do not include naturalizing. While the bulbs, under garden culture, may be kept in good condition year after year, by far the majority of them will *run out* unless taken care of. A few of the species, however, are adapted to naturalizing, under favorable conditions. These are mentioned later in this chapter in the list of tulip species described.

TYPES OF TULIPS

The beginner, unfamiliar with bulb-catalogue parlance, will be somewhat confused by the various types which he finds mentioned therein, and differentiated from each other, if at all, by very abbreviated descriptions.

Some knowledge of the various tulip types is essential if the best results are to be had from them as material for garden making. So I shall briefly describe the dozen or so distinct types which are commonly available, even though the average bulb gardener may be likely to make a selection from but three or four of them. As more familiarity is gained, however, any bulb enthusiast will get the keenest pleasure from increasing his collection until he has at least one variety from each type grown. They differ so greatly in their individual merits that where space allows you will surely want them all eventually.

Single Earlies. These are the first to flower and they were formerly largely used for "design" beds. They include the most brilliant colors to be found among tulips, blossom during early or late April, and have an average height of from ten to fourteen inches. The various varieties are remarkably uniform in their season of bloom, making them ideal for "bedding" purposes. They are also the best for early "forcing" or growing indoors. One of the best-known varieties of the single earlies is the Keizerskroon (Grand Duc), a very bright crimson with a broad band of yellow, making it one of the most conspicuous of all tulips.

Early Doubles. The double form of the early tulips is entirely different from the singles, the blooms much resembling a small peony in appearance. They are sometimes desirable where a large mass of color is wanted, as the flowers last considerably longer than the singles; they are, however, somewhat squat in appearance, and to many people, much less attractive than the single sorts. They come somewhat later, do not average as tall in growth, and are less brilliant in coloring. They are, however, excellent for forcing, particularly where several bulbs are grown together in a bulb pan. Murillo, a soft rose pink, shaded white, is probably the best-known variety.

Cottage Tulips. These come into bloom somewhat later than the single earlies; have much larger flowers; and grow taller, averaging eighteen to twenty inches in height, with slender but stiff, strong stems. They include the widest range of colors and variations of flower forms of any of the several classes. They are not, on the whole, as good for "forcing" as either the Earlies or the Darwins, although some of the varieties are excellent for indoor growth. If one were restricted in the planting of tulips to but a single type, the Cottage tulip would be the one to choose; but, fortunately, no such limitation is imposed. (The term "May Flowering" is often applied to the Cottage or "Cottage Garden" tulip, but it is somewhat confusing, as it is likewise applied to other types which also flower in May.) Picotee, white, with narrow margin of rose, is one of the most popular Cottage tulips.

Double May Flowering or Cottage. These are double forms of the above type. Personally I consider these more beautiful than the early doubles, but they have never become popular in this country. Most of the American catalogues do not list them. Bleu Celeste (Blue Flag) is an example of this type.

Darwins. These are the most popular of all tulips and are distinguished by their enormous flowers, their vigorous growth, thick foliage, and heavy, thick stems 24 to 30 inches tall. The flowers are "cup" or "egg" shaped, with no pointed petals, and with no shade of yellow; they are almost invariably "selfs" or single-colored, although the shadings in the coloring may vary considerably. Clara Butt, a clear pink with salmon shading, is the best known of all Darwins, and probably the most popular tulip in the world. In many Darwins, the "base" formed by the lower ends of the petals is of a color contrasting with the body of the flower.

Rembrandt. These are similar in every way to the Darwins excepting that the colors have "broken," so that the petals, in place of being "self"-colored, are striped, "feathered," or "flamed" with contrasting colors. Victor Hugo, white feathered with bright carmine, is one of the best-known sorts.

Breeders. These are similar to the Darwins in many respects, being, if anything, even more robust in growth and stature. Like the Darwins, they are mostly self-colored, but are noted for their peculiar dull, artistic color tones, which range through what artists call the "pastel" shades. Many of them are distinctly sweet-scented. Louis XIV, bronze purple with broad margin of dull gold, "the most beautiful tulip in the world," is one of the best known of the Breeders, but because of its two-toned coloring is not so characteristic of the type as Bronze Queen (Clio), another very popular sort, a dull buff golden brown.

Old Dutch. These are broken forms of the Breeders, holding the same relation to them as the Rembrandts do to the Darwins. Those in which the background of the coloring is brown or yellow are known as Bizarres; and those in which the background is white are known as Bybloemens—rose Bybloemens or violet Bybloemens according to the nature of the striping or the feathering. They are not quite so tall as the Darwins and Breeders, averaging twenty to twenty-two inches in height. "Black Boy," yellow, feathered dark brown (Bizarre); Lady Stanley (violet Bybloemens), with dark violet feathering; and Reine de Hollande (rose Bybloemens), white, feathered bright red, are examples of this type.

Parrot. These are entirely distinct from all other tulips in being deeply laciniated or fringed, and generally irregular in form, often with raised blotches or pimples on the outer petals. They grow about fifteen inches high and have rather weak stems; but they are the most conspicuous flowers of the tulip race. Lutea Major, a clear yellow, with crimson and green blotches and stripes, is a typical variety.

Lily-Flowered. This is a new and very beautiful class, resulting from crossing tulip Retroflexa with a Darwin variety. As the name suggests, the flowers are lily-shaped. Sirene, a soft satiny rose, is an example.

Bunch-Flowered. This is a comparatively new type, with several flowers to a stem. It is very distinct and pleasing, and likely to be developed more extensively in the near future. The most available variety at present is Mons. Mottet, which has ivory-white flowers, four to six, on each stem.

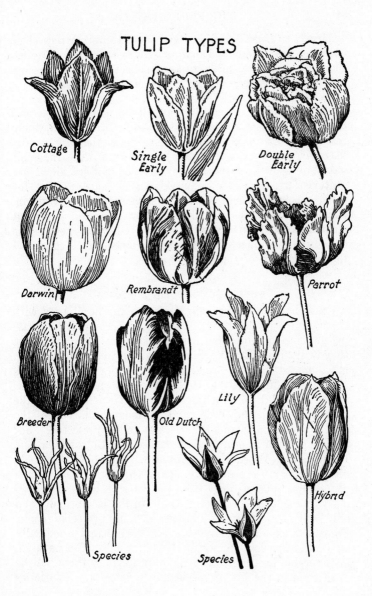

TULIP TYPES

Cottage

Single
Early

Double
Early

Darwin

Rembrandt

Parrot

Breeder

Old Dutch

Lily

Species

Species

Hybrid

Mendel or Hybrid Tulips. Here is yet another new class, resulting from crossing Darwins with the Cottage varieties. They are well worth adding to any collection. Dido, orange red, bordered orange yellow, is one of the most outstanding sorts.

Tulip Species. In addition to all the above types, and the many varieties available under most of them, there remain the Species or "Botanical" tulips, as they are usually listed in the catalogues. These are in a wide range of habit of growth, form, and color. Several of them are quite dwarf, and can be used in rock gardens and for other purposes where most tulips would not well fit in. Clusiana, sometimes called the "Lady Tulip," a small but striped pointed flower with cherry red outer petals and creamy white inner ones, giving a striped effect, is one of the best known of the many Species.

TULIPS FOR SPECIAL PURPOSES

Once the bulb gardener has gained some familiarity with the various types of tulips available, it becomes a fascinating game to employ them in and about one's garden, where they will "just fit in." For group planting, for instance, in a mixed border practically all types can be used, although the doubles and the "broken" forms—Rembrandt, Bizarres, and Bybloemens—are less satisfactory than the others. For design beds, and various formal beds, the Early, both single and double, are to be preferred. For a mass of color in a large bulb garden, the Cottage Garden, Darwin, and Breeder varieties are preferable. For bold bits of color in the shrubbery, against hedges or other points of vantage some distance from the house, tall, strong-growing varieties of the foregoing and also the Rembrandts and old Dutch types; some Parrots also, in protected spots. For the rock garden, some of the Earlies and practically all of the Species. Some of the latter may also be used, in favorable locations, even for naturalizing—these will be mentioned in the list of species given later on. (Varieties suitable for forcing are described in Chapter XVIII.) For growing out of doors for cutting, varieties should be selected which will give a constant succession, from the Early, May-Flowering, Darwins, and Breeders. As a rule, varieties with rather long pointed flowers, with not too stiff stems and not too solid colors, are the most satisfactory for this purpose. The Lily-flowered type and the Parrots are also excellent for house decoration, the latter being most unique and effective. Fragrance is also very desirable in flowers for cutting. A list of the fragrant varieties is given at the end of this chapter.

CULTURE

The general details for preparing the beds for planting, when and how to plant, and so on, as given in the preceding chapter, apply with practically no alterations or additions to the handling of tulips, and, therefore, need not be repeated here. In mild locations, where freezing weather is not to be expected until toward the end of December, the planting should be held off until late October. Early varieties should be planted three to four inches deep; and the later sorts, an inch or two deeper, depending upon the size of the bulbs which vary greatly with the different varieties. Some of the species, notably Clusiana and Kaufmanniana, should be planted very deep, six or eight inches. The Parrot tulips, which are rather shy bloomers, may well be planted somewhat closer together than the other large-flowered sorts, such as Darwins and Breeders, which may be spaced six or seven inches, or even a little wider if ground-cover plants are to be set or sown between them.

All tulips, with the exception of a few of the species, such as persica, kaufmanniana, daisystemon, should be lifted annually, even if they are to be replanted in the same position. (For suggestions concerning propagation, see page 240.)

SOME GOOD VARIETIES

It would be impossible, without increasing the size of

this book, to attempt to give any detailed description of the majority of the worth-while tulips; nor would it serve any vital purpose, as new sorts are being constantly added to the list in commerce; and as detailed descriptions are to be found in the catalogues. As a guide to those unfamiliar with tulips, I have made selections of a few varieties under the most important types. To be sure these represent largely my own personal preference, but they are also the result of experience with tulips in many gardens, under widely varied conditions, and may, I think, be safely followed. I have been at particular pains to select varieties which will give a succession of bloom, as this point is generally neglected. These have been indicated as Early, Medium, and Late, under the several types.

SATISFACTORY TULIPS

Single Early.

Early.   Proserpine, rose and carmine.
Mon Tresor, clear deep yellow.
Keizerskroon (Grand Duc), scarlet-edged yellow.
Pelican, new pure white, extra fine.

Medium. Moonbeam (Yellow Queen), pale primrose.
Thomas Moore, terra cotta.
White Hawk, pure white.
Chrysolora, golden yellow.
Ibis, rose and white.
Rising Sun, deep yellow.

Late.   De Wet, golden orange.
Diana, pure white.
Kohinoor, darkest red.

Very Late.   White Swan, pure white.
Rose Luisante, pink.
Couleur Cardinal, flaming scarlet.
Le Reve (Hobbema), old rose and buff.

Double Early.

Schoonoord, best white.
Vuurbaak, flaming scarlet.
Mr. Van der Hoef, golden yellow.
Peachblossom, pink, flushed white.

Cottage.

Early. Moonlight, canary yellow, tall, earliest.
Avis Kennicott, yellow, black base.
Inglescombe Pink (Salmon Queen), salmon
pink.

Medium. Picotee, white, margined rose.
Gesneriana spathulata (*G. major*), scarlet.
Hammar Hales, old rose and apricot.
Grenadier, flaming orange, most brilliant
of all.

Late. Zommerschoon, salmon rose and white.
Inglescombe Scarlet, bright vermilion.
Walter T. Ware, deep yellow.
Geseriana Lutea, glowing yellow.
Mrs. Moon, purest yellow, tall, very late.
(NOTE. The last three are all excellent
for planting with Darwins, which include no
yellows.)

Double Cottage.

Bleu Celeste, violet purple.
Yellow Rose, deep yellow.

Darwins.

Early. La Candeur (White Queen), pearl white.
Sophrosyne, silvery lilac rose.
Bartigon, deep carmine.
Spring Beauty, clear scarlet.
William Copland (Sweet Lavender), lav-
ender.

Medium.   Zwanenburg, pure white, black anthers.
Princess Elizabeth, clear deep pink.
Mr. Farncombe Sanders, deep cerise, white base.
Pride of Haarlem, deep purplish rose.
Rev. H. Ewbank, lavender violet.
La Tulipe Noire, "the black tulip."

Late.   Flamingo, soft shell pink.
Clara Butt, salmon pink.
Baronne de la Tonnaye, bright rose, lighter margin.
Afterglow (Katherine Havemeyer), orange-shaded old rose.
Dal Ongaro, pale lavender, shading to violet.

Rembrandts.

Victor Hugo, white, feathered carmine.
Eros, white-shaded lilac, striped rose.
Semele, white, feathered old rose.
Caracalla, white base, carmine flames; most striking.

Breeders.

Early.   Turenne (McMahon), brownish purple and yellow.
Heloise, reddish brown and plum.
Chester Jay Hunt, bluish purple, white base.
Coridion, pure yellow, with violet vein; most striking.

Medium.   Abd-el-Kadir, dark bronze, lighter margin.
Panorama (Fairy), orange mahogany, robust.
Indian Chief, copper, with purple shades.
Vulcan, ruddy apricot and buff, distinct.

Louis XIV, rich purple, bronze, and gold.

Bacchus, grape purple, white base.

Dom Pedro, dark mahogany, lighter edge, vigorous.

Old Times, yellow, shaded purple.

William the Silent, deep purple, extra tall and strong, new.

Late. Bronze Queen (Clio), golden bronze, yellow base.

Cardinal Manning (Goliath), wine red and bronze.

Lucifer, dark scarlet orange, light edge, yellow base; extra late.

Old Dutch (Bizarres and Bybloemens).

Bizarre. Black Boy, purplish brown, feathered clear yellow.

Le Duel, dark mahogany, flashed yellow.

Rose Bybloemen. Admiral Van Kingsbergen, deep rose, feathered white.

Perle Schaep, cream white, flamed rose.

Violet Bybloemen. Glory of Holland, pure white, feathered purple.

Amphion, rosy lilac, feathered yellow and white.

Parrot.

Fantasy, a "parrot" sport of Clara Butt, clear pink, strong stem, extra fine and distinct.

Cramoisie Brillant, carmine and black.

Lutea Major, yellow and crimson, green marks.

Perfecta, golden yellow, scarlet blotches.

Lily-Flowered.

Retroflexa superba, pure light yellow.

Sirene, bright cerise, paler at edges, white base.

Bunch-Flowered.

Mons. Mottet, ivory white; fine for cutting.

Mendel or Hybrids.

(Darwins and Cottage.)

Argo, deep golden yellow, edged orange.
Alaska, pure soft yellow, long pointed flower.
Dido, orange red, shading to yellow.
Carrara, purest white, most beautiful.

Species.

Most interesting additions to the tulip list, particularly for the rock garden. Not sold by all bulb dealers, but well worth looking up. All kinds below are offered in American catalogues. Unless otherwise noted, they bloom in May.

Acuminata (*cornuta*), scarlet and gold, laciniated, April, 16 inches.

Australis (*celsiana*), yellow brown shades.

Clusiana (the Lady Tulip), cherry red and white, very dainty, 8 inches.

Dasystemon, yellow and white, small, bunch-flowered, 3 to 4 inches.

Eichleri, large scarlet, with black and gold base, April, 12 inches.

Greigi Aurea, brilliant orange; reflexed; gorgeous; hot, dry location; April–May; 9 inches.

Kaufmanniana, cream, carmine, and yellow, extremely beautiful; for naturalizing; late March or early April; 9 inches.

Kaufmanniana varieties: Aurea, yellow and scarlet; Brilliant, scarlet, yellow center; Gaity, dwarf, white, red stripes.

Linifolia, old, but only recently offered in this country; tiny, brilliant scarlet; most effective; naturalizing; April–May; 6 inches.

Marjolleti, soft primrose and carmine, distinct; mid-May; 14 inches.

Oculus-solis, crimson, black center; early May; 14 inches.

Persica (*breyniana*), yellow and bronze, bunch-flowered, fragrant; very graceful; May; 6 inches.

Polychroma, violet and rose, very dainty; May; 8 inches.

Praestans, brilliant orange, bunch-flowered; late April; 14 inches.

Primulina, like Clusiana, but fawn and pink; 9 inches.

Sprengeri, bright orange scarlet; latest of all; flowering in June; 15 inches.

Sylvestris (*florentina odorata*), wild English tulip, yellow and bronze, somewhat fragrant.

Turkestanica, white and rose, yellow inside, twisted petals; six to ten flowers on a stem; early April; 6 to 10 inches.

Viridiflora Praecox, "the green tulip"; pale green, narrow petals; edged cream, April–May; 8 inches.

NOTE. Of the above the beginner will do well to try first the following: Kaufmanniana, the earliest tulip; Sprengeri, the latest; Clusiana, Florentina, and Greigi.

Fragrant Tulips.

Altogether too little attention has been given to the character of fragrance in tulips, possibly because they were so long considered primarily as a flower for bedding. Many varieties are as deliciously fragrant as any other flower which grows; and, fortunately, the fragrant varieties are to be found among several types. The following list, while by no means complete, will give a very good selection. So far as I am aware, it is the first list of fragrant sorts ever presented.

Early Singles.

De Wet; Prince of Austria; Proserpine; Thomas Moore; Yellow Prince; Goldfinch.

Cottage.

Miss Ellen Willmott; Orange King; La Merveille; Mrs. Moon; Dido (hybrid); Vitellina; Elegans; Yellow Rose (double).

Darwins and Breeders.

William Copland; Pride of Haarlem; Mattia; Dom Pedro.

Species.

Florentina odorata; Persica.

CHAPTER VII

DAFFODILS

DESPITE all that has been written and said on the subject, many beginners are still confused between the words "narcissus" and "daffodil." Let it be understood, at the outset, that the two are synonymous. Narcissi are daffodils, and daffodils are narcissi. Narcissus is the Latin word, and daffodil the English word for the same flower, including all its species and subspecies.

The confusion concerning these names has arisen from the fact that, merely through practice among gardeners, and in the "trade," the word narcissus has been used as applying to some types, and daffodils to others. This practice is, however, by no means standardized or uniform. With the increasing popularity of the daffodil in this country it is more than likely that an American Daffodil Society will be organized in the not distant future; then we may hope to have something done in the way of standardizing the terminology. At the present time, the best thing we can do is to follow the English system of classification, which is given later on in this chapter.

Like the tulip, the narcissus has been handed down to us from gardens immemorial. Its culture seems to have antedated the Greek legend of Narcissus, who, too greatly enamored of his own reflection in a stream, pined away and died. If his beauty was at all comparable to that of the flower which bears his name, it is quite possible to "psychoanalyze" his state of mind! The ancient Egyptians, who were very thoughtful for the comfort of their dead, gladdened the dark recesses of their tombs with narcissus flowers.

Notwithstanding its long historic lineage, however, the

63

daffodil's modern vogue is a matter of comparatively recent years; and while many of the original or natural species are still cultivated, as they well deserve to be, most of the varieties now found in the average garden are the result of the work of the hybridizers of the present generation. Only a few things from the hands of their immediate predecessors still hold their own.

This popularity of the daffodil is no passing whim of the garden public. It is easy to understand and will endure. No flower, bulbous or otherwise, has more to offer to the amateur. It will succeed under the greatest range of conditions; and at least moderate success is certain if it is given any kind of a chance. Moreover, the bulbs may be left in one place for years without lifting or digging, so that its culture is extremely simple. And with careful selection of varieties, the beautiful flowers may be enjoyed for a full two months, from late March until late May.

DAFFODILS FOR MANY USES

The variety of uses to which the daffodil may be put in garden making covers practically the entire range. It is preëminently the bulb of all bulbs—if not, indeed, the flower of all flowers—for "naturalizing." This form of planting, which is described on page 18, is fortunately becoming more popular in America. While daffodils, under the present enforced American production, will for some years to come probably be scarcer than they were under foreign importation, some varieties will still be available for this purpose. Also, as the bulbs in one's garden or flower bed will increase fairly rapidly under good care, naturalizing offers a very happy use for any surplus of the hardier varieties which may be accumulated. In the hardy border, daffodils are beautiful indeed. They present the feature of the flower display during early spring. With them, one need not worry about "color combinations," because all the varieties "go" perfectly with each other and with other flowers. In the mixed border, of course, the lower-grow-

Try to imagine this scene in color, in sunshine and shadow! Fortunate indeed is the gardener who possesses a bit of woods where daffodils may be naturalized.

Every morning, our little "Daffodil girl" made an inspection trip to get acquainted with the new varieties. (*Lower*) Three of the new giant trumpet super-giants—Olympia, VanWaveren's Giant, and Treserve.

ing varieties should be kept at the front, and taller ones to the center, or back. Some of the finest new things, under favorable conditions, will attain a height of well over two feet. For solid beds, for early masses of color, the daffodils are not used so generally as are tulips. Save for the expense of the bulbs, however, there is no reason why they should not be. Mixed with any of the early-flowering white or blue plants, they make a wonderful display. For the rock garden, the species and the dwarfer-growing garden varieties are not only ideal from a cultural point of view, but in habit and form of growth present a most pleasing contrast to the low growing, spreading, and trailing Alpine, and other rock-garden plants. For forcing also, many of the "daffs" are quite ideal. These are discussed in Chapter XVIII. As cut flowers from the open garden for decoration indoors, they last for a long time, and are beautiful either by themselves or combined with other flowers.

The beginner, in making his or her selection of daffodils for any of the purposes suggested above, will do well to include as many as possible of the different types. Do not select too many varieties of one type. Owing to the fact that they are so easily preserved from year to year, one's collection of daffodils can be very easily built up to satisfactory proportions by adding a few new things each season. Where the gardener is fortunate enough to number other daffodil enthusiasts among his garden acquaintances, it is an excellent plan to compare notes in making selections, so that as wide a variety as possible can be obtained. In the course of two or three years, there will be extra bulbs of each for "swapping." This exchange of material is not only an economical way of building up a collection, but is, in addition, one of the happiest of garden pleasures.

DAFFODIL TYPES

Unfortunately, we have not developed yet in this country any real daffodil shows such as are held in England and on the Continent. The nearest approach we have to them are the exhibits, mostly commercial, at the big spring flower shows. The educational value of the various flower shows, staged by the National Dahlia, Gladiolus, and other flower societies, is beyond estimate. It is to be hoped that the day is not far distant when we may have the same thing with daffodils.

In the meantime, the beginner who wishes to familiarize himself with the various types of daffodils will have to do the best he can by visiting gardens, and by studying books and catalogues. No printed word or photograph, however, can take the place of actually seeing the flowers themselves. The best way of all, of course, is to have them in one's own garden.

The classification given below was adopted by the Narcissus and Tulip Committee of the Royal Horticultural Society of England. Up to that time, the classification had been based on the size of the "trumpet" or "cup" of the flower, as Giant Trumpet, Medium Trumpet, and Small Trumpet, or Chalice Cup. This classification, however, was found to be insufficient and difficult, and the following was adopted in 1909.

CLASSIFICATION OF NARCISSUS

The central, cup-shaped part of the flower is called the "trumpet," the "crown," the "cup," the "chalice," or the "eye" of the flower, depending upon its shape and size. The petals are sometimes called the "perianth segments," the "perianth" being that part of the flower which joins the stem. The varieties mentioned in parentheses are well-known sorts typical of the several classes.

Division I.

Trumpet Daffodils: trumpet as long as or longer than petals.

A. Yellow Trumpet: all yellow (King Alfred).
B. White Trumpet: white petals, and white or nearly white trumpet (Mme. de Graaff).

C. Bicolor Trumpet: white petals and yellow trumpet (Spring Glory).

Division II.

Incomparable, or Large-cupped or "Star" Daffodils, the cup being less than the length of the petals, but at least one-third as long.

A. Petals yellow; cups with or without red (Sir Watkin).

B. Petals white; cups with or without red (Will Scarlet).

Division III.

Barri, or Short-cupped Daffodils, the cup being less than one-third as long as the petals.

A. Petals yellow, with or without red in the cups (Barri Conspicuus).

B. Petals white, cups yellow (Albatross).

Division IV.

Leedsi, large-cupped and short-cupped flowers with white petals, and cup white, cream, or primrose.

A. Similar to Incomparabilis, but with coloring as above (Lord Kitchener).

B. Similar to Barri, but with coloring as above (Queen of the North).

Division V.

Triandrus and *Triandrus Hybrids:* Cyclamen-flowered daffodils, with petals reflexed and flowers more or less drooping; dwarf growth and more graceful than the preceding. Some of the hybrids, however, are much like other types (Queen of Spain).

Division VI.

Cyclamineus and *Cyclamineus Hybrids:* reflexed petals and tubular yellow trumpets; dwarf growth; very early (February Gold).

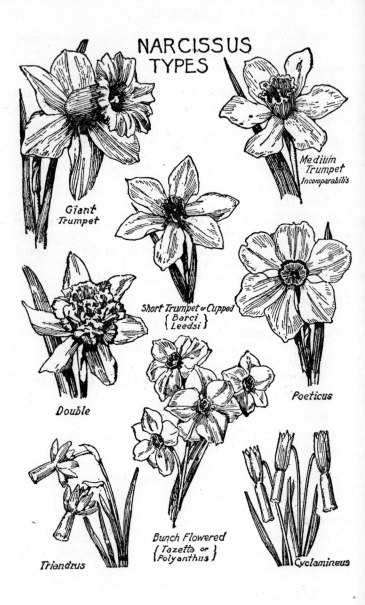

NARCISSUS
TYPES

Giant Trumpet

Medium Trumpet
Incomparabilis

Short Trumpet or Cupped
{ Barci
Leedsi }

Double

Poeticus

Triandrus

Bunch Flowered
{ Tazetta or
Polyanthus }

Cyclamineus

Division VII.

Jonquilla and *Jonquilla Hybrids:* clustered fragrant, small bright yellow flowers (Odorus Campanella; Buttercup).

Division VIII.

Tazetta and Tazetta Hybrids (Poetaz): the polyanthus or bunch-flowered daffodils, three or more flowers to each stem (Soleil d'Or, old Polyanthus type; Elvira, Polyanthus-Poeticus hybrid or Poetaz type).

Division IX.

Poeticus: snow-white petals; shallow cup or eye; yellow-edged crimson or scarlet (sometimes all crimson or scarlet), and sweetly scented: (Poeticus recurvus; King Edward VII [Almira]).

Division X.

Double Varieties: (Double Van Sion, double trumpet; Doubloon, double incomparabilis; Jonquilla flore pleno, Double Sweet Jonquil; Double Poeticus).

Division XI.

Various: including such miscellaneous minor species as Bulbocodium, or "Hoop-petticoat"; Gracilis; Minimus; mostly dwarf growing, early flowering, and particularly suited to the rock garden.

DAFFODILS FOR SPECIAL PURPOSES

As with tulips, the varieties of daffodils which the beginner will do best to invest money in will depend first of all upon the purpose for which they are to be used, and secondly upon personal taste in the form of flower, color, and so on.

In the mixed border, practically all of the hardy type can be used, and most of the species. This will exclude only the few tender and half-hardy sorts. It should be kept in mind, however, that the "white-blooded" or white-flowering forms of the trumpet daffodil (Class I-B, above) such as Mme. de Graaff and Alice Knights, are not so vigorous in growth as the yellows and the bicolors.

In solid beds, the yellow trumpet and the leedsi, barri, and poeticus type give the best effect, and are the most certain to grow satisfactorily.

For grouping among or against low-growing shrubs, practically all of the hardy types may be employed; but the tallest growing varieties will best answer the purpose.

For naturalization in grass or under trees the poeticus varieties, barri conspicuus, incomparabilis, Sir Watkin, and Autocrat, and the Trumpets, Golden Spur, Emperor, Empress, and King Alfred, are particularly good.

For the rock garden, use and make selections from the jonquils and jonquil hybrids, and also cyclamineus, bulbocodium, triandrus albus; to which may be added some of the small-growing trumpets such as minimus, lobularis, nana, and that little creamy white gem with naturally drooping blossoms, W. P. Milner; and the small golden Cervantes.

POINTS ON DAFFODIL CULTURE

While the cultural requirements of the daffodil are in general similar to those of the tulip and of other fall-planted bulbs, which have already been described, there are nevertheless some points which may be given particular attention.

Plant Early. To get the best results from your daffodil bulbs it is more important that they be got into the ground earlier than is the case with tulips. If you have your own bulbs for planting back, they may be put in as early as August. New stocks from the seed stores or bulb specialists are usually not received until September. But the planting should, if possible, be completed before the end of September, or early in October at the latest. Two years ago I had occasion to plant some bulbs of several varieties quite late in the season. They were planted in the same field and under exactly the same conditions as other bulbs of the same sorts planted about three weeks earlier. The result was illuminating. The late-planted bulbs made hardly more than half the volume of foliage and length of flower stalk which the earlier planting produced, although the late-planted bulbs were, if anything, even better than the others. Both had come from the same Holland grower. It was difficult to convince many people who saw them that the varieties were the same. The poeticus type, particularly should be planted as early as possible, as it is their nature to begin to make their new roots in the soil almost as soon as the bulbs have thoroughly dried and become dormant after the spring's growth. They start the formation of new roots almost as persistently as onions in a moist place.

In planting, don't be afraid to cover your daffodils too deeply. Most beginners err in the other direction. There should be a good four inches of soil above the shoulder of the bulb; and varieties which are inclined to form a long, tapering top or "neck," such as some of the incomparabilis and poeticus sorts, may go even an inch or two deeper, unless the bulbs themselves are smaller than the average. Ordinarily, the bulbs are placed four or five inches apart, but where they are to be used in groups, in the border, they will make a more pleasing effect, particularly the first season, if placed about three inches apart.

Winter Mulching. While most varieties will come through all right without a winter covering, two or three inches of light manure may well be put over the beds containing any choice or expensive sorts. In addition to the protection from alternate freezing and thawing, rain will carry the fertilizing elements from the manure to the roots. The mulch should, of course, be removed as growth starts in the spring.

Cultivate. Shallow cultivation in the spring and the removal of any weeds which may be starting are desirable, but care should be exercised not to cut or bruise the foliage. If extra choice flowers are wanted, an application of fine ground bone and tankage may be made, or liquid manure applied when the foliage is a few inches tall, and again just before the buds begin to develop.

Do not Cut the Foliage. If blooms are wanted, they should be removed just as the buds begin to open, carefully cutting the flower stalk at the surface, but without removing any of the foliage. If foliage is desired, it is a good plan to grow some cheap variety just for this purpose. All flowers should be removed, cutting them off at the top, as soon as they begin to wither.

After the flowers have perished, every reasonable effort should be made to keep the plants growing vigorously and for as long a time as possible. I always work a dressing of bone meal into the soil as soon as the blooms have gone by, and if a "dry spell" is encountered, as is quite likely to be the case at this time of the year, I give one or two thorough irrigatings. If the bulbs are neglected and the ground allowed to bake hard after flowering, the plants will not have the opportunity to make the normal growth which is essential if fine blooms are to be expected another year. The plants should by all means be left undisturbed where they have flowered, if possible. If it is absolutely necessary to remove them, to use the space for something else, take them up with a fork, when the ground is moist, with as much soil and as little damage to the roots as possible. They will not, like many other plants, make a quick, new root growth after shifting to carry them along.

Lifting. As soon as the tops have turned yellow, they begin to die down. The bulbs, if they are not to be left in their positions for another season, should be taken up in a short time after this, as otherwise a new root development may be started, particularly if a hot, dry period is followed by rainy weather. Get them out without delay, or else leave them alone. Personally, I prefer a short-handled, flat-tined potato hook to the ordinary digging fork for getting the bulbs out of the ground; but without the "knack" which experience gives in using one of these, a fork, perhaps, would be safer.

Separating the Bulbs. After the newly harvested bulbs have been dried and stored, as described on page 43, they will be ready for going over and being cleaned and separated. Remove only the small-sized bulbs or "splits" which come off easily almost at a touch; never pry or tear off those which still firmly adhere to the old or "mother" bulb, after drying. For further information on this point, see Chapter XX, which deals with Propagation.

VARIETIES OF DAFFODILS

It is quite likely that, for a few years to come, the list of varieties available, with American production, will be somewhat limited. It is equally certain, however, that it is only a matter of time when all the best of the finer new things from abroad will be avaliable to American gardeners. In all probability, also, the production of new varieties will be undertaken by American hybridizers. We cannot, however, look for such quick results as we have had with gladiolus, dahlias, and other things of that sort. As it takes many years to work up a commercial stock of a new variety of daffodil, even after the variety itself has been obtained, patience is a virtue which the daffodil hybridizer must develop to a degree. The daffodil "specialists" are, however, beginning to appear, and one may look to them for many varieties not available through the ordinary trade channels where they were obtainable in the past.

DAFFODILS

(Refer to classification, page 66, for general description)

Giant Trumpets.

Yellow.

King Alfred, very tall, deeply frilled; best all round sort.

Golden Spur, fine extra early.

Cervantes, small, but earliest of all.

Emperor, very good; excellent for naturalizing.

Van Waveren's Giant, Tresserve, and Olympia are three of the newer giant sorts, much larger even than King Alfred; all of lighter yellow color, representing a distinct new type.

White.

Alice Knights, medium size, earliest.

Mme. de Graaff, trumpet pale primrose, the standard, extra fine.

Mrs. Robert Sydenham, both petals and trumpet pure white.

Mrs. H. D. Betteridge, trumpet wide and fluted; very refined.

W. P. Milner, small and dainty, and Moschatus of Harworth, "The White Daffodil of the Pyrenees," are the best whites for naturalizing.

Pink. A distinct new type, with rosy or pink shading, and as yet very scarce.

Mrs. R. O. Backhouse, "the pink daffodil."

Lovenest, trumpet pure white, flushed pink.

Bicolor.

Spring Glory, extra fine, early.

Duke of Bedford, pure white and soft yellow, extra early.

Empress, standard bicolor, better than Victoria.

Mrs. Walter T. Ware, very long lasting flowers, sulphur white trumpet.

Robert Sydenham and Remembrance are newer "giant" bicolors, still quite scarce.

Incomparabilis.

Sir Watkin, very fine and always satisfactory, is the standard yellow-petaled variety.

Homespun, very free flowering, a honey-yellow gem.

Autocrat, extra fine all yellow.

Crœsus, very large frilled flower, new.

Lucifer, with glowing orange red cup, one of the best known of the white-petaled sorts.

Will Scarlet has large wide flower and fiery red cup.

Bernardino, fluted cup, stained deep orange, is exceptionally beautiful.

Gallipoli, Red Cross, and Great Warley are three wonderful new varieties, the latter with clear yellow crown an inch and a half across; all still scarce.

Barri.

Conspicuus, old but as popular as ever, is the standard yellow-petaled sort.

Brilliancy, very large, deep gold petals, and golden cup.

Nannie Nunn, rounded petals, with vermilion cup, edged red.

Seagull is one of the best known of the white-petaled varieties.

Albatross, very tall, *"floating" above the foliage*, has a frilled, orange-edged cup.

Sunrise is distinct, with a primrose bar down each petal.

Leedsi.

Lord Kitchener, giant flower with large pale primrose crown, with fluted edge.

Mrs. Langtry, white cup, edged yellow.

Evangeline, pure white with lemon yellow cup.

Sirdar, very tall and striking, cream-colored, frilled crown.

Sir E. Carson, pure white with salmon rose cup.

St. Olaf, four-inch flower, with cup more than an inch wide, with sulphur yellow fluted margin.

Czarina, giant flower on tall stem, five inches across, with twisted petals and citron crown an inch and a half deep; is one of the finest new varieties. Mrs. Francis King, pure white, is another.

Triandrus—Hybrids.

Queen of Spain, delicate canary yellow, most distinct and graceful; excellent for naturalizing.

Albus, the "Angel's Tears Daffodil"; a cluster of small creamy white flowers on a slender stem, grows but six to eight inches tall.

Calathinus; the flowers are twice the size of Albus; two or three to a stem, drooping; extremely pretty for rockery.

Cyclamineus and Cyclamineus Hybrids.

Nanus, the yellow cyclamen-flowered daffodil; little gem for naturalizing in damp, peaty soil, in semi-shade; six inches tall, and the earliest of all to bloom.

March Sunshine, golden yellow and very free flowering.

February Gold, a fine companion to the preceding.

Jonquils and Jonquil Hybrids.

Single Sweet-Scented Jonquil, the old fragrant yellow favorite.

Odorus Campernelle rugulosus maximus, a terrible name, but a beautiful flower, rich deep yellow, nearly twice as large as the old rugulosus.

Buttercup, an Emperor × Jonquilla cross, broad stiff petals, slightly reflexed and fine color.

Golden Scepter, a Monarch × Jonquilla cross; deep color; very free flowering and fragrant.

Tazetta and Tazetta Hybrids (Poetaz).

Polyanthus type.

Grand Monarque, white, citron cup.

Grand Soleil d'Or, yellow orange cup.

Grand Primo, primrose, light orange cup.

Poetaz type.

Aspasia, pure white, yellow cup, very tall.

Elvira, fine white flowers with yellow, orange-edged cup, fragrant.

Laurens Koster, white, deep yellow cup.

Admiration, sulphur yellow petals, and cup with scarlet rim.

Poeticus.

Ornatus, pure glistening white, with yellow cup, rimmed scarlet, early.

Recurvus (Pheasant's Eye), pure white with deep orange-red cup; the finest of all daffodils for naturalizing; very late.

Glory of Lisse, an improved form of Ornatus.

Almira (King Edward VII), snow white with canary-yellow cup, rimmed red; extra large and tall; one of the finest Poets.

Epic, one of the largest and finest.

Horace, especially beautiful; purest white with dark red cup.

Homer, scarlet cup; very late.

Firetail, creamy white with broad cup, deep red to bottom; extra fine but still scarce.

Double.

Von Sion (*telamonius plenus*), the old "double yellow"; not a good variety for America, as it opens irregularly and half green in many sections.

Argent, a cross between the above and Poeticus ornatus, is a reliable sort; creamy white with yellow petals.

Doubloon, deep yellow, shaded orange, is an extremely free flowering, handsome yellow double.

The Pearl is similar, but cream colored.

Golden Phœnix, golden yellow, is very fine.

Mary Copland, new, is pure white, splashed with scarlet petals, most distinct and effective.

Twink is similar, sulphur yellow and bright orange.

There are double forms of Jonquila, Campernelle, and Poeticus.

CHAPTER VIII

HYACINTHS

The very name, with all that it suggests, with its connotation of delicious fragrance, is in itself "a little poem of completeness."

Unfortunately, in some respects, perhaps, when the hyacinth began to be "developed," the bulb "vogue" being for design bedding, the patient and painstaking Dutch bulb growers were led to "create" a flower which would be ideal for this purpose—short, stocky, absolutely uniform and formal; far removed, probably, from the flower which the singing tent maker of Persia had in mind when he wrote:

> I sometimes think that never blows so red
> The Rose as where some buried Cæsar bled;
> That every Hyacinth the Garden wears
> Dropt in her Lap from some once lovely Head.

For many years the Dutch breeders discarded entirely the double hyacinth. The double form was developed quite accidentally, and then became quite "the rage" for a period. During the last few decades, however, the single-flowered varieties have again become more popular.

For those who like solid beds of color, or design beds, they make ideal material. Because of this fact, however, and unfortunately, many gardeners are prejudiced against them. It is the misfortune and not the fault of hyacinths that they are thus condemned.

As a matter of fact, hyacinths, if given a chance in the creation of your garden, will surprise you with many of the most lovely and charming effects. They do not *have* to be planted in straight and formal rows or circular beds. Use them in small groups, in the mixed bulb border; in

78

See what hyacinths will do for you when you give them the opportunity! Don't feel that you must crowd them in tight in a bed of geometric design.

A few of the less known, but not less beautiful, early spring flowers. (*Left*) The checkered lily (*fritillaria meleagris*). (*Center*) The delicately graceful snowdrop (*galanthus*). (*Right*) The curious and extremely graceful decorative feather hyacinth (*hyacinthus plumosa*).

larger, irregular patches against early low-growing shrubs or in among the evergreens; in the foundation planting around the house, and see what they will do for you! Where, in the composition of a more formal garden, a real mass of color is wanted early in the spring, no other flower is quite equal to the hyacinth. If you were among the thousands of visitors who saw the wonderfully charming formal bulb garden which comprised Mr. John Scheeper's exhibit at the spring flower shows in New York and Cleveland, two years ago, you will not be likely to forget how effective was the bed of lavender blue Grand Maitre which surrounded the tranquil little pool that formed the center of the picture. But—and what an important "but" it is!— how different would have been the effect of those same flowers, mixed with another color, and stuck out in a round bed in the center of an otherwise beautiful lawn! In the first instance they were in harmony with their surroundings; in the other they would not have been. It is not the amount of money that is spent for planting material, but the amount of brains that goes into the planning of the planting, which determines the real value of the result in the garden picture!

Whether hyacinths are planted in beds by themselves or in small groups in the mixed border, and even though care may be taken to select those varieties which are not stiff and ungraceful in their habit of growth, they will almost always be greatly improved by having mixed in with them other spring-blooming plants. We prize them, after all, for their rare color and delicious fragrance rather than, or perhaps in spite of, their form!

Most of the early-flowering plants which have already been mentioned for use in bulb beds may be planted among the hyacinths. Those which are rather loose and graceful in form will give the prettiest effect. Some thought, of course, should be given to color combinations; for instance, a blue hyacinth such as Grand Maitre, interspersed with some white flower such as Arabis, or with potted plants of annual sweet alyssum. The hyacinth bulbs may be set from nine to twelve inches apart, if they are to be interplanted; and the saving on the bulbs will usually pay for the other plants.

TYPES OR "GRADES" OF HYACINTHS

Among hyacinths, there is not such an endless multiplication of types and varieties to confound the beginner, as is the case with tulips and with daffodils. Nevertheless, he is often confused by the catalogue listings of "Exhibition," "Bedding," "Dutch Roman," and "Miniatures." These are not, in fact, different types at all, but represent merely different sizes or ages of bulbs, or those which have received some special form of treatment in their culture or "curing." The varieties are exactly the same, but there is a very considerable difference in the size of the flower head, and some difference in the density of the spike. Personally, I always prefer the smaller or more open spike to the enormous very dense one. The former look like real flowers, the others give much the impression of being artificial; but they naturally appeal to those who consider that size is the greatest merit which any flower can possess.

"Exhibition" hyacinths are the largest bulbs. They are sometimes described as "mother bulbs" or as "top root" bulbs. Most of the American catalogues do not specify the exact size, but a few do; then you can tell exactly what you are getting. Exhibition bulbs should measure 19 to 20 centimeters (2½ inches) in diameter or even larger. They are particularly suitable for forcing in pots or bulb pans for show purposes. They will bloom equally well out of doors, but are likely to be top-heavy and easily beaten down by rain or wind. Naturally, they are the most expensive grade of hyacinth to buy.

"Bedding hyacinths" are smaller bulbs, but should give the best results and a uniform effect; they should run 17 or 18 centimeters (2¼ inches) in diameter. They are often sold "to color" instead of in named varieties; but it is always best to pay the slightly higher prices which named varieties command, because if you buy by color only you will get several different shades and a variation in type of flower and in season of bloom, which will produce a very unsatisfactory effect, either in solid beds or in small groups.

"Miniature hyacinths," also called "Dutch Roman," are still smaller. They should measure 14 to 15 centimeters (just under 2 inches); they are younger bulbs (usually three years old), and are quite ideal for forcing for home use, being easily grown and producing flower spikes which have smaller bells and a more open habit of growth than the larger sizes. (For suggestions concerning growing indoors see Chapter XVIII.)

French Roman hyacinths are of about the same size as the Miniatures or Dutch Roman, but are of a distinctly different type. They are produced in France, instead of in Holland, and flower considerably earlier. The individual flowers are smaller, but each bulb will "throw" several spikes of bloom. The flowers are dainty, and the fragrance, while delicate, is most delicious. The white variety is the one ordinarily used and is the most reliable, but the rose and blue shades are also available.

"Prepared" hyacinths, which are sometimes described as "treated," are used exclusively for forcing. The ripening process of the bulb is hastened by special treatment so that they will flower considerably earlier. I have grown them and have found the claims made for them in every way substantiated, but the special early flowering is of more value to the commercial florist, who wishes to bring them in in time for Christmas. Naturally they cost considerably more than the ordinary bulbs.

"Prepared Miniatures," however, are quite reasonable in price, costing about twenty cents apiece, and a pan of these coming into flower makes an out of the ordinary, most attractive decoration, and a charming Christmas present.

Jacinthes de Paris are the daintiest of all; somewhat similar to the Roman hyacinths, but quite distinct. Like the Roman hyacinths, they are not hardy save in the milder sections.

HYACINTH CULTURE

From the legend connected with its name, one might assume the hyacinth to be a water-loving plant. To the extent that an abundance of moisture is essential to develop it to its best, it is; but nevertheless hyacinth bulbs are less tolerant of water standing in the soil about them than almost any other bulb except certain of the hardy lilies. Good drainage, or rather *extra* good drainage, is, therefore, the first requisite for the growing of good hyacinths. If your soil is naturally somewhat low and wet, it will be safest to plant them either in a raised bed or on a slope. For other suggestions, read again that part of Chapter IV, Making the Bulb Garden, which deals with the subject.

Hyacinths prefer a sunny situation; the sunnier the better they will like it. A really shaded situation should be avoided if at all possible. Protection from beating winds and storm, if it may be provided, is desirable, particularly if large-sized bulbs are planted.

A comparatively light soil best suits the hyacinth— lighter than it is necessary to have for perennials and for most other bulbs. If your soil is of the clay type, or even a "heavy loam," add plenty of sand or sifted coal ashes where the hyacinths are to be planted. Humus or peat they take to very kindly, as these materials are great moisture holders. While hyacinths prefer a rather light soil, it can hardly be made too rich. But as the flowers are much deeper rooting than most other bulbs, any plant food which is added should be kept well below the surface. Where it is not too much trouble, an excellent plan is to dig out eight or ten inches of soil, put it to one side, and then to mix thoroughly with the soil below this well-rotted cow manure. Such treatment, if bone meal be added also, makes an ideal preparation for the hyacinth bed. Put a layer of sand on top of this, place the bulbs in position, and refill the bed with soil, adding plenty of humus and peat, and you can look forward to splendid results from your hyacinth bulbs for years to come. Where it is not possible to do the work as thoroughly as this, dig the soil as deeply as possible, adding humus or peat.

Cover the bulb deep—four, five, or six inches, according to the size of the bulb, is none too much in light soil.

Early planting is of no particular advantage. Late September or early October is the best time. Following planting, however, the soil should, if possible, be kept thoroughly moist, so that the root system will be developed before freezing weather. After the ground freezes, the bulbs should be mulched. Dutch peat, humus, or coconut fiber are all good for this purpose; although, of the three, I prefer the latter. In beds where other flowers are planted in the fall between the hyacinth bulbs, some lighter material, such as leaves or hay, can be used. In this case, the mulch must be removed in the spring; otherwise, it will not be necessary.

The tops of the flower heads should be removed as they fade, and if it is necessary to lift the bulbs after blooming, take them up with as much soil as is possible, and keep them well watered and partially shaded until they have recovered from the moving. If the bulbs can be left where they are, which is the preferable way, give the bed a good top-dressing with thoroughly rotted, sifted cow manure, or stable manure, and bone meal. Work this into the soil with a small, narrow fork as deep as it is possible to get it without injuring the bulbs. It may be applied just after the flowers are removed; or, if other flowers are being grown between the plants, at any time between then and September, when the beds will be bare.

Harvesting or "lifting" hyacinth bulbs is managed in much the same way as for tulips or for daffodils; but they should be given, if anything, more care, as they are softer and more prone to "sweating" after being stored. Take them up after the foliage turns thoroughly yellow, twist off the leaves, and store them only one layer deep, or, better, upside down on a piece of chicken wire. If a vacant frame is available they may be laid in that, covered with two or three inches of *dry* soil, and allowed to cure—with the glass on, but raised for ventilation—for fifteen or twenty days before being stored; this extra curing is especially desirable if a wet spell has preceded the time of harvesting.

VARIETIES

There is really much more variation in the varieties of hyacinths than the catalogue descriptions might lead one to suppose. The colors are, for the most part, clear and charming, and any one to whom color *tones* mean as much as the colors themselves will find a wide field for choice. There is also a considerable range in the "density" or shape of the flower spikes. To the beginner with hyacinths, I would suggest that, for the first season or two, every reasonable effort should be made to become familiar with as many different varieties as possible, either by visiting the exhibits at the spring flower shows, or, better still, gardens or bulb-testing grounds; or by buying for his own garden a few bulbs each of several different varieties. Then, when he has been able to select the things which particularly appeal to his own taste, he can plan a restricted list. As with most other bulbs, it is possible to stretch the season of bloom over a much longer period than is usually enjoyed, by selecting early-, medium-, and late-blooming sorts. In making up the following lists and suggestions, I have given particular attention to this point.

DUTCH HYACINTHS (*Hyacinthus orientalis*)
Singles.
> *White.*
>> L'Innocence, pure white, very *early*.
>> Hein Rozen, loose spike, large bells, pure white, *early*.
>> Queen of the Whites, extra large bells, pure white, *early*.
>> La Grandesse, fine, pure color, extra fine, *late*.

Rose.

　Lady Derby, clear rose pink, extra fine, *early.*
　General De Wet, soft light pink, *medium.*
　Queen of the Pinks, clear rose pink, large bells, *late.*

Red.

　Nimrod, deep rose, *extra early.*
　La Victoire (Victory), rosy red, *early.*
　Marconi, bright rose pink, *medium.*
　Roi des Belges, crimson scarlet, *medium.*
　Etna, dark rose, *extremely late.*

Pale Blue.

　Schotel, soft light blue, large bells, *early.*
　Dr. Leibler, pale lavender, *medium.*
　Lord Derby, small flowers but extra fine, *late.*
　Queen of the Blues, bright porcelain, *late.*

Dark Blue.

　Grand Maitre, dark porcelain blue, extra fine, *medium.*
　Menelik, entirely dark, the best "black," *medium.*
　King of the Blues, *extra late.*

Yellow.

　Yellow Hammer, creamy yellow, *early.*
　Buff Beauty, one of the most artistic, pale yellow, narrow spikes, *medium.*
　Orange Boven, pale salmon, distinct in both color and form, *late.*
　City of Haarlem, best pure yellow, *late.*

Doubles.

　Double La Grandesse, pure white.
　Chestnut Flower (*Kastanjebloem*), bright rose.
　Prince of Orange, rose, *early.*
　Bloksberg, porcelain blue.
　Garrick, dark lavender.
　Sunflower, yellow.

CHAPTER IX

OTHER SPRING-FLOWERING BULBS

WE American gardeners are rather prone to concentrate on one thing. If we are dahlia, gladiolus, peony, or rose "fans," the chances are that other flowers will receive scant consideration at our hands. We have not yet learned as fully as they have on "the other side" to be gardeners first, and hobbyists afterward.

Making a specialty of one flower, becoming expert in its culture, and an enthusiastic collector of old and new varieties is, without question, one of the most exciting, thrilling, and pleasurable ways in which to garden. No matter how enthusiastic we may be about our favorite flower, however, there is no excuse or reason for ignoring everything else. Who does not know the "dahlia bug," for instance, in whose garden(?) you will find not a single timid blossom of any sort peeping forth from April to July, and where, after the first sharp frost, there is a relapse again to barrenness? And who would attempt to maintain that such a person, no matter how enthusiastic and skillful he may be with his hobby, gets as much pleasure as the owner of a real garden, to which the circling seasons bring their gifts of beauty, one after another, no matter on how small a scale the stage may be set?

If you happen to be one of these single-track specialists, get out of the rut! You can do it without in the least neglecting your chosen flower, and your garden pleasures may be multiplied ten or a hundredfold. I know it, because I have so often seen this same thing happen; sometimes, I have been so fortunate as to have had a hand in bringing it about, and never yet have I seen the one-flower hobbyist return to one flower, once he or she had been induced to try other things.

What has all this to do with "other spring-flowering bulbs"?

It has a great deal. It is this regrettable tendency toward lopsided gardening which has been responsible for the undeserved neglect which so many of the less well-known spring-flowering bulbs receive in American gardens. And they have been neglected, not merely by the one-flower gardener, but to a great extent, also, by the amateur who has learned the enjoyment which tulips and daffodils bring so generously through the weeks of early spring. To any such gardener, who is ready to take up and follow new suggestions, this chapter holds the key to as many worth-while new garden opportunities as any other in the book.

A WIDE RANGE OF BEAUTY IN THE SPRING BULB GARDEN

If for no other reason than for their extreme hardiness and the fact that, once planted, they practically take care of themselves for years, many of the less well-known spring-flowering bulbs have a just claim for a position in every garden. Add to this, however, the fact that many of them bloom even before the earliest of the ordinary daffodils, and long before the tulips; and the further fact that most of them possess a rare and graceful beauty even though they may not be enormous in size; and on top of this, their very moderate cost, a fraction of what the larger bulbs command; and it becomes difficult to understand why they have remained obscure so far as the general public is concerned. The different species and varieties make it possible to enjoy their flowers from earliest April or March—sometimes even February!—until early summer. The range of colors available is also all that any one might desire.

In the following pages, the various lesser spring-flowering bulbs will be discussed in several groups: crocuses, the "minor bulbs," and hardy bulbous spring plants. For the purpose of conserving space, the cultural directions are necessarily condensed as much as possible.

CROCUS

Next to tulips, daffodils, and hyacinths, the crocuses are undoubtedly the best known of the spring bulbs.

While they are widely known, however, they are not well known. The average person, even the amateur gardener, thinks of crocuses merely as gay but rather gaudy-colored flowers to be naturalized in the lawn, where they will give a bit of spring cheer; but, later on, be most annoyingly in the way of cutting the grass when it should be cut. Naturalized under proper conditions, where they will *look* natural, crocuses are decidedly attractive; but there are other and better ways of using them than to spot them here and there in the lawn, where they decidedly do not look natural.

On the small place, there are three quite distinct ways of using them, all easily employed and all charming in effect. The first is to plant them in broad, irregular groups well toward the front of the mixed border; for this purpose, at least twenty-five bulbs should be used in a place. The second is to naturalize them in patches or "drifts" under or at the edge of trees, or along the front of the shrubbery border, with stray bulbs running out into the grass; here a hundred or more bulbs should be used in one place, and the number of varieties should be resolutely held down. The third method is to use them for narrow edging or "ribbons" for borders or beds; for this purpose, it is best to plant them in a broad, somewhat irregular row, three or four inches wide, rather than in a severely straight, narrow line. When crocuses are used in this way, that excellent little edging plant, the white dwarf Stonecrop (*sedum album*), makes an ideal thing to combine with them. It flowers after the crocuses are gone, and its foliage is attractive during the balance of the season, turning to a pleasing coppery bronze in the autumn; in addition to which it affords protection to the crocus bulbs during both summer and winter.

For larger and more pretentious places, crocuses may, in addition to the suggestions given above, well be used by the thousand for naturalizing; they are particularly effective on sloping banks.

So far we have been speaking only of the "Dutch crocuses" which are the ones most commonly known and ordinarily offered. From a few bulb specialists, and through the more energetic bulb dealers, there are available a number of the "wild crocuses" or crocus species. These, for the most part, have smaller flowers, but bloom very much earlier—some of them, in fact, almost forcing themselves up through the snow; they are most graceful in habit and form, and are, if anything, hardier and longer lasting than the Dutch crocuses when used for naturalizing, for which purpose they are quite ideal. They are also among the choicest of all plants to use for the rockery, for the rock garden, or any picturesque gardening of a similar type. (For suggestions concerning varieties of crocus, see the list on page 91.)

The *autumn-flowering crocuses* are still another group entirely distinct from any of the foregoing; there are several species, all different from the spring-flowering sorts in that the flowers are produced before the leaves. The bulbs should be planted as early as possible, July or early August. The flowers will appear a few weeks later, but the foliage and the seed pods do not develop usually until the following spring. Except for the necessity of extra early planting, their culture is similar to that of the other sorts.

POINTERS ON CROCUS CULTURE

While growing satisfactorily in a wide range of soils, crocuses prefer, like hyacinths, a rather light sandy soil thoroughly well enriched. The wild varieties, or species, both spring and autumn flowering, particularly like a sandy or gritty, thoroughly drained soil. Unlike hyacinths, they will do equally well in full sun or in rather heavy shade; they bloom earlier, of course, in sheltered nooks, and by planting some bulbs in such a location, and others of the same variety in shade or a northern exposure, the season of bloom may be considerably lengthened.

Plant crocuses in early September or October, covering the bulbs a full three inches deep, and place them about three inches apart.

As the bulbs have a natural tendency to work up out of the soil, mulching is desirable to keep them from alternate freezing and thawing, which increases the danger of their doing this. The mulch should not be applied, however, until after the ground has frozen, as it may make a harboring place for mice, and these little rodents are particularly fond of crocus bulbs.

Planted deep in soil that is not too wet nor too heavy, the crocuses will establish themselves, and may be left for many years undisturbed. If, at the end of three or four years, the bulbs have worked up too near the surface of the soil, or the tops have begun to crowd, they may easily be lifted, after the foliage dies, dried off, sorted, and replanted later, in the same way as tulip bulbs. The crocus, like the gladiolus, forms the new bulb on top of the old, which tends to bring them near the surface of the soil each year; but in light soils, the long anchor roots which they send down will keep them in place, if they are protected from frost action. Often they seed freely, and it is not difficult to grow them from seed. (See Chapter XX.)

SOME GOOD CROCUSES

White.

    Kathleen Parlow.

    King of the Whites.

    Tilly Koenen, pure white with bright orange anthers; striking.

Blue and Purple.

Baron von Brunow, dark mauve.
Maximilian, pure porcelain blue.
Purpurea grandiflora, purple.
Harbinger of Spring, dark purple, extra early.
Julia Culp, purple-blue, extra late.

Yellow.

Grand Yellow (Large Yellow), pure golden yellow.

Striped.

Pearl, white-shaded lilac, early.
Mme. Mina, grayish violet, striped purple, early.
Albion, blue-striped purple.
Sir Walter Scott, white and pale lavender.
Pallas, white with fine lavender stripes and orange
    anthers; extra fine.

Species.

Spring flowering.

Imperati, mauve with fawn on outer petals.
Sieberi, lavender, with most striking orange anthers.
Susianus, pure deep yellow, shaded brown outside;
    extra fine.
Tommasinianus, mauve to richest purple; very vig-
    orous.

Autumn flowering.

Sativus (the Saffron Crocus), deep lilac, with lighter
    shadings and orange stigma.
Speciosus, violet blue, with yellow throat and orange-
    red anthers; most attractive, and good for natural-
    izing.
S. Albus, white form of above.
S. Artabir, pale blue, with dark stripes.
S. Aitchisoni, unique shape, having pointed petals;
    lavender, with darker shades and silver sheen;
    extremely late.

Zonatus, lilac rose, with yellow and orange center "zones"; most striking.

THE MINOR SPRING-FLOWERING BULBS

Grape-hyacinths, Snowdrops, Scillas, and the like

The so-called "minor bulbs" comprise a group of half a dozen or so spring-flowering bulbs, the supply of which comes mostly from Holland, although a few are now being grown commercially in this country. This group includes chionodoxa (Glory-of-the-Snow), eranthis (Winter-Aconite), fritillarias ("Crown Imperials," and Trout Lilies), galanthus (Snowdrops), leucojum (Snowflakes), muscari (Grape-hyacinths), and scillas (wood hyacinths, and bluebells).

We may be thankful that the Federal Horticulture Board, which had at first expected to include all of these bulbs under the quarantine which prevents the further importation of daffodils, finally decided that it was not necessary to do so, with the result that a full supply is still available from the customary sources of production.

The phrase "minor bulbs" is a trade term and refers to their importance in the bulb trade and in no way to their merits as plants. It is true that most of them are also "minor" in size as compared with the larger-flowering Dutch bulbs, such as daffodils and tulips; but they are not minor in beauty. If the narcissus quarantine results in our becoming better acquainted with these less-known spring-flowering bulbs, it will, to that extent at least, have been a blessing in disguise to American gardens. I will never forget the thrilling surprises I received from my first plantings of these minor bulbs! Infinitely more graceful than hyacinths, tulips, or even than most of the daffodils, their brilliant colors lend to the spring garden that cheer and intense enjoyment which none of the season's later flowers can possibly bring. The minor bulbs have remained without the recognition which they really merit, chiefly because they mean less in profit to the bulb dealer, and consequently have been given comparatively little space in the catalogues. In addition to their rare and charming beauty, however, they possess two distinct advantages: the first is their extreme hardiness and ease of culture; the second, their very reasonable price.

All the bulbs above mentioned are extremely hardy and may be left undisturbed for years, becoming more beautiful each spring, as the "colonies" increase in size. They are therefore quite ideal for naturalizing, and for planting in a rock garden or other permanent and informal use. They are delightful, too, in small clumps in front of shrubbery or low evergreens, or scattered here and there irregularly along the edge of the mixed bulb border or perennial border. Many of them, once established, will remain not merely for years, but for generations, and a number of them self-sow from seed, as well as making new bulbs; so that a very moderate original investment in these little gems is almost sure to yield dividends at compound interest.

IN THE SHADOWS OF THE SNOWDRIFTS

Another characteristic which endears several of the minor bulbs to the heart of any one who has ever grown them is their extreme earliness. We are wont to think of the crocuses, which "woo the nipping air in loveliness," as among the earliest of spring's bright harbingers. But long before they dare to venture forth, some of these others have pushed up through the chill, icily cold soil to flaunt their frail banners against the still unconquered battalions of winter. Add to your collection at least two or three of these extra early things; plant them in some sunny, sheltered nook, where they can unlock for you the gates of spring, days or even weeks sooner than you have been expecting to get your first peep through them.

Bulbocodium. The bulbocodium, otherwise known as the spring Colchicum, has cheery little rosy purple flowers, valuable from the fact that they bloom two weeks before the crocuses. It seeds well under ordinary conditions, and in grass. Vernum is the standard variety.

Chionodoxa (*Glory-of-the-Snow*). The chionodoxas attain a height of eighteen inches or so, and are excellent for edging as well as for massing or naturalizing, and for the rockery. The charming little star-shaped flowers are borne in clusters; the earliest variety to bloom is Sardensis, which the late Rev. Joseph Jacob, who wrote so delightfully of bulbs, called "the first real blue flower of another year." Luciliae, which is, perhaps, the most popular variety, is a lighter blue with a conspicuous white eye or center, and comes on a bit later. There is now a pure white form of this variety, Luciliae alba. Gigantea, a large-flowering variety of Luciliae, is also blue and white and blooms still later. It thrives well in any good garden soil, and in sun or half shade, or partial shade. Plant three or four inches deep, and from two to three inches apart. The flowers will not begin to show at their best until the planting has been established two or three years, but even the first spring's display will be full reward for the slight expense and trouble necessary.

Eranthis (*Winter-Aconite*). Eranthis hymenalis is not a large flower, but is well worth including in the spring-flower collection because of its extreme earliness; and also it contributes a bright, clear yellow to contrast with the colors of the other early bulbs. It has two other advantages in that it remains in bloom for a considerable period and has really attractive foliage which enhances the beauty of its own flowers and also of the flowers of other extra early-blooming things which are associated with it. Plant two to three inches deep as early as possible, and, if there is any choice in soil, in a rather moist location, even if that involves considerable shade.

Erythronium (*Dogtooth Violet*). In their native haunts the erythroniums, most of which are American species, grow in shade or partial shade and in soil that is largely leafmold. These conditions should be reproduced, so far as possible, when planting them in the garden; but they will succeed in any ordinary garden soil which is not too heavy or too dry. They are particularly fine for the rock garden, but merit a location in any garden. These quaint, miniature lilies have a range of color from the yellow of the ordinary American variety of cream, rose pink, and light purple. The beautiful light green, or conspicuously mottled or marbled foliage, give them an added attraction. Grandiflorum robustum is a bright buttercup yellow; hartwegi is a strong grower of a beautiful rose pink in color. With dens-canis, purple or white, it is the earliest to bloom, flowering in March. Californicum, one of the best-known sorts, bears a cluster of cream-colored flowers, and hendersoni is similar but with purplish bloom, having very dark centers. The above should be planted, as soon as received, four to five inches deep, and the soil above them mulched with leafmold every winter or early spring; unlike most other bulbs, they do not need to dry out in the soil to "ripen," but should be fairly well supplied with moisture throughout the season. This is one reason why a continuous mulch is helpful.

Fritillarias. Various types of the fritillaria are Checkered Lily, Crown-Imperial, and Mission Bell. All are considerably larger and later to bloom than the other minor bulbs.

The best known of these species and the most vigorous in growth are the Crown-Imperials (*fritillaria imperialis*), which have long been a favorite in perennial gardens in the Old World, and quite generally used here. The flowers which do not usually appear until the end of April, after really cold weather is over, are borne in clusters on the ends of stout stems three or even four feet high, which grow up with amazing rapidity. The variety most generally offered is Maximus, a dull red, "the color of boiled lobster." There are also single and double yellow varieties, and some very beautiful orange shades, as in Imperalis Orange Brilliant. In the variety "Crown-On-Crown" there are several sets of blossoms, one above the other, and it is most striking in appearance. Aurea, yellow, is one of the several low-growing European varieties, which prefer sun and light sandy soil, and are good for the rockery. The bulbs should be gotten into the ground just as soon as they can be obtained in the fall, and covered four or five inches deep. A rich border soil is desirable; as is also an annual mulching of leafmold, although the plants are perfectly hardy.

The Guinea Hen Flower, or Checkered Lily (*fritillaria meleagris*), produces early in April pendant bell-shaped flowers of various shades which are checkered and striped in the most amazing fashion. The colors in the mixed bulbs and in the several varieties include yellow, white, dark purple, and almost black tones; the white variety, alba, is particularly beautiful. The plants are rather dwarf in growth, only about twelve inches high, and unlike the Crown-Imperials are well suited for naturalizing and for the rock garden as well as for groups in the mixed border. Plant early, three to four inches deep, and mulch. In Elwesii shades of dull purple and dull yellow are combined, giving an exceedingly rich effect.

In addition to the above sorts, all of which are from Europe, there are several American species, including lanceolata, growing two feet or more in height, with mottled green and brown flowers, and recurva, similar but with orange-colored flowers, very closely resembling a miniature lily. Both of these prefer a rather stiff soil. Pudica, with flowers of a clean light yellow, a unique color among fritillarias, on the other hand prefers a rather dry, sandy, or gravelly soil. As the fritillarias may remain undisturbed for years, it is an easy matter to gradually accumulate several varieties. Imperialis maximus, meleagris mixed, meleagris alba, and pudica will do well to start with, adding some of the others later.

Galanthus (Snowdrop), one of the most welcome because of its extreme earliness, and the gracefulness and cheer of its little bell-like flowers with three outer petals and an inner cup of three more. Given a rather light soil, in sun or shade, and left to themselves, they usually become well established and will need no further attention for years except an annual four months' mulch where the soil is likely to "heave" from alternate freezing and thawing during the winter. One of the best of all bulbs for tucking away in sunny or shady little corners, under the edge of evergreens or other trees, against a hedge or in the rockery; and also for naturalizing. Plant in groups, or "drifts," placing the bulbs irregularly an inch to three inches apart, and about three inches deep; secure the bulbs as early as possible, and plant immediately. The variety usually offered is nivalis, of which there are both single and double forms. But it is necessary to obtain only the former, as they will soon produce a generous percentage of double flowers. Another species is represented by galanthus Elwesii, which is more vigorous in growth, has larger flowers, growing eight to ten inches tall, or nearly twice the size of nivalis, and is particularly beautiful; it is to be regretted that it is not more generally known and offered in American catalogues.

Leucojum (Snowflake). Another attractive and very early little flower closely related to the snowdrop. The dainty flowers, white with green tips, nod gracefully on frail stems seven or eight inches tall. They are of somewhat stronger growth than the snowdrops, and better for cutting. An extra supply for this purpose may well be planted, as there are few things to be had from out of doors so early in the season. Their cutural requirements are about the same as for the snowdrops. The larger bulbs may be planted somewhat deeper. The Spring Snowflake (L. vernum) is the best known. This flowers in March or early April, and may well be followed by the Summer Snowflake (L. æstivum), which blooms in May or early June, and grows almost twice as tall as the former. There are several other early-flowering varieties, and also autumn-flowering sorts; the former are not generally available, and the latter not always satisfactory.

BLUE LANTERNS THROUGH THE MISTS OF SPRING

Nature, for reasons which even the scientist has not been able to fully fathom, has seen fit to weave the garment of the changing year in different colored patterns for the several seasons. In early spring, yellow and white predominate; but with an unerring sense for the artistic, Nature has seen to it that other colors are also present, to add accent and contrast to heighten the beauty of masses of white and yellow. So, when you add blue, real blue, to your spring garden, you are making the whole picture more beautiful. You know the effect of a single bluebird flashing across the tapestry of spring!

And so it is with blue flowers; you will look in vain for them among the daffodils and tulips—the crocuses and hyacinths come nearer; but, for the real singing blues that will add an entirely new and lyric note to your spring garden, you must turn again to the minor bulbs. There are several which give this most desired color; you should possess at least one of them, no matter how small your garden may be.

Muscari (*Grape-Hyacinth*). No garden should be without at least one or two varieties of these charming little flowers with their slender spikes of diminutive little bells. They come into bloom just after the crocuses, and may be used equally well for naturalizing, for planting under the edges of shrubs or trees, in fairly large clumps—twenty-five to fifty bulbs in the mixed border—or in smaller groups in the rock garden. Once established, they persist like weeds, and while preferring a rather open, "gritty" soil, they will grow practically anywhere. I came across a colony of several thousand bulbs last spring in rather heavy soil, with the surface packed almost as hard as a pavement, which had not received the slightest attention in a generation.

Here are three which any gardener may grow and which most gardens should possess. (*Left*) Spanish iris. (*Center*) A clump of snowflakes (*leucojums*). (*Right*) The easily grown and extremely imposing crown-imperial (*fritillaria imperialis*).

(Left) *Brodiaea coccinea*, or the "floral firecracker." (Center) Because of its beautiful metallic sheen and brilliant coloring, the *calochortus* is known as the "butterfly tulip." (Left) The graceful, brilliant ixias.

Plant before the first of October, if possible, putting the bulbs three to four inches deep, and the same distance apart. Mulch at least for the first season or two. The groups will increase rapidly, not only by the formation of new bulbs beneath the soil, but from self-seeding upon the surface.

The one variety of grape-hyacinth to plant, if you can plant but one, is "Heavenly Blue." To any one familiar only with the old, rather clouded blue grape-hyacinths (*muscari botryoides*), the much larger and more beautiful spikes of Heavenly Blue will be a revelation. And it is heavenly in fragrance as well as in color, which is a softer tone than the older sort. Much earlier to bloom is muscari (*hyacinthus*) azureus, which comes in with the snowdrops and snowflakes and makes a most charming companion to them. Moschatum and heldreichii come a bit later. All three are very fine for the rockery. The latest to bloom is amethystinus (*hyacinthus amethystinum*), rather pale blue but exceptionally dainty with drooping bells. This variety takes rather more kindly to shade than the others. In addition to the above, there is a white form (*botryoides album*) and several other species, including the feather hyacinth (*plumosum*), the musk hyacinth (*moschatum*), the decided odor of which some people like and others do not, and the tassel hyacinth (*comosum*).

Scillas (*Bluebells*). While there are white and rose-colored forms of some of the scillas, their several clear shades of blue are what make them so charming and desirable. The plants are small, growing only half a foot to a foot in height, but are of a charming and graceful habit of growth. The earlier and lower sorts are quite ideal for the rock garden, and are all right for the mixed border if not overgrown or crowded out by other things. The later sorts, which are of more vigorous growth, are well employed either in the rock garden or in the mixed border, or for naturalizing, particularly along the edges of shrubbery groups or in not too thick woods. They can also be most happily associated with other bulbs. Their being planted with tulips is sometimes recommended; but this is a rather doubtful practice, as the tulips should be dug annually, and the scillas are much better if left undisturbed for years. The cultural requirements of the various bluebells is most simple; the larger bulbs, which are not unlike the grape-hyacinth bulbs in appearance, should be covered about four inches deep and placed about four inches apart; the smaller ones three inches deep, and two to three inches apart. The several species are quite distinct in their appearance and in their habits of growth. Most of them will thrive equally well in full sun or in considerable shade. The earliest to bloom are bifolia, some of the varieties of which will flower in March or even in late February when it is possible for them to do so; and sibirica (the Siberian squill). This is of a glorious color, one of the most singing blues among all bulbs, and, for that matter, among all flowers. Both are dwarf, usually not over six inches in height. Both species, and their varieties, bloom with or just after the Snowdrops. Later and taller growing are the English Blue-bells or Wood Hyacinths (*scilla festalis, nutans,* or *non-scripta*) and the Spanish Bluebell (*scilla hispanica* or *campanulata*), the more vigorous growing of the two, pro-ducing, under favorable conditions, spikes considerably over a foot in height. While not quite as hardy as the earlier squills, the wood hyacinths will naturalize themselves in almost any location if their simple wants are met. As they grow naturally in woods, the soil above them is largely leafmold, and they receive annually a mulch of decaying leaves; give them the same in your garden.

Still later than the wood hyacinth are the Italian Squill (*scilla italica*) with more open bells, and growth about a foot high; and the "Cuban Lily" (*scilla peruviana*) which, though less hardy than some of the others, is all right, except in very severe climates, if thoroughly mulched.

All of the scillas should be planted in October or early

November, placing the bulbs three to four inches deep, according to size, and half as far again apart.

If the early blue chionodoxa canadensis, the sardensis, and the later-flowering luciliae are used, along with the grape-hyacinths, the squills and the wood-hyacinths, the spring garden will not lack its bluebird note of "happiness" from the time the snowdrifts melt 'til after the drifts of apple blossoms fade. And the beauty of it is that once you have them, you will probably not be without them again, even though you never make out another order for these bulbs!

OTHER HARDY BULBS AND BULBOUS PLANTS FOR SPRING FLOWERING

In addition to the spring-flowering bulbs described in the preceding paragraph, which are ordinarily spoken of as comprising the "minor bulbs," there are a number of other spring-flowering bulbs and bulbous plants which are easily grown and well worth including in any garden where space is not too limited. Do not disregard these bulbs entirely because you may not have room for all of them. Try at least one or two; and another year add a couple more. They are hardy and most of them will stay with you and go on multiplying by themselves once they are given a chance within your garden's bounds.

Lily-of-the-Valley (*Convallaria majalis*) has so many points of recommendation that no garden, even the smallest, should be without it. No other bulb or bulbous plant has flowers of more dainty and graceful, if modest, beauty; none are more easily grown; none possess a more universally pleasing fragrance; none demand less space; and very few will thrive so well, even in quite dense shade. Where a shady position is not available, lilies-of-the-valley will thrive in the open, and will make themselves at home in a very wide range of soils from hard-packed, heavy loam to almost pure sand, provided well-rotted manure, peat, or humus is mixed with the latter so that it will hold sufficient moisture.

For outdoor planting, either clumps, or single roots or "pips" should be used. They are best employed in rather large groups, or solid beds, or as a solid ground covering under trees. Where clumps are used, they should be set a foot to two feet apart each way, as they will spread very rapidly and close up the intervening space. Single roots should be set six to twelve inches apart. "Cold storage" Lily-of-the-Valley pips, which are used in enormous quantities for forcing, should not be planted out of doors, but clumps or newly imported pips may be obtained in late October or November, and may be planted immediately; or the planting may be delayed until very early spring. In either case, if good roots are used, they will flower freely the first season. The use of manure, if it is well rotted, is not dangerous, and the bulbs will make a more vigorous growth and give larger spikes of flowers if an annual mulching of finely pulverized manure is applied to the bed. No further attention is required until the plants have become so thick that they overcrowd and begin to flower rather sparsely. The entire bed should then be dug up, and the larger "clumps" pips, or roots replanted, or transferred to a new place. This work is best done in October, or just as soon as the ground can be dug in the spring. Lily-of-the-Valley is also an exceptionally satisfactory plant for flowering in the house, or under glass. (See Chapter XVIII.)

Alliums. There is no denying that the allium is but a more highly cultured cousin of the humble garden onion. More than that, if unduly disturbed, it will, in spite of its pretty dress and garden manners, reveal the relationship. Fortunately one does not often need to disturb it, and it possesses so many good points that it is well worth including in the bulb-garden list. The various alliums are most easily grown and the large umbels of flowers which cover quite a range of colors are very attractive, and bloom throughout a longer season than many other bulbs. They require the same general culture as the grape-hyacinths, and they will thrive in any ordinary soil. Neapolitanum, and N. grandiflorum, which has larger flowers, are both white, and bloom quite early. Moly, a bright yellow, perhaps the best known sort, and caeruleum (or azureum) blue, flowers considerably later. Acuminatum has flowers of an attractive pink shade, as has also roseum. Cyaneum is blue and very dwarf growing, being only six inches or so in height, and is excellent for use in the rock garden. While they may be flowered indoors, their odor is more objectionable there than in the open.

Camassia. Attaining a height of from one and a half to two feet, with very attractive, star-shaped blossoms, borne in loose spikes and with a very attractive range of colors, including pure white, light blue, and very deep purplish blue, it is rather surprising that this well worth-while group of flowers has never taken the popular fancy to a greater extent. I know that I considered I had made quite a distinct "find" when I first grew them. Although they do not look like shady-place flowers, they thrive in fairly heavy shade as well as in the open, and they may well be used where most other fairly late-flowering bulbs cannot. They bloom in late May or very early June, and are very beautiful when planted in the hardy border back of groups of some of the very latest flowering tulips. Cover about four inches deep, and plant several in a group, three to four inches apart. They may be left undisturbed for several years before replanting will be necessary.

Esculentea, with flowers of a rich purple color, and growing about two feet in height, and leichtlinii, a beautiful azure blue, attaining about three feet high, are the two sorts most generally offered. Esculentea alba, white, and fraseri, a very pale blue, make good additional varieties, if one cares to go beyond the two mentioned above.

Star of Bethlehem (Ornithogalum). Though by no means imposing plants, the several hardier species of the ornithogalums are very attractive with their large, loose clusters of cheery star-shaped flowers borne on stems a foot to two feet in height. They are most valuable, perhaps, for naturalizing and for planting in small clumps under shrubbery or in any "half wild" location. They have a rather strong fragrance which some people find pleasing, and others are not enthusiastic about. Any well-drained soil suits them. Plant in September or October, in small groups, placing about three or four inches apart, and covering three to four inches deep.

Nutans, which has orange-colored flowers and blooms in April, grows only about six inches high and is good for rockery work as well as for naturalizing. Umbelatum, with white and green flowers, blooms in May, and reaches a height of a foot or so. Arabicum, with white flowers, on stems about a foot and a half high, flowers in June, and parymidale, with white flowers with a greenish stripe, reaching a height of two feet, is the latest of all to flower.

Puschkinia. The puschkinia, or "striped squill" as it is often called, is an extremely dainty little April-blooming flower somewhat resembling the squills, but with more open blooms, in a loose spike, white or pale blue in color, with a unique blue stripe through the center of each petal. It is quite ideal as a rockery plant, growing only five to six inches high, and preferring a rather light, sandy soil. It is also very effective when used at the very front of a "close-up" border, but not so good in masses. Puschkinias should be planted in September three inches deep, and three to four inches apart.

NOT STRICTLY BULBS—BUT MOST DESIRABLE

If this book were built along strictly botanical lines, most of the following plants would have to be omitted, as they are neither true bulbs, tubers, nor corms, but rather hardy perennials with fleshy or clumplike roots. However, as my aim has been rather to help the amateur bulb enthusiast to make an attractive and successful garden than to please the botanically minded critic, I am including them.

Most of these plants flower along with the spring-blooming bulbs, and are beautiful when planted in association with them; also they should be planted in the fall. Moreover, many of them are offered in the catalogues which are devoted to the spring-flowering bulbs. So there are practical, if not botanical, reasons for including them here.

The culture of the few species to be mentioned is not difficult. For the most part, they should be planted in September or early October, covering the "crowns" or tops of the clumps one to three inches deep, and, after the ground freezes, given a winter mulch. The soil which is to receive them may be prepared in the same way as for the other fall-planted bulbs. They will establish themselves quickly and no further particular attention is required, except taking up and dividing and replanting the clump, after several years, if they begin to crowd to an extent which interferes with their flowering.

Bleedingheart (*Dielytra or Dicentra*). Bleedingheart (dielytra or dicentra), sometimes called the "Seal Flower," is an exceptionally graceful and pretty spring-flowering plant, with its pink flowers borne on long-curved and drooping racemes; the individual flowers are heart-shaped, giving the plant its name. The foliage is attractive throughout the season. Two varieties are ordinarily offered, spectabilis and exima, the latter being known as the plumy bleedingheart on account of the finely cut plumelike foliage which is not excelled for decorative effect by any other hardy perennial. Both varieties are extremely easy to grow, flourishing in any good garden soil, but preferring plenty of moisture and some shade. The fact that they will grow in shade should be taken advantage of.

Dicentra (*Dutchman's Breeches*) are miniature, graceful little flowers with finely cut foliage, 6 to 9 inches high.

There are three native species (cucularia, white flowers tipped yellow and very quaint), "squirrel's corn" (canadensis), quite similar to the above in appearance, but with small cornlike tubers, and "Golden Ear Drops" (chrysantha), with golden yellow flowers. All of these are particularly good for naturalizing, or for planting in the rock garden or among ferns.

Spirea. To most people, the name "spirea" will call to mind the plant which flowers during the winter months, and is sold in pot or pan by the florist. However, a number of these are perfectly hardy and will grow out of doors as easily as any of the other hardy perennials.

The spireas have finely cut, fernlike foliage which is very decorative, and pyramidal panicles of numerous small flowers which give a very plumelike effect. The colors range from pure white through pink to dark crimson, and the various species and varieties are from eighteen inches to six feet in height; they bloom from June on. They associate finely with other flowers, and will thrive in considerable shade as well as in the open; shade is preferable, especially for the pink varieties, which fade out somewhat in full sunlight.

The cultural requirements of the spireas are simple. Plant in ordinary soil, adding plenty of peat or humus to hold moisture, which they must have to do their best. Cover the crowns one or two inches deep; water freely at the roots during dry weather, especially during the flowering period; divide the clumps and replant them, every three or four years, in late summer or fall when growth is dormant.

There are two general types: the true spireas (Meadow Rue or Goatsbeard—*spirea arancus* and *s. filipendula*) which are of rather coarse, scrubby growth; and the Astilbes, which are more refined and of smaller growth—eighteen to twenty-four inches or so—and used largely for forcing, grown in shallow pots for florists' sales during the winter months, but also equally valuable for the garden.

The Arendsi and japonica hybrid astilbes now include a wide range of wonderfully beautiful varieties, such as Gladstone and Avalanche, pure white; Peach Blossom, light pink; Queen Alexandra, deeper pink; Gloria, brilliant pink; Rubens, red; Granat, dark crimson, extra fine; and America, lilac. Moerheimi, white, and Salland, red, both grow five to six feet tall, and are wonderfully effective in the background of the hardy border, with the earlier blooming hardy lilies.

SOME LITTLE WILDLINGS FOR WOODSY NOOKS

Entirely distinct from the above are three or four little native plants which may well be used in the rock or semi-wild garden, or with spring-flowering bulbs wherever there is some shade and protection from drying winds. These somewhat bashful little beauties are woodland natives, but easily grown; well worth while for their intrinsic value, and not merely as garden "curiosities" as many people seem to think. They should be given plenty of peat or humus, mixed with leafmold if it is available; planted about three inches deep; and, if convenient, mulched with half-decayed needles from pine, cedar, or some similar evergreen. In other respects, they will take care of themselves. The Ladyslipper (*cypripedium*) belongs to the orchid race and is desirable because of its quaintness, and because it is so very distinct from all other hardy spring flowers. The "red" Ladyslipper—it is really dark pink—or "Moccasin Flower" (*acaule*); the showy Ladyslipper (*spectabile*); and the yellow Ladyslipper (*pubescens*), while not listed in many catalogues, may be obtained without difficulty, where one cannot gather them from the wild, and will repay the effort.

The Wakerobins, or Trilliums, which belong to the lily family, throw up from their tuberous roots a clean round stem, six to eighteen inches tall, supporting three pointed leaves and a distinctive three-petaled flower of pure white, red, or pink. They are easily grown, and most interesting and attractive. A half dozen or more species are available, but the white Wakerobin (*Trillium grandiflorum*) and the Painted Trillium (*erythrocarpum* or *undulatum*) with its many edged petals and crimson stripes at the base of each, are the most desirable.

Bloodroot. Bloodroot (*Sanguinaria canadensis*) which throws up its small white flowers from fleshy roots—which "bleed" profusely when broken—just ahead of the young deeply cut leaves, and looks like a tiny lotus lily, will thrive in dense shade, with a leafmold mulch. The flowers are fragile and short-lived, but very charming; and it is well worth growing for the handsome foliage alone.

Virginia Bluebells or Cowslips. Virginia Bluebells or Cowslip (*Mertensia virginica*), eighteen to twenty-four inches tall, and bearing clusters of little bright bluebells, is one of the most charming of all our native early flowers, and splendid for the bulb garden or rockery, in sun or shade.

Solomonseal. Solomonseal (*Polygonatum*) is another bulbous-rooted native unlike any of the cultivated plants. The bell-shaped little whitish green flowers hang in pairs from the long, gracefully arching leaf stalk, and are followed by conspicuous bluish black pendant berries. There are two forms: the smaller, biflorum, growing a foot or so high, is excellent for the rock garden; the larger or "Giant Seal" (*majus*) in rich soil grows several feet tall, and is extremely decorative when not crowded by other plants, so that the pendant clusters of little bells may be seen clearly.

I have given some space to these native plants because they bring variety to the garden, and deserve much wider use than they now enjoy. We are too prone to use none but exotics in our gardens, thinking that only those things are good which come from a great distance; and overlooking equally beautiful things from nearer home. In the Connecticut hills and woods which I roamed as a boy, all of these flowers, except the Virginia bluebells, were to be found; but no one, in those days, even thought of bringing these "wild" things into the garden. Now they are beginning to become "popular" and, as a consequence, more available. Plant at least one or two of them, and enjoy a new garden adventure!

CHAPTER X

THE HALF-HARDY SPRING-FLOWERING BULBS

THERE are a number of very beautiful and desirable bulbous plants, brought from climates less rigorous than ours, which are not quite "hardy" enough to go through our winters safely with the same treatment accorded the bulbs which we have discussed thus far.

These fine things are, however, perennials in their natural habitats, and with some slight extra protection may be grown out of doors along with the other hardy favorites of the bulb garden. They are, therefore, generally described as the "half-hardy" bulbs.

The terms "hardy," "half-hardy," and "tender" are often confusing to the amateur. It should be kept in mind that they are really relative. A canna, for instance, might be "hardy" at Charleston, S. C., "half-hardy" at Washington, D. C., and "tender" at New York, although these locations are not great distances apart. As generally used in catalogues, however, the terms "hardy," "half-hardy," and "tender" apply to the cold resistance of plants when grown where the winter temperatures frequently get down to zero or lower. In the growing of bulbs, as with other plants, consideration should be given the fact that temperature is only one factor. Plants actually suffer less in many places where winter temperatures are very low, but where the *protective blanket of deep snow remains through the winter*, than they do in more moderate zones, with alternate freezing and thawing. Proximity to the seacoast, or to large bodies of water, is another modifying factor.

A WIDE RANGE OF UNUSUAL BEAUTY

If the addition of some of the half-hardy bulbs to our gardens meant merely the multiplication of species and varieties, there would be no good reason for the amateur gardener's giving them consideration. But a number of them are quite distinct from any of the hardy bulbs and of great beauty. The gracefully charming bulbous irises, and the gayly colored anemones and ranunculus, for instance, have no real equivalents among the hardy things, and are well worth the slight effort needed to grow them.

In emphasizing the fact that there is a place in the garden for the half-hardy bulbs, I do not mean to advocate that the beginner should feel bound to try them. Let the start in bulb gardening be made with the hardiest and easiest things; and then, as one gets a bit familiar with bulbs and their ways, those which require a little more difficult culture may be added—and with them the keen pleasure which the gardener of growing skill always gets with the addition of some beautiful new flower to his or her increasing circle of little friends.

The half-hardy bulbs may be utilized in several different ways.

First comes planting in the open garden, along with the hardy bulbs. Here they may be employed in the same way as the hardy bulbs, other than that the extra protection required must be given, except in southern sections; most of the half-hardy bulbs are "hardy" south of Washington, D. C. In planting select, so far as possible, the nooks and corners most sheltered from strong spring winds, and the best drained soil. Or, for general garden use, in cold sections, the half-hardy bulbs may be treated as "tender" bulbs—planted in the early spring and taken up in the autumn for safe storage during winter.

Most of the half-hardy bulbs are particularly desirable for cutting; for this purpose, they may be either planted in sheltered, protected beds or in a low frame. They are also most desirable for planting indoors, for early spring—not really "forced" but brought through the winter in a frame, and flowered early in the moderate warmth of the average living room. (See Chapter XVIII.)

THREE WAYS OF HANDLING HALF-HARDY BULBS

Wherever one's garden may be, then, from the moderate climate of the more southern states to the extreme north, the half-hardy bulbs may be enjoyed, in one way or another.

Planting in the Open. Prepare the soil as for other bulbs (see page 31), except that, most of the half-hardy sorts being more tolerant of manure, this material may be more freely used; it should, however, be thoroughly rotted. Most of the bulbs, which run rather small as compared to daffodils and tulips, will want covering about three inches deep. Mulch very thoroughly, as soon as the ground *begins* to freeze, with from four to six inches of leaves or other light material, or from three to four inches of coconut fiber—the best material if readily obtainable—coarsely sifted leaf-mold, or coarse peat. (Very fine peat or humus may become water-soaked, and freeze in a solid mass which is not desirable.) The mulch may be held in place neatly and permanently by an edging of light, narrow boards, or a strip of chicken wire. Do not remove the mulch in spring until just as the plants begin to break through the soil, thus holding them back as long as possible.

None of the half-hardy bulbs are well suited to naturalizing; and, while some of them may be left in the ground for two or three seasons where conditions are favorable, they are much better lifted and replanted each year, as with the Dutch tulips.

Planting in Frames. The most certain method of growing the half-hardy bulbs is to build a light, shallow frame, similar to a coldframe, but less substantial (see illustration on page 112). This may be removed entirely in the spring, or left, as desired. Mulching, as described above, should be put on in the frame as the ground freezes. It will not be necessary to provide a glass covering: a few old boards will answer every purpose during the winter. In the spring, if extra early and perfect blossoms are wanted, a regular coldframe sash or sash covered with "glass cloth" or with

HALF HARDY BULBS

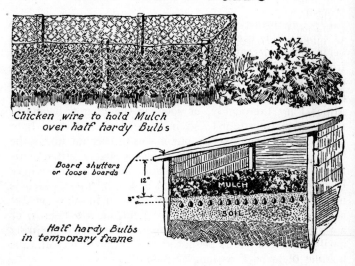

Chicken wire to hold Mulch over half hardy Bulbs

Board shutters or loose boards

12"

3"

MULCH

SOIL

Half hardy Bulbs in temporary frame

"celloglass" may be placed over the frame, after the mulch is removed, several weeks before outside bulbs are coming up.

The bulbs may be placed in pots or pans, several in each, and then buried in the soil in the frames. In early spring, transfer them, pots and all, to any spot in the garden. After blooming, the pots may be transferred to another spot and buried to the brim, allowing the foliage to mature naturally.

Planting in the Spring. Many of the half-hardy bulbs, such as anemones, ranunculus, and montbretias, are offered in the spring catalogues. Or they may be obtained in the fall, and kept over winter along with one's tender summer-flowering bulbs, and planted out the first thing in the spring. So treated, they will not bloom quite so early. as when planted in the fall, but there is no danger of winter killing, and one saves the bother of winter mulching, or of making a temporary frame. On the other hand, there are always more things than one can attend to in the spring, so that fall planting has its advantages. Whether it will be best to plant the half-hardy bulbs in the open garden or in a frame in the fall, or wait until spring, will depend both upon local climatic conditions and upon convenience; possibly a combination of two or all these methods will be best. Experience is the only true criterion for the individual gardener.

THE BULBOUS IRISES—"ORCHIDS OF THE GARDEN"

While the flowers of the bulbous irises look unmistakably like those of the hardy garden species (see Chapter XVII), the roots, foliage, and habits of growth are entirely distinct. They grow from small bulbs, something the size and appearance of a crocus bulb, but more pointed; and the foliage is slender or even grasslike; in fact, so scanty looking during its early growth in the spring that one growing them for the first time will scarcely believe possible the flower show they will later produce. They are, for the most part, moderate in height, a foot to a scant two feet.

For planting in groups in protected spots in the mixed border or the rock garden, the bulbous irises are very distinctive and charming; and as an early flower for cutting they are certainly unsurpassed, perhaps unequaled, by any other flower. As they may be set quite close together, they are ideal for planting in a frame for cutting.

While the bulbs are small, this type of iris gives a much

better display if not crowded too close together. In the garden, give them from eight to twelve inches each way. In a frame, they may be put in rows from twelve to eighteen inches apart, the bulbs spaced six inches or so in the row. The English iris will grow in a fairly heavy soil, but the others prefer plenty of sand or ashes mixed with it; all must have excellent drainage.

It is of great importance to get these irises in as early as possible—during September, if the bulbs are to be had. They will begin growth at once, and a well-developed root system will help both to take them safely through the winter, and to give fine flowers the following spring.

TYPES AND VARIETIES

Dutch Iris (*I. xiphium hybridium*). These are the earliest to bloom of the three best-known sorts—"Spanish," "English," and "Dutch." The Dutch are nearly two weeks earlier than the Spanish irises—from which they were developed—stronger growing, and with much larger flowers; but they are generally considered not quite so hardy. White Excelsior (Voerman), pure white; Hart Nibrig; clear blue; Arie Scheffer, very dark blue; Cornelius Troost, pale yellow, and J. W. De Wilde, deep yellow, are a few of the many wonderfully colored varieties.

Spanish Iris (*I. xiphium*). One to two feet tall, flowering in early June, after the "Dutch." Queen Wilhelmina, extra early, and British Queen, pure white; Excelsior, light blue, late; King of the Blues, dark blue; Chrysolora, pale yellow; Cajanus, deep yellow; Thunderbolt, dark bronze, and Bronze Queen, terra cotta, are but a few of many good sorts. Golden Lion, a rich yellow with frilled petals, is of a distinct new type of Spanish iris; but, so far as I am aware, it has not yet been offered in America.

English Iris (*I. xiphioides*). These are still later, but, for the beginner, perhaps the most satisfactory of the bulbous irises to try. Some of the good-named sorts are: Mer de Glace, white; Tantalus, light blue, shaded darker; Princess

Juliana, deep blue; Prince of Wales, deep purple; Queen Alexandra, lavender.

Iris filifolia, especially the variety Imperator, a wonderful clear blue, with extra large flower, and Iris Tingitana, growing three feet tall, especially the variety "The First," a very dark blue of splendid large bloom, are largely used for winter forcing, being extra early. I have grown them in frames, with the same care as given the English and Dutch Irises, with success, but have never tried them in the open. In mild sections, with thorough mulching, they would undoubtedly come through satisfactorily. *Iris reticulata* is the earliest bloomer of the lot, flowering in March if conditions make it possible. To add to its charm, the deep violet and gold flowers are quite fragrant.

ANEMONES AND RANUNCULUS

These two little treasures—among the gayest, cheeriest, and most brightly colored of all flowers—we are taking together because they are a good deal alike in general appearance and usefulness, and even more so in their cultural requirements.

While ideal as cut flowers, and increasingly popular as commercially grown for florists' use, they are too seldom encountered in the amateur's garden—not so much because of any great difficulty in growing them, as because they require somewhat different treatment from the ordinary run of spring-flowering bulbs. Given the special but simple conditions which they require, they may readily be grown out of doors as far north as New York or Cleveland; farther north, it is safer to grow them in frames, or to plant in early spring.

The anemones or "wind flowers" grow from eight to twelve inches high and the ranunculus a bit taller. Both are extremely effective in sheltered nooks in the mixed border, the bulb border, in front of the foundation planting about the house, or in the rock garden. The anemones prefer rather full sunshine (unless planted in spring, when they bloom later); but the ranunculus do better in partial shade.

Plant *late*. Unlike most of the early spring-flowering bulbs, anemones and ranunculus *should not be planted until October or early November*. The reason for this is that earlier planting will result in top growth in the fall, which is almost certain to be killed back during winter or early spring, or smothered if given a mulch sufficient to protect it. While new growth will usually be made, even then the plants will have been weakened by the wasted effort.

The anemone bulbs closely resemble a tiny dahlia tuber, and should be covered about three inches deep, and placed six inches apart. The ranunculus is a cultivated cousin of the common wild (but not, as most persons suppose, native) Buttercup or "Crowfoot" (*R. acris*). The peculiar claw-shaped roots, hard and dry, appear absolutely lifeless; but, nevertheless, should be put in dry sand if kept out of the soil for any length of time. In planting, place them with the points or prongs down, and cover *firmly* with two inches of soil; placing them from four to five inches apart.

After planting, cover the spot with small evergreen boughs, oak branches cut *with* the leaves, marsh hay, or loose litter; decaying leaves or other material which might pack should not be used. This winter protection serves the double purpose of preventing "heaving" during the winter, and of protecting the young growth in spring from driving cold winds. When this protection is removed, a two-inch mulch of peat, humus, coconut fiber, or fine rotted manure, worked in around the plants, is beneficial but not essential. After the foliage dies down, the bulbs may be taken up and stored in a cool cellar in dry sand, until time for replanting. If the seed from the plants is saved, this may be planted in July or August, as raising anemones from seed is not very difficult. Purchased seed may be started under glass in January or February. Germination is very slow, but usually sure, and the young plants are readily handled.

TYPES OF ANEMONES AND RANUNCULUS

St. Brigid anemones, semi-double and double, are the best known and most generally offered. They are a strain or selection of the coronaria type. The colors include pure white, pink, rose, crimson, scarlet, lavender, violet purple, and deep maroon. They prefer a rather moist situation, such as may be found in a slight depression, natural or artificial; or frequent watering during early spring and the flowering season. An extra quantity of peat or humus to hold moisture will make ordinary soil suitable for them.

The Poppy-flowered, or Giant French, singles, with similar colors, and also near-blue, are even more brilliantly colored. The Excelsior type or strain is especially vigorous in growth. The flowers, under suitable conditions, are borne on stems nearly a foot long. Anemone flowers should, by the way, be cut with a knife, and not pulled out from the bulb, as other buds are forming. The Poppy-flowered anemones, and also the two described below, should be planted in soil containing *plenty of sand or cinders;* a bank, or along the edge of a bed raised slightly above the general level, makes an ideal location. Even more than most bulbs, they are particular about perfect drainage, although enjoying abundant water about the roots while growing.

The *Scarlet Windflower* (*A. hortensis fulgens*) and the brilliant "Peacock Anemone" (*hortensis pavonia*) which is a double form of it, are two of the most strikingly effective of all bulbous flowers, but not quite so hardy as the others. Put plenty of sand about the roots when planting, and give a sheltered situation. These two, if happily situated, will need replanting only every second or third season.

"Turban" Ranunculus are the hardiest type; the double flowers, looking something like little pompon dahlias, are of pure self colors, in white, rose, crimson, scarlet, orange, and pure yellow.

The *"Persian"* section with white, red, and yellow semi-double flowers, resembling tiny roses, are more dwarf in habit of growth.

The *Giant French* type include a wide range of colors and are also attractively striped and variegated; the flowers, which somewhat resemble giant English daisies, are held well above the foliage. This type, while well suited in rather heavy soil outdoors, *should not be planted until spring*.

MONTBRETIAS

Montbretias—or more correctly speaking, perhaps, Tritonias—which have been well described as "little fountains of bright color"—might almost be termed hardy gladiolus. In bulbs, foliage, flower spike, and general appearance they resemble somewhat that popular flower except that the wiry flower stalks and the flowers themselves are of looser, more open structure. The newer hybrids have flowers four inches across, but the color range is quite distinct from that of the gladiolus, covering exceptionally rich shades of orange, apricot, chrome yellow, and scarlet. One of their great merits is that they flower for a very long period, which makes them especially desirable both for the hardy border, or for planting in groups along the shrubbery border, and for cutting. The varieties vary in height from two to four feet, and flower from July until September.

A light, well-drained soil, with plenty of rotted cow manure, humus, or peat, best suits the montbretias. Plant from four to five inches deep, and about six inches apart, in groups of at least half a dozen, but better a dozen or twenty-five. Give full sun. Mulch thoroughly with leaves or manure. In heavy soils or in very cold sections, plant very early in spring, as with gladiolus. In fairly light soils, the bulbs may remain undisturbed for two or three seasons, but in heavy soils it is better to lift annually, keeping the bulbs through the winter with the "glads."

Varieties. While many American concerns still list montbretias only in mixture, a few of the more progressive offer the newer named hybrids, such as King Edward, deep golden yellow, with mottled throat; Lord Nelson, deep orange, shading to crimson outside; George Davison, pale orange, deeper outside; Hereward, similar to above, but much later to bloom; Prometheus, deep orange with crimson center; and King Henry VIII, bright orange, shaded darker, one of the largest of all. Crocosmaeflora, the "type" of the above varieties, is pure yellow, orange outside; Speciosa is a burning scarlet.

IXIA AND SPARAXIS

This little pair, while they may be brought through the winter safely, with generous protection, in moderate climates, are among the most tender of the half-hardy bulbs. If we had a "quarter-hardy" class, they would belong in that. The ixia, sometimes called the African Corn Lily, hails from Africa; the sparaxis, known as the Harlequin Flower, from the Cape of Good Hope. Both are extremely brilliant in color. Most catalogue makers use the adjective "gorgeous" in describing the ixias, and in this instance, at least, it is entirely merited. Blues, purples, yellows, intense scarlet, and vivid carmine and cerise are all present, usually combined with a boldly contrasting shade; and there are metallic bronzes, coppers, and greens found in few other flowers. The narrow pointed foliage is also very attractive. Equally brilliant are the splashed and mottled blooms of the sparaxis, which grows to a height of nearly two feet—six inches or so taller than the ixia. Plant both in October or early November, in a protected, thoroughly drained or raised bed of sandy soil, or a sheltered nook in the rock garden; mulch with peat or humus, which should be left on, and cover this with marsh hay or evergreen boughs, to be removed in the spring, when some growth has been made. Plant the bulbs three inches deep, and from three to four inches apart; or plant in early spring.

SOME OTHER HALF-HARDIES

While there remain a considerable number of half-hardy bulbs which we have not touched upon, they are not, with the exception of the few mentioned below, generally available through the ordinary seed and bulb catalogues; and their culture, for the most part, is similar to that of the bulbs already described.

Here are, however, briefly, a few more:

Brodiaea, sometimes called the "California hyacinth," is another beautiful thing which this State has contributed. The long tubular flowers are borne in June in clusters held on thin, wiry stems a foot or more above the mass of narrow pointed leaves, and last for a long time. The colors are striking. They do well in shade, and are excellent where a rather sandy or gravelly soil is encountered, in a protected place, under trees; and in raised locations in the rock garden. Plant four inches deep, when the bulbs are received—usually in early September—and from four to six inches apart. Mulch every fall with rotted cow manure, and replant every three or four years. In cold sections, plant early in spring.

Varieties. *Uniflora*—sometimes catalogued as Triteleia uniflora, the "Spring Starflower"—is much the hardiest, and will succeed under ordinary garden culture: the star-shaped blossoms are white, shaded blue, and fragrant. *Coccinia* (more correctly *Brevoortia ida-maia*), known as the "Floral Firecracker," has a cluster of bright red, green-tipped flowers, unique but pretty. Crocea is light yellow; Lactea is creamy white; Hendersoni, yellow. Grandiflora, six inches tall, purple; and Laxa, eighteen inches tall, clear blue —and often called the Blue Milla—are both quite hardy, and two of the best for ordinary garden conditions.

Babiana. Charming little flowers somewhat resembling freesias in growth, from six to nine inches high, and mostly sweet scented. Plant in October about four inches deep and the same distance apart. The varieties include Plicata, violet and blue, Ringens, bright scarlet, Disticha, bright

blue, and Macrantha, purple and yellow, the strongest
growing.

Calochortus, Mariposa Lily or Butterfly Tulips, which
include the "Star" tulips, are tuliplike flowers from California. The gayly colored cup-shaped flowers, often several
on a stem, are so marked, veined, and spotted as to bear
quite a resemblance to a butterfly's wings—"Mariposa" is
the Spanish for butterfly. The colors include delicate lilacs
and lavenders as well as pale yellow, rose, white, and
orange. They vie with the orchids in exquisite coloring.
Although these fine flowers are natives of America, they are
much more widely grown in Europe than here; there many
named varieties are offered in the leading catalogues. Here
they are offered mostly in mixtures only. Some of the new
varieties grow well over two feet tall, but the average is
from one to one and a half feet; they flower during June,
July, and August, and as this gives them a considerable
period of growth before blooming, they may be planted in
spring more successfully than many of the half-hardy bulbs.
For fall planting, put them in in September or October, or
very early November, in full sun in rather open, gritty soil,
but not too loose—the harder the subsoil the better. Place
from four to eight inches apart, and cover three inches
deep; mulch thoroughly, removing in early spring. Give
abundance of water during growth, and then withhold
entirely, as the bulbs need to dry and "bake" in the soil
to mature properly. The largest flowers are those of the
Mariposa type. The "Star Tulips" (formerly cyclobothras)
are the earliest, grow about eight inches tall, and have
drooping flowers, somewhat like a fritillaria; the "Globe
Tulips" or "Fairybells" prefer partial shade.

Cooperia, or "Evening-Star," is another little American
plant, from Texas, about ten inches high, with sweet-scented
wax-white flowers, some two inches in diameter. The individual blossoms last but a day or two, but the plants flower
continuously from early June to September, which make it
extremely well worth while for the sheltered border or

rockery. Plant in September or October, or early in April, three inches deep and three inches apart in groups of a dozen or so; the bulbs cost but about a dollar a dozen. Pedunculata, tinged crimson outside, and Drummondi, pure white, are the varieties.

Zephyranthes, "Fairy Lilies" or "Zephyr Flowers," with grassy foliage, are very pretty, graceful, starry flowers of white or rose pink, growing from six to ten inches tall, and blooming all summer. They are quite tender, but very easily grown in any well-drained ordinary garden soil, by planting in April or early May, and lifting and storing before frost.

For planting outside, select a sheltered nook in the rockery or mixed border and put the bulbs in in October, three inches deep and from three to four inches apart. They are also ideal for growing in pots or boxes, in which they may be carried over winter. Of the half dozen or more varieties, carinata, rosy pink, and candida, white, tinted rose, are usually offered.

Eremurus, the Giant Asphodel, Foxtail Lily, or Spire Lily, is entirely distinct from any of the other bulbous plants. In general appearance, it is something like a century plant or a gigantic tritoma, the flower spikes thrusting up boldly from a dense clump of narrow pointed leaves to a height of from six to twelve feet, the upper three feet or so being densely clothed with starry tubular flowers, the whole making an enormous plume not unlike a fox's brush in general effect. The colors range from pure white, through pink, to yellow, copper, and orange. While these tremendously effective plants come from cold localities—Asiatic Russia and the Himalayas—their great trouble in our climate is the danger of frost injury after growth, which is extremely rapid, starts in the spring. The critical point in their culture, which otherwise is not difficult, is to hold back and protect this early spring growth. Mulching thoroughly after the ground freezes with cinders, and over these with leaves, or leafmold, and planting in a *northern* exposure,

If the average gardener knew how easily beautiful little snowdrops (*left*) and early tulips can be forced, few homes would be without them.

Eremurus—giants of the bulb family; their common name of "spire-lily" is fitting. (*Right*) The Peruvian daffodil (*ismene*), a handsome, fragrant flower—one of the best to add to your list.

such as north of a tall wall, or of evergreens, will help in the first respect; while a cylinder of poultry wire, about two feet in diameter, placed over each plant and filled with leaves or straw, will accomplish the second.

The spreading, fleshy roots, which themselves are enormous affairs a foot and a half or more in diameter, should be planted in autumn, or as soon as the ground opens in spring, in prepared holes, containing plenty of sand and rotted cow manure, or peat or humus. Cover the roots about three inches deep, bringing the crown near the surface. Often the plants will not flower until the second or third season, but they are well worth waiting for.

Tritoma (Kniphofia), the "Torch Lily," Flame Flower, or Red-hot-poker Plant, is, like the Eremurus, not a true bulb but usually offered and handled with bulbs, and therefore mentioned here. In habit of growth, too, it is somewhat like the giant "Spire Lily," but attaining a height of only four to six feet. The older types flowered only late in autumn, but some of the newer hybrids bloom from May through the season, making them one of the most desirable of all plants for the background of the mixed border, or of the rock garden. Plant in full sun in well-drained soil in fall or early spring, keeping the crown level with the soil, and mulch thoroughly with strawy manure or leaves for winter. In very cold sections, the roots may easily be taken up, packed closely together in sand in a box, kept in the cellar, and set out again in the spring; and the summer-long display of gorgeous spikes is well worth the slight trouble. Tritoma Pfitzeri, the "everblooming Flame Flower," dazzling scarlet shading to orange toward the base of the spike, is the best known sort; but the newer Early Perpetual Flowering and Perry's Hybrids begin flowering much earlier—the former will, in fact, flower the first season from seeds started under glass. Royal Standard and Lord Roberts are splendid new English sorts, two of the few named varieties offered in any American catalogue; they are three feet tall, and very free flowering. C. M. Prichard, bright golden yellow, is taller; while Nelsoni is a dwarf-growing scarlet. Uvaria grandiflora is the old-fashioned, late-flowering type, which I have had bloom even into December. Quartiniana is the hardiest, and blooms in May or June.

CHAPTER XI

SUMMER- AND AUTUMN-FLOWERING BULBS

In summer- and autumn-flowering bulbs, I have included those which, generally speaking, begin flowering, or have the greater part of their flowering season, after the middle of June.

Among the summer- and autumn-flowering bulbs, and near-bulbous, or fleshy-rooted plants, are many of our finest and most popular flowers. Every bulb enthusiast will wish to include some of these in his plantings, so as to continue the pageant of beauty from bulbs, so wonderfully begun during the spring months, throughout the summer and far into the fall.

HARDY, TENDER, AND HALF-HARDY

There are three distinct classes or groups of summer- and autumn-flowering bulbs; first, those which are perfectly hardy, and which remain year after year, with little attention, such as the strongest growing hardy lilies; second, those which are too tender to remain in the ground over winter, even with protection, such as dahlias or cannas; and third, those which are "half-hardy" and which may, in mild sections or with adequate protection, remain in the ground over winter, such as the bulbous irises and anemones. (The half-hardy bulbs have already been considered in the preceding chapter, and no further mention of them need be made here, except to describe their culture when treated as "tender" bulbs.)

The great majority of the hardy and tender summer- and autumn-flowering bulbs are much taller in habit of growth than are the spring-blooming bulbs. Many of them bear their flowers on tall, slender stems or "spikes"; they are, therefore, best suited to planting against walls, evergreens, or shrubs; at the back of the mixed border, especially where a "lane" or "vista" between two long borders is to be created, or as low screens or hedges in front of objectionable views. The species which bear tall spikes are particularly effective against flat walls, either structural or of living green; and giving them such a position has the further advantage of protecting them from wrecking winds, thus rendering the practice of "staking" unnecessary.

Staking plants in garden use always looks unnatural and

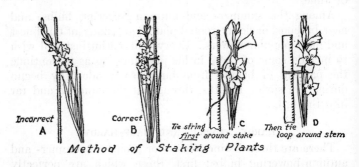

Incorrect
A

Correct
B

Tie string *first* around stake
C

Then tie loop around stem
D

Method of Staking Plants

decidedly objectionable, to say nothing of the extra work involved. By using slim, green-stained bamboo canes, which are very cheap and will last many seasons if cleaned and taken indoors over winter, and green raffia, staking may be made quite inconspicuous; but it is better to avoid it altogether, if possible. Where it must be resorted to, put the stakes in early—as soon as growth starts, in the case of hardy bulbs; and, preferably, *before* planting, for tender ones. The stake should be placed as close to the bulb, or vice versa, as possible; this will avoid the necessity of bending the stalk from an upright position when tying it to the stake. For tying, use raffia; it is soft, ties readily, and stays tied. Raffia is a dried grass, imported largely for florists and market-garden use, and is sold by most seed houses. Soft twine or strips of cloth may be used instead of raffia. The great secret in "staking" plants successfully is to tie the raffia or twine *tightly about the stake first*; this prevents the tying material from slipping down; then the two ends may be tied loosely about the plant, holding it firmly in position without cutting or bending it. Plants should be tied *as they grow,* using two or even three loops, if necessary; it is unsatisfactory to attempt to fasten them up once they have fallen over.

Naturalizing. Some of the hardy summer- and autumn-flowering bulbs, especially among the hardy lilies, are excellent for naturalizing; but the great majority of these, as well as the tender and half-hardy things, are best handled in the garden border; they look out of place in a "naturalistic" setting, as well as being culturally unsuited to it. This does not mean, however, that they must be used only in garden rows and "formal" planting. Such is too often the case; and many fine garden effects are sacrificed merely because we have got into a rut in planting such tender and half-hardy bulbs as gladiolus, cannas, tuberous begonias, Spanish iris, anemones, etc. The picture facing page 141, showing gladiolus used in an informal planting, illustrates more clearly what is meant than a page of argument.

For Cutting. For the rock garden, also, most of the summer- and autumn-blooming bulbs are not suited, though there are a few exceptions, noted later. As flowers for cutting, however, almost all of them are excellent, and a goodly number are quite ideal. They should be freely planted for this specific purpose. (See Chapter XVI.)

CULTURE OF THE LATE-FLOWERING BULBS

As the summer- and autumn-flowering bulbs include species which differ as widely as possible botanically, and in their natural habits of growth, no broad set of cultural directions can be applied to them, excepting as concerns the general preparation of the soil in which they are to be planted, and here the instructions given for the spring-flowering bulbs may be repeated. (See Chapter IV.) Otherwise, they may best be considered in the three groups already mentioned—hardy, tender, and half-hardy.

Hardy. The hardy late-flowering bulbs may, almost without exception, be planted in either late fall or very early spring; in the latter case often merely because the bulbs cannot be obtained before the ground freezes. Frequently this may be overcome by covering the spot or the bed where they are to be put with several inches of fresh stable manure, which is replaced after the bulbs are planted. This will give them a chance to start root action. Strange though it may seem to the beginner, a bulb which is actually growing in the soil and has developed its new root system will withstand much more in the way of freezing than will one which has just been planted and is merely lying dormant. Where bulbs must be kept over winter for spring planting, take the slight trouble to cover them with sand, which should be dry enough so that it does not feel moist to the touch.

Planting and Replanting. In planting all large bulbs, it is particularly important not to leave holes with empty air spaces below the bulb (see page 37); and in planting very late, it is especially important that sand, for extra good drainage, be placed about the bulb.

When replanting becomes necessary, by far the best time of the year to do it is just after the foliage turns yellow and dies. Small bulbs which may have formed around the base of the larger ones should be separated and planted either in the "nursery" (see page 239) to grow to larger size, or set out in a permanent position where they are to flower a year or two later.

An *annual mulch* in winter or early spring is desirable, not so much for protection from cold as to hold the very early growth in check and to *keep the soil cool and moist during summer.*

Tender. The tender summer- and autumn-flowering

bulbs are handled in either of two ways: first, planted out directly where they are to bloom after the weather has become settled and warm, usually about May 1st or 15th in the latitude of Philadelphia to New York; second, started early indoors or under glass, and set out as growing plants, after *all* danger of frost is past—usually May 15th to June 1st. By buying the started plants in pots, or starting the plants yourself, you can have them in flower four weeks or more earlier than by setting out the dormant roots or bulbs. Plants which may be handled in this way include cannas, tuberous begonias, caladiums, etc. A few of the "tender" bulbs, while not hardy enough to be left out over winter even with protection, are, nevertheless, sufficiently hardy to be planted out as early in the spring as the soil can be worked. Where this is the case, mention is made of the fact in the cultural directions in the succeeding chapters. Gladiolus is an example of this type of "tender" bulb.

Starting Plants. The more "tender" bulbs are best started in heat, in February or March; but if only an unheated coldframe is available, they may be started in that, in late March or April, three or four weeks before it would be safe to plant them outdoors. The best method is to start them in a "flat" first, burying the bulbs level to the surface in a mixture of thoroughly decayed screened manure and peat or humus—or one of the latter alone, if the manure is not available—and then shifting them to three-, four-, or five-inch pots when the tops and roots have begun to grow. In the pots, use rich light soil—say equal parts screened manure, peat or humus, or leafmold and sand, with a little bone meal added. As hot weather comes along, and the pots are inclined to dry out rapidly, "plunge" them in the frame, as suggested in Chapter XVIII.

I have just been experimenting with a new type of pot made of compressed ground peat, which has the vital advantage of absorbing and holding a great amount of water; and the further advantage that *pot and all* may be planted out in the soil, where the pot gradually disintegrates, with the result that there is little or no "transplanting shock" to the growing plant. If the manufacturers can make these pots a practical commercial proposition, they will possess very great advantages over the ordinary clay pots for this type of work. The bulbs may also be started in "flats" set four or five inches apart each way, and carefully cut out, in squares, when ready to transplant outdoors, but this method is less satisfactory. Growing plants of many bulbs, such as cannas, caladiums, and tuberous-rooted begonias, may be bought from florist or seedsman.

Fertilizers. The tender, bulbous plants are as a rule gross feeders, and will thrive on manures and nitrogenous fertilizers which would be excessive for most other classes of bulbs. Generous amounts of manure, dug into the soil before planting, and the use of dried blood or tankage, in equal parts with fine ground bone, will give them a quick start, and keep them growing vigorously. Watering with liquid manure (made by diluting stable manure, preferably cow manure, with water) or with nitrate of soda (at the rate of a large tablespoonful dissolved in hot water, to a twelve-quart watering can) will also stimulate vigorous growth in meager soils; liquid manures should always be applied when the soil is fairly moist.

Harvesting or Lifting. Many of the tender bulbs will not have completed their natural cycle of growth when the early frosts cut short their season of bloom. When the tops have been "blackened" by the first severe frosts, cut them off six inches or so above the soil, and carefully "lift" the bulbs with a spading fork. Place them, carefully tagged, in flats or shallow boxes, and let them dry off for two or three weeks in a coldframe or in some well-ventilated shed, safe from frost; after which they may be put into winter quarters—some place that is not too dry, and where the temperature will be, preferably, around 38 to 45 degrees—a cool, frost-proof cellar being the best place for such things as cannas, dahlias, "glads," and others of that type; while the more warm-blooded tuberous begonias, caladiums, callas, etc., should be kept somewhat warmer— 45 to 50 degrees; these are best stored in dry sand, sawdust, or peat to prevent shriveling. Of course, it is not always possible, under average home conditions, to maintain just the temperatures suggested above; but they may be kept in mind as a mark to aim at, and the bulbs will remain in good condition even though there may be considerable variation from this mark.

Half-Hardy. This group, which includes those bulbs which must have protection to come through the winter safely, such as montbretias, tritomas, and colochortus, has already been discussed in Chapter X (page 110). All of them may, however, be treated as tender bulbs, and planted in the spring; and as they are quite hardy, the planting may be made as soon as the soil can be worked, instead of waiting for warm weather. It is quite remarkable how early they will start to grow; and, of course, the sooner they begin growth, the more nearly they approximate their natural condition of remaining in the ground over winter, and the better the results which may be expected. In wet soils, a handful or so of sand or leafmold, peat or humus, placed under each bulb, will prove beneficial.

KEEP ALL LATE-BLOOMING BULBS WELL CULTIVATED

One thing more, in the way of culture, which applies to all the summer- and autumn-flowering bulbs, hardy, tender, and half-hardy, and which is so important a point in their successful growing that I have put it the last thing in this chapter, for emphasis.

Unlike the spring-blooming bulbs, which are ceasing growth or lying dormant in the soil during late June, July, and August, the late-blooming bulbs are at just this season making their maximum and most important growth, coming into flower, or developing bulbs for the coming season. *Their requirements for moisture and plant food, therefore,*

*are greatest just when that of the spring-flowering bulbs
is least.*

Thorough and frequent surface cultivation is, therefore,
most important. During prolonged periods of dry weather,
watering may be necessary, but remember that *watering
does not take the place of cultivation;* it should merely
supplement it. When water is given, it should be a thorough
soaking, followed immediately by a surface cultivation. If
the plants are not making satisfactory growth, a top-dressing of fine bone meal and nitrate of soda, in the proportion
of six parts bone to one or two of nitrate, should be applied
just before watering or rain; use the larger proportion of
nitrate if the foliage is somewhat off color, or of a yellowish
tinge, indicating a lack of available nitrogen in the soil.
*Lilies and other plants, in positions where soil around them
cannot readily be cultivated or hoed, should be given a
mulching, several inches deep, of strawy manure or leafmold, or one to two inches of peat, humus, or coconut fiber.*

CHAPTER XII

THE HARDY LILIES

WITHIN the entire range of garden plants, there are probably no flowers more universally admired than are the hardy lilies, and yet the gardens in which one finds them are comparatively few!

Why?

Well, let us admit the truth at the beginning. There are very few plants with which the amateur is more likely to meet failure at his first attempt to grow them. Nevertheless, success is not only possible; it is, with at least a very satisfactory range of varieties, quite easy, if one knows and caters to their simple requirements.

No other flowers are so striking in the garden picture; so stately and yet so graceful; so charming in their combinations of form, color, and fragrance; or less trouble to take care of, year in and year out, once they have become established. Is it not, then, well worth a little study on the part of the amateur to learn the "secrets"—which really are not secret at all—of their successful culture? Particularly so as their requirements, once understood, are easily met, so far as many of the most beautiful varieties are concerned. There is hardly a garden, no matter how small, which will not furnish suitable conditions for at least a half dozen or more varieties; for, fortunately, the various species succeed, in nature and under cultivation, over a remarkably wide range of conditions of soil and climate, running from full sun to quite dense shade, from extremely dry to very wet locations, and in soils from very acid to fairly "sweet," and from heavy loam to almost pure sand. The one big secret of success with hardy lilies is to select

133

varieties which will be happy under the conditions which you have to offer them! It is for this reason that I shall devote most of this chapter to the endeavor to make plain how the beginner can succeed in growing lilies rather than to the usual elaborate description of species and varieties. The more I learn of plants—and the God of Chance has been so considerate as to grant me experience with a great many different kinds, under many widely varied conditions —the more I become convinced that Nature is a teacher whose lessons all gardeners may always study with profit. But she never urges us to come to her school. Her book is free, but he who would learn from it must open it himself. If there are sermons in stones, they are only for the sharp eye and the keen ear. And the old Dame never gives you a diploma; the longer you study under her tutelage, the more you realize you are merely a sophomore.

Now the lilies, more than almost any other important class of plants we have, are, and remain, wildlings, even in the captivity of the garden. There are many natural species which have been brought together for our enjoyment from many parts of the world, but there are very few manmade varieties. And so, in considering the lilies, we will particularly do well to turn to the pages of Nature's old but still very reliable herbal.

TAMING A WILD LILY

Still clear in memory are my own first attempts at lily growing. In a field on our Connecticut farm which was called the Long Mowing—a name handed down through generations with the farm—the yellow Field Lily grew in scores along the sides of a little stream which drained the lot. But every year, just as their slender golden bells began to open, would come the mowers, with their long lean scythes, each one following with his wide swath and parallel row of heel tracks, close behind the other; and, in their wake, my towering beauties, arrayed even as Solomon was not, lay prone with the plebeian herd's grass and timothy. To this day I never see one of these lilies without having spring to mind Rosamund Mariott Watson's lines:

> They are mowing the meadows now and the whispering, sighing
> Song of the scythe as it falls on mine idle ear,
> Whispers of summers dead, and of this one dying—
> Roses on roses fallen, and year on year . . .

For the pale and beautiful wild roses fell with the towering candelabra stalks of the lilies before the circling scythes.

We wander, it may seem to the reader, somewhat afield in search of lily lore. But that is just where it must be looked for, as I found out in trying to "tame" some of the lilies described above. I decided to transfer them to my garden, thinking that, on the richer soil there, they must thrive even more wonderfully than they did in the meadow. To omit the sad details of three years of disappointments, I found out that they would not grow in richly manured soil; nor in wet soil, where I tried them the second year— attempting to imitate the conditions I had found them in, but failing to realize, until after I had lost another season, that their natural growing place, while quite moist, was *well drained* by the little brook flowing through it, so that the bulbs were actually above the winter water level. And, thirdly, I found that they did not like lime. The last discovery was an accident; in seeking material to improve the drainage of the bed where they were growing, I used some old plaster rubbish as far as it would go, and finished out with hard coal cinders and coarse ashes. The difference was most marked. Since then, I have often used coal ashes as a drainage material, and have always had lilies of many varieties do excellently with them, although I have never found them recommended in any articles or books on lily culture.

CONSIDER THE LILY—WHERE IT GROWS

After my first experience in trying to get lilies to grow, I began to take particular notice, wherever I found them, of the exact conditions under which they grew. *And I always discovered good drainage around the bulbs,* no matter how moist the soil seemed. Sometimes it was a near-by stream or ditch; sometimes a gravel subsoil. Also I never found any *growing in bare soil.* Always there was grass, low-growing shrubs or plants, or a thick layer of leafmold covering the spot where they flourished. These facts were true of all the lilies growing wild in my locality—the yellow Meadow Lilies (*canadense*), *and canadense flavum,* the "Turkscap" (*superbum*), and the orange-red Wood Lily (*philadelphicum*).

My next experience was the making of quite an elaborate bed of lilies, of many varieties, in a low spot of rather rich soil, where several former attempts had resulted in failure. The system which I worked out for this bed gave excellent results from the first. The soil was dug out to the depth of a foot; an eight-inch layer of coarse coal ashes and rotted cow manure was put in; then four inches of soil mixed half and half with "run-of-bank" gravel (about half coarse sand); and over this eight inches more of soil, leafmold, and sand mixed together in equal parts, a moderate dressing of coarse bone meal being added. This raised the bed about eight inches above the ground level, the sides being sloped and sodded. The entire surface of the bed was covered, after planting, with a thick mulch of strawy, spent horse manure.

In this bed some fifteen varieties of lilies were planted, and grew to perfection, without further attention except an annual dressing of bone meal and a winter mulching of manure, which was left on in the spring, for many years. The location was naturally anything but an ideal one for lilies; but by taking a few hints from Nature, we were able to get them to do finely. Since then I have frequently found that the generous use of coal ashes and a raised bed, where the ground is likely to remain wet during the winter, will always bring success; other conditions, of course, being right.

I consider these two things, although I have never happened to see them recommended in any bulb literature, the first essentials, where conditions for bulb growing are not naturally favorable. Where the soil drainage is already very good, it is not necessary to dig out the bed, but even then a generous amount of coal ashes dug deep into the soil is, I think very helpful, as it gives the soil that open calcareous character in which most lilies seem to thrive; and at the same time, the ashes *hold moisture,* which gravel or coarse sand will not do.

CONDITIONS FOR SUCCESSFUL LILY CULTURE

And now as to the other conditions.

Most lilies prefer an acid, or at least a neutral, soil, and this should be provided except in the case of a few varieties which are lime tolerant (and which are noted later). The simplest way of providing this condition is to use plenty of leafmold in the soil where lilies are to be planted. Peat, which is inexpensive and easy to obtain, is also splendid. An excellent mixture for lilies is one part loam, one part leafmold or peat (or better both), and one part sand and rotted manure, with a sprinkle of coarse bone added. Dig out the loam to a depth of from one to two feet, fork coal ashes into the subsoil, mix the soil as above, and replace. Then you may be sure you have laid the foundation for success.

This is not as much trouble as it sounds. A large shallow box, similar to the sort used for mixing cement or mortar, may be used "on the job" for mixing up the soil and keeping the lawn clean. A good-sized bed may be prepared with a few hours' work, and as it will not need to be touched again for years, lilies really require much less time on the part of the gardener than do most other hardy flowers. Where lilies are grown in groups, or clumps, in the hardy border or among shrubs, prepare a "hole" for them from two to three feet in diameter, just as suggested above.

To the gardener who will not employ the precaution suggested above, but would prefer to "take a chance" and plant in his or her soil as it is, I can only say this: at least lift out a spadeful or two of soil, where each bulb is to go, and put in coal ashes or sand an inch or two under each bulb; and mulch the soil above it after planting.

Remember also that the *soil should be covered,* where lilies are growing. Low cover plants, low shrubs, spreading perennials which will shade the bases of the lilies, or a constant mulch are essential to success.

EASILY GROWN SPECIES AND VARIETIES

And now, before we discuss briefly the various species and varieties of lilies available, a word as to their place in the garden picture. Remember that they are among the most striking of all garden plants. Unlike many other flowers, you do not need a "mass effect" with them to enjoy their great beauty. In nature, they are seldom found in great quantities together. A single lily, standing out against a background of evergreens, a hedge, among tall shrubs, or making a charming contrast with a group of some other tall flower, such as delphiniums, may add more to the real beauty of the garden than an entire "bed." Study your garden most carefully to select the spots—not too many— where lilies are to go, and then plant not over six or a dozen, under ordinary circumstances, in a place; two or three will often look as well. Spend the extra amount on more varieties, which will give you a longer season of these beautiful flowers; they may be had from early June until October.

In the following brief descriptions, arranged with the view of helping the beginner to select intelligently, rather than to do justice to the wonderfully varied beauty of the many sorts, the distinction is made between "base-rooting" and "top-rooting" species. The former, forming roots at the base of the bulb, should be covered comparatively shallow —about twice the vertical diameter of the bulb, or four to six inches; the latter, which form a circular mass of roots *above* the bulb, as well as at the base, should go deeper—

three or four diameters, or eight to ten, or even twelve, inches deep.

As it is well to select varieties differing in season of bloom, three groups have been made—early, medium, and late.

Early Lilies. Hansoni, one of the earliest, prefers some shade; bright orange, stem rooting. Candidum, the popular white Madonna lily; one of the finest and easiest to grow; secure north of France bulbs; plant in August *as early as possible;* cover only two inches deep. Canadense, and canadense flavum (yellow) one of the most graceful of all, very hardy, base rooting. Testaceum (the "Nankeen lily") somewhat similar to candidum, but delicate buff shade; tall and very graceful; plant same as candidum, base rooting. Monadelphum, free bloomer, strong grower, shades of yellow; medium height, base rooting. Browni, pale yellow; good for very light soils, plant eight inches deep; stem rooting. Umbellatum and its varieties, orange, apricot, crimson; medium height. Martagon, six feet, deep purple, base roots. Croceum, any soil; full sun or shade; orange flowers and extra good foliage; stem rooting. Elegans (*thunbergianum*), orange red, and elegans varieties, blood red, apricot, brilliant orange, and buff colored, all dwarf, beautiful varieties, thriving in sunny locations. E. Prince of Orange grows less than a foot high; plant eight inches deep; stem rooting. Tenuifolium, dazzling red, is also medium height, extra early, loam soil and semi-shade, stem rooting: Golden Gleam is an apricot yellow variety.

Mid-season. Regale (*myriophyllum*), finest of the mid-season group and one of the most beautiful and satisfactory of all lilies; large white with golden centers, and reddish brown bands on outside of petals; stem rooting. Regale may be raised from seed without great difficulty. A new race of regale × sulphurum hybrids, introduced as Sulphur-Gale Hybrids, is now available. Sargentiae, somewhat similar to regale; but blooms later; fine to follow; very hardy. Superbum, reddish orange, very hardy; moist location preferable, but not necessary; base rooting, chalcedonicum, Scarlet Turkscap, brilliant color, very easily grown. Pardalinum, the "Leopard Lily," very striking, bright orange with maroon spots; six to seven feet; very hardy, but requires excellent drainage; base rooting; there is a bright yellow form, Roezli. Willmottiae, quite new, orange-red, vigorous grower; plant in wind-protected position, eight inches deep; stem rooting.

Late-flowering Lilies. Auratum, the "gold-banded" lily of Japan; huge, but artistically shaped white flower, with crimson splashes and golden band through each petal; vigorous grower, but likes heavy mulching and some shade; plant very deep—a foot is not too much; stem rooting: macranthum is a still more vigorous growing form of auratum, with white flowers spotted yellow. Speciosum and its various forms are among the most satisfactory of all lilies for the average garden; the irregularly waved recurved flowers are most artistic, and the season of bloom is quite long; rose, red, white, and deep ruby-colored varieties, of which the latter, *speciosum magnificum,* is the finest. Album Kraetzeri is snow white, with yellowish green band through each petal. Tigrinum, the well-known Tiger Lily, is the hardiest of all; grows like a weed, often escaping to form colonies on dry banks; base rooting, several varieties, of which *splendens* is one of the latest flowering of all lilies. Henryi, vigorous grower, six to eight feet, is one of the most distinct of all; a rich, orange yellow, of graceful form; extra fine; prefers shade and wind shelter; plant extra deep, ten to twelve inches; stem rooting. Batemannia, pale orange, shading to pink, medium height.

TWO PINK LILIES

The two pink lilies which do best with garden culture are not so rugged as most of the above. If attempted, they should be surrounded with sand, and well mulched. A surer way is to plant in large pots, seven or eight inches, and plunge for the winter in a frame, then set out, pot and all,

(Upper left) Japanese gold-banded lily (*auratum*) from American-grown seedlings. *(Upper right) Speciosum,* most satisfactory for general use. *(Below)* The Madonna lily, pure white, effective against evergreens.

(*Upper left*) Large-flowered type of gladiolus. (*Upper right*) The new lacinated type (*lacinatus*). (*Below*) Gladiolus used for land-scape effect in the general garden planting.

in the spring. They are japonicum (*krameri*), three feet tall, a beautiful clear pink; and rubellum, growing but eighteen inches tall, deep rose to light pink, with conspicuous yellow anthers. Both are stem rooting, should be planted deep—seven to eight inches; give *plenty of peat* in the soil and place in partial shade.

The lilies which will grow in a neutral or ordinary garden soil include candidum, speciosum, regale, tigrinum, testaceum, henryi, hansoni, martagon, monadelphum, and croceum; but even these, as well as the others, do better in an acid soil.

CHAPTER XIII

GLADIOLUS

OF the several flowers which are in keen competition to-day for the favor of the amateur gardener, probably none has made so much progress during the past few years as the gladiolus.

As a definite measure of its triumphant advance, there stands out the remarkable fact that the membership of the Gladiolus Society of America has increased from 274 to 3,265 during the past four years—an achievement unequaled, so far as I know, by any other flower organization.

And, incidentally, these members have voted to give the much disputed pronounciation of the name of this flower as gladi-ó-lus, both singular and plural, for which the amateur owes them much thanks!

Any flower, to make a showing such as that indicated above, must have some very decided advantages to offer its votaries. The gladiolus has them, beyond question. First of all, perhaps, is its unequaled certainty of results, even for the beginner. The old reliable "glad" can be counted upon to come through with flying colors ninety-nine times out of a hundred. I have grown gladiolus commercially and in my garden for twenty years and in several different states, and I have never noticed injury by any insect pest. There are a number of diseases or "scabs" which occasionally give the commercial grower some trouble; but these usually show in the bulb, which is sorted out before the crop is passed on to the home gardener.

That the gladiolus is preëminently the amateur's flower is often shown at the gladiolus shows, where some beginner will carry off the prize for the best spikes of a variety in competition with professional growers.

HOW TO USE "GLADS"

The gladiolus has so long been grown primarily as a flower for cutting that it seems difficult to disabuse the public mind of the erroneous belief that it is not suitable for any other purpose. Just as the unfortunate crocus is almost entirely relegated to spotting up the front lawn, instead of being utilized, as it may well be, in the general garden scheme, so the helpless gladiolus is outlawed, by general practice, from association with other flowers, and condemned to an unsightly bed by itself, or a space in the vegetable garden. And even those who supposedly champion this beautiful flower lift no voice in protest!

The gladiolus *can* be used for planting in the mixed border, where groups of a dozen or twenty-five bulbs of one variety are exceedingly effective. Because of its tall, imposing form, long lines or small groups planted against walls or tall hedges, or in the shrubbery border, where there will be some protection from high winds, make a wholly pleasing picture. The foliage itself, which gives the plant its popular name of "sword lily," is beautiful until the flowers open, and remains attractive for a long time after the faded flower stalks are cut off. The clear, self-colored varieties are by far the most effective for either border or landscape planting. Two or three hybridizers whom I know have seen the possibilities of the gladiolus for landscape use and are systematically working toward the development of a distinct type for that purpose. The new reflowering or "cut-and-come-again" type will also doubtless extend the use of the gladiolus in this direction. By planting, at the same time, some of the bulbs two inches deep, others four, and still others five or six, a "succession" of bloom may easily be had from one planting.

FOUR MONTHS OF "GLADS"

Another great appeal which the gladiolus possesses is that it may easily be had in bloom continuously for weeks on end. The bulbs are extremely hardy and may be planted as soon as the ground can be worked in spring—March or early April. The earliest varieties will bloom in from seventy to eighty days, bringing them in the latter part of June. From then on, by using later-flowering varieties and by succession plantings, which can be made up to early July, it is possible to have a constant procession of bloom until hard frosts.

This is a fact which, to my mind, the catalogue makers have never stressed nearly enough. My own practice has been to plant the choice new varieties early so as to get a good crop of bulblets or cormels—the little "seed" bulbs which form in a cluster around the base of the old bulb— and to reserve a supply of the cheaper or more plentiful kinds for later plantings.

The midseason and late varieties take from eighty to a hundred days, so that it is possible to secure a month of bloom from one planting. And thus by making four plantings—about April, May, June, and July 1st—including in each some early, midseason, and late varieties, it is easily possible to have four months of flowers.

If strong second-size bulbs are planted, they will produce flowers almost anywhere; but to get the finest spikes, and to have a new bulb as good as the old for "carrying on" for next season's planting, a fairly deep, rich soil should be provided. As most varieties of gladiolus increase rapidly, a good system of growing is to plant a number of bulbs each spring in a rich bed, or in the vegetable garden, where the varieties may readily be kept separated and marked. If the spikes are cut with only one or two leaves, leaving the rest of the foliage, the new bulbs and bulblets will develop satisfactorily. Surplus bulbs, which will rapidly accumulate, may be used for planting in the flower garden and about the grounds, and either left unharvested in the fall, or taken up and thrown into a general mixture, for cutting with extra long spikes, which will practically stop the growth of the new bulb, the following summer.

For growing for flowers or for increase of stock, plant the bulbs in rows about four or five inches deep, in light soil; but only three to four inches in heavy soil. In stiff clay, two inches is quite enough. The rows are usually made twenty-four inches apart, but eighteen is sufficient if space is limited. The bulbs should be spaced three to six inches apart, according to soil, size of bulbs, and vigor of growth of the variety.

The growers of gladiolus bulbs always grade them into

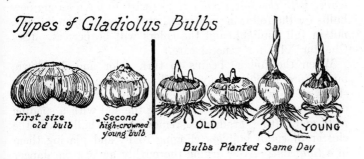

Types of Gladiolus Bulbs

First size old bulb

Second "high-crowned" young bulb

OLD   YOUNG

Bulbs Planted Same Day

several sizes, No. 1's being one and a half inches or over; No. 2, one and a quarter to one and a half; No. 3, one to one and a quarter, etc. But size is not the only thing to consider. I would much rather have, either for propagating or merely for bloom, a young, well-rounded, or "high-crown" bulb, of No. 2 or even No. 3 size, than a several-year-old flat or concave bulb two inches in diameter. They will start more quickly, grow more vigorously, and "stand up" much better against winds than the old bulbs. The illustration drawn from a photograph, shows the result of one of several experiments I made some years ago with old and young bulbs of the same varieties—America, in the case illustrated. They were planted at the same time, and under identical conditions.

The gladiolus, even more than most plants, appreciates thorough cultivation during the growing season, and plenty of moisture. For "show" blooms, a top-dressing of liquid manure or nitrate of soda may be given just as the flower spikes are developing. Staking the individual plants, or supporting with string stretched between stakes, is sometimes resorted to; but if the bulbs are planted deep, and the stalks well "hilled up"—like corn or potatoes—as they grow, this will seldom be necessary.

Flowers for cutting should be taken just as the first two or three buds are well opened. Remove *only one or two leaves with the flower spike* if you wish to have strong new bulbs for the following season. Let the spikes open indoors, not in full sunlight, and the colors will be perfect. (See Chapter XIX for general care.)

When the foliage begins to turn color and die down, but before it pulls away readily from the bulb, cut the stems off to within three inches or so of the soil, and take up the bulbs carefully by loosening the soil with a spading fork and lifting gradually, removing the bulb with the cluster of small bulblets clinging to it, and placing them in a *tight* flat. After drying thoroughly away from danger of frost, separate and store for winter (see Chapter XX).

TYPES AND VARIETIES

The development of the gladiolus in its modern form is a comparatively recent achievement; and we are now in the midst of the greatest activity, on the part of the hybridizers, that this flower has ever enjoyed. Every season sees scores of new varieties displayed at the "glad" shows and many of them are better than, or distinctly different from, their predecessors.

The gladiolus has "broken" in so many different directions, in form as well as in color, that the new things are not merely improvements on existing varieties, but are entirely distinct and different. When, for instance, the Kunderd or "ruffled" type was introduced, less than ten years ago, it gave rise to an entire new race.

Then came the primulinus hybrids, which gave us a whole new range of orange, salmon, and yellow shades.

And still more recently, we have the laciniated or serrated type, entirely distinct from anything preceding it.

And the breeders are still at it. Types which will throw several spikes of bloom, one after another, and which are especially adapted for landscape planting, now seem assured; and the sweet-scented gladiolus, which will be a wonderful improvement, is at least within sight.

The varieties of gladiolus are multiplying so rapidly that any attempt to cover the latest would require an annual supplement to a book! Those given below, which in some instances are quite recent introductions, have been thoroughly tested in general use and have made good.

As the average planter selects his "glads" by color, as a first consideration, I have grouped the varieties on that basis.

Many of the finer sorts may be had at from seventy-five cents to two dollars a dozen; the rarer ones being from twenty-five to fifty cents up to several dollars a bulb.

Pink. Pink is, undoubtedly, the most favored color for "glads"; and certainly no other flower offers such a wonderful range of shades and combinations in this color. The best-known pink is America, comparatively old but still the most popular "glad" in the world. Mrs. Frank Pendleton, rose pink with rich carmine blotch on lower petals, is one of the closest contestants for second place. Halley is a very early salmon pink; and Marshal Foch, later, is a splendid ruffled salmon pink. Panama is similar to America but considerably deeper in color. Of the newer pinks, Mrs. Dr. Norton has probably won the greatest popularity —cream colored with light pink shading, and particularly beautiful for cutting. E. J. Shaylor, very early, a pure, deep rose, was awarded a certificate of merit by the Royal Horticultural Society of England.

Other good pinks which have made places for themselves are Evelyn Kirtland, shell pink; Byron L. Smith, an orchid or lavender pink, with fine, wide-open flower; Richard Diener; Mrs. H. E. Bothin; 1910 Rose; and Pink Wonder.

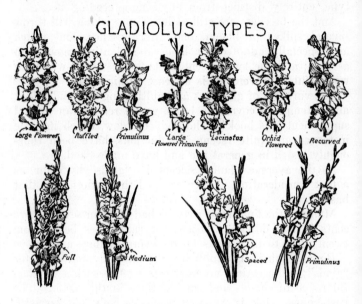

GLADIOLUS TYPES

Large Flowered Ruffled Primulinus Large Flowered Primulinus Lacinatus Orchid Flowered Recurved

Full Medium Spaced Primulinus

Not so well known, but extremely beautiful, is Dorothy McKibben, which, personally, I consider one of the very finest of all "glads." It is a beautiful apple-blossom pink with graceful ruffled flowers. I noticed this fine flower first in the Chicago cut-flower market, where among thousands of spikes of scores of other varieties, it stood out distinctly as the most artistic in form and color of the lot.

Red. Under this head I have included a considerable range of colors. Mrs. Francis King, a brilliant vermilion, and War, a late, deep blood red, are two of the best known. Empress of India is an old dark maroon, which has been largely superseded by Mrs. Watt and Goliath. All of the same type, these are the nearest to black among the "glads."

For a great trio of the newer reds, try Early Sunrise, very early, salmon scarlet with yellow overcolor; Joe Coleman, midseason, the most effective red for massing I have yet seen; and Scarlet Wonder, a gigantic, late scarlet.

Yellow. The pure yellow "self"—that is, without markings—still remains an ideal for the hybridizers; but great progress has been made with this color during the last few years. Schwaben, a canary yellow, has long been the standard, with Niagara, splashed with carmine, as a companion.

Now we have Golden Measure, a glorious spike; Flora, one of the purest yellows; and Gold, the very deepest yellow.

Among the newer yellows, fighting for position, may be mentioned Golden Swallow, Yellow Treasure, and Piccadilly, the last with a rating of 98.

Among the ruffled yellows, Golden Glory is probably the best known.

Orange. Several varieties, usually classed with the reds or the yellows, are of quite distinct color, and with the wider spread of primulinus blood throughout our new hybrids this color will increase in importance. Orange Queen; Pride of Lancaster, orange salmon, ruffled; Orange Glory, and Lustre, a strong growing orange vermilion, are among the class to which I refer. Sheila, with large distinctly triangular-shaped flowers; J. A. Carbone, and Pola Negri, apricot, are three splendid newer ones.

CHOICE WHITES AND BLUES

White. Almost all of the whites have at least a trace of lavender, crimson, or yellow as a throat color, or as veinings or feathering on the lower petals. Nevertheless, marked advancement has been made recently, and the old standards, such as Augusta, Shakespeare, and Peace, are now out of the running. For a quartet of splendid whites, plant Lily White, L'Immaculee, White Wonder, and Europa, blooming in the order named.

Joerg's White is probably the largest of all. Albania is another fine one. Carmen Sylva, with its lilylike blooms, is very distinct.

Of the creamy whites, Helen Franklin, extra early, Mary Pickford, and Fern Kyle are very choice. Anthony B. Kunderd, cream with a pink flush, is most effective for cutting.

Blue. I say "blue," as that is the term commonly used; lavender and purple shades would be more accurate, as there is no true pure blue. Baron J. Hulot, fairly early, is the old standard, and still one of the bluest. Bluejay is later. Mr. Mark, nearer a "self" color, and Mary Fennell, deep lilac, are preferable in many ways. The "blue" which I consider the finest I have ever seen, is a new European variety, Mrs. Van Konynenburg, with flowers as large and well-opened as those of America.

It is among the lavenders, however, that the choicest shades are to be found—colors which can compete with the orchids themselves for delicate beauty. Sweet Lavender is the very earliest. Herada, a delicate mauve, belongs in every garden. Louise and Muriel, lavender and light blue respectively, are two of the prettiest.

"SMOKES"

Certain varieties of an indescribable blending of dark colors, wine-reds and lavender purples, which they inherit from the old Empress of India, are known as "smokes." Roseash is, perhaps, the most striking, and a fine, strong spike; London Smoke, Ross Valley, and Ulysses are others.

THE INDISPENSABLE "PRIMS"

No other section in the wide range of "glads" has gained so rapidly in public favor during the last few years as the primulinus hybrids. Mark first and foremost of all for your list Alice Tiplady, and get enough of them to make several plantings if you love cut flowers. The color is a delicate orange saffron.

Maidens Blush, a most dainty flower of exquisite light pink; Souvenir, canary yellow; Salmon Beauty, and Orange Brilliant comprise four splendid additional shades. Among the best of the ruffled prims are Dorothy Wheeler, rose pink; Gold Drop, deep yellow; and Primunella.

Typical of the large-flowered Prim. hybrids, which will hold their own with any of the other large-flowered types, are Myra, a deep salmon with yellowish throat; Ming Toy, a most peculiar Chinese yellow; and Gladdie Boy, undoubtedly one of the finest "glads" yet developed in any section, and likely to prove one of the most popular of all.

Gladiolus growing for the amateur is treated more fully in the author's Homegarden Handbooks series in the volume "Gladiolus" to which the reader, if he or she is particularly interested in this flower, is referred.

[NOTE: For a much more complete discussion of gladiolus, including hybridizing, growing for exhibition, and growing for profit, the reader is referred to the author's book "Gladiolus" in the Home Garden Handbook Series.]

CHAPTER XIV

DAHLIAS

WITH the dahlia holding the leading position, so far as popular favor is concerned, of all bulbs grown in American gardens, one naturally hesitates to raise a dissenting voice in the general chorus of approbation.

In the first place, to take any stand whatsoever in the matter, other than the usual one of unlimited approval without any reservations at all, immediately lays one open to the accusation of being a "highbrow," who can see no beauty in anything that is popular, merely because it *is* popular. And, in the second place, it is difficult to explain that any disapproval one may wish to express is not directed against the flower itself, but against the way in which it is used.

If the dahlia is to be judged upon its merits as a cut flower alone, then, of course, any method of growing it which produces the best flowers for cutting is the best method to use—and there is nothing more to say in the matter. If, however, it is to be thought of as a flower for the garden, and worth while considering in the general garden picture, there is much to say. The dahlia, as usually grown, does not belong in the garden, although one so frequently sees it there. In spite of the great beauty of its individual blossoms, the stiff and ungainly plant, tied up to a stake, is a blemish and not a beauty spot in the garden picture. I never see a dahlia under such conditions without recalling the exclamation of a friend of mine which was called forth by similar circumstances, "Another beauty gone wrong; but more to be pitied than blamed!"

There is, however, still hope for the dahlia, or rather for

the dahlia grower. When its admirers once learn that mere size is not the ultimate of perfection which a flower may attain, and that a Giant Russian sunflower is not necessarily more beautiful than a New England aster, then we may hope that the dahlia will be, as it deserves to be, seriously considered as a possibility for the garden.

This beautiful flower is comparatively a newcomer among the garden's occupants. It was not until very late in the eighteenth century that it was discovered, and the only result of the first fifty years of the hybridizer's work with it was the development of the "ball" type of flower, in not too attractive colors, or shades of coloring. The ball dahlia is, perhaps, the most perfect masterpiece of a stiff, stilted, and absolutely artificial-looking bloom that has ever been created by the infinitely patient hand of the hybridizer from a timid, simple little blossom torn out of Nature's garden.

But, then, what happened? The gardening public finally revolted against this "man-made" dahlia, and the popularity of the flower waned to such an extent that it was rapidly disappearing. The result was the development of new types, beginning with the "cactus," which was later followed by the "decorative," "show," "century," and others. Along with the new forms came new and remarkably beautiful colors and shades of coloring. No other flower in all the annals of horticulture has even shown itself more fluid material in the plant breeder's hand; and in little over fifty years more, there have been developed the amazing variations in form, now covering well over a score of distinct types and sub-types; and a range of colors, shades, tints, and blendings which, perhaps, is unsurpassed by any other flower. The dahlia, moreover, flowers over a long period— three months or so under proper culture; and is a vigorous grower, fairly free from insects and diseases; and multiplies rapidly, even in the hands of the amateur grower.

Is it to be expected that a flower which has proven itself capable of such infinite variation in form, color, and habit of growth, and possesses so many other advantages, must permanently be denied a real place in the garden, as well as in the plot for cut flowers? I, for one, refuse to believe it, and I feel certain that the next great step in the development of the dahlia will be in the breeding of a type or types especially adapted to garden and landscape work—even though little has as yet been done in that direction.

USING DAHLIAS IN THE GARDEN

Even with the types which we now have, however, adapted primarily though they are to the production of beautiful blooms for cutting, it is possible to use dahlias in the garden.

For this purpose, only the most free-flowering and *sure*-flowering varieties should be selected. By placing the plants at the rear of the border behind other flowers, so that only the blooms and tops of the foliage will show, it is possible to use many of the well-known varieties ordinarily grown for cut-flower or exhibition purposes. Even though the plants be staked, and given at least the minimum amount of pruning and disbudding which those sorts require, they will present, from the front, quite the appearance of a plant growing naturally. Between groups of shrubs and in corners, where there is not too much shade, they may often be used with excellent effect. For actually planting in the border or in the beds, however, it is best to use the more dwarf or bushy-growing varieties, particularly among the singles (St. George is especially fine for this purpose), the pompons, and the "decorative pompons" —which are really not pompons at all, but miniature "decoratives." The pompons, and other small-flowered, free, and constant-blooming, dwarf-growing varieties are becoming more popular each season, as must be plain to any one attending the annual dahlia shows and noticing the increasing interest which they command.

It is to this type, and to the still more recently popularized "star" type, when the hybridizers begin to give them the really serious attention they merit, that we may look for some real garden dahlias. The small-flowered sorts, however, are no less beautiful for cutting; some of them bloom so freely that they may be cut in sprays, and with other flowers, or with something light and airy in the way of foliage, such as gypsophila, they are, indeed, beautiful. These quite double the use of the dahlia as an indoor flower, for the immense blooms of the standard sorts, wonderfully beautiful as many of them are, are unsuited to many forms of room or table decoration.

There is yet another method of planting dahlias which is immensely effective, though one seldom sees them so employed. That is to set them out in a long narrow bed or row, where they may form a hedge, or bank, of foliage or blossoms; or be held against a wall or fence. So planted, and kept within a few harmonizing varieties, they will command universal attention, and be truly beautiful. Save up the bulbs of a few of your most reliable freer-flowering varieties, until you have sufficient to give this method of planting a trial, and see how you think the result compares with the row of stakes in the average dahlia garden!

DAHLIA TYPES

The dahlia enthusiasts have worked out a system of classification for this mercurial flower which is quite as elaborate, if not quite so definite, as that employed for daffodils. It is difficult, however, to make the dahlia "stay put" in any system of classification, because each type constantly merges into the others, and new varieties keep coming along which do not exactly fit into any. To help the beginner, however, in making selections of the sorts which appeal to his particular taste, I will endeavor to give some idea of the differences between them.

Cactus Type. Double flowers with the petals (or more correctly speaking "the floral rays") long, narrow, and "rolled," usually curved or twisted, such as F. W. Fellowes or Ambassador.

DAHLIA TYPES

Cactus

Hybrid Cactus

Decorative

Ball

Peony Flowered

Collarette

Dahlia grown without
staking by proper
system of pruning

Star

Single

Pompon

Hybrid Cactus Type. Similar to the above but with shorter petals, less rolled or flat; such as George Walters and Attraction.

Decorative Type. Double flowers, full to the center, rather flat with broad, loosely arranged petals, often with rounded tips, such as Insulinde or Jersey's Beauty.

Ball Type. "Show dahlias," double flowers of globular or ball form, full to center, with regular spiral arrangement of florets and evenly rolled petals—the perfect artificial flower. How fashions change! Once this was the only dahlia considered worth while, and now you seldom find one listed. A. D. Livoni and Dorothy Peacock were, and still are, the best of the "balls." I may mention, in passing, that my friend L. K. Peacock, one of the "daddies" of the dahlia game, told me recently, at a show where we were judging, that in his opinion the ball type is "surely coming back."

Peony-Flowered Type. Semi-double, with open center or heart, inner petals usually twisted or curled; outer ones broad and often twisted; the most artistic in form of all; as, for instance, the old but ever popular Geisha and John Wanamaker.

Pompon Type. Ball shape, but with the tight flowers quite small—less than two inches in diameter, and mostly of dwarf habit of growth; such as Belle of Springfield and Sunbeam. Most of the miniatures are included in this class. Keep one eye on the pompons!

Collarette. Open centered, with single row of broad outer petals and "collar" of shorter inner ones, usually of sharply contrasting color; a "freak" type, but very attractive, nevertheless. Maurice Rivoire and Queen Anne are typical.

Singles. Flat, open-centered flowers, with outer row of broad petals. Most of those listed are of the "New Century" class, extra large and very fine, such as Ekford Century and Snowflake.

Star Type. Last, but, in my opinion, by no means least. The small, anemonelike blooms, with open centers, are borne, in extravagant abundance, on long, lean, wiry stems, and the plant has a neat, compact growth. Here is a type to try by all means; it will give you an understanding of what the dahlia will yet do for our late summer gardens. Keep both eyes on the "stars"!

Other Types. The above by no means exhausts the "sections" of the dahlia classification, but will serve for a working program. Other classes include the Duplex (semi-double); "Anemone-Flowered"; Tom Thumb or Mignon; single Cactus; Bedding Type, and several more.

GROWING GOOD DAHLIAS

The dahlia is popular, in spite of, rather than because of, its cultural requirements. There is no denying the fact that it requires more care than most other bulbs. Not that it is not worth the trouble, for it is, by all means; but there are more chances to "go wrong" with it than with most of the plants mentioned in this book. Any one who has ever belonged to a local dahlia society—and the country is now full of them—knows of the heated discussions on the fine points of culture!

Very often it is a case of the Pinaforian cat that was killed by too much care. Not infrequently the "rank beginner" has very good luck; and then becomes so expert that he fusses his plants into flowerlessness if not to death. Some seasons are much better than others for flower development—there is no question about that; but, ordinarily, good blooms can be had each year, if the following points are absorbed—and applied.

First of all, dahlias need plenty of sun, air, and room; and prefer a rather light, warm soil. These things are more essential than to have an extremely rich soil.

Next, the dahlia is a vigorous grower and a very gross feeder. In fact, it is something of a pig, and will overeat very quickly if allowed to do so, with the result that there is a tremendous production of stalks and foliage and few, or imperfect, flowers. *Don't give dahlias too much nitro-*

gen. If this is avoided, there is no danger of getting the soil "too rich," provided the plants are vigorously pruned.

Use plenty of old, well-rotted manure in your dahlia soil, if it is to be had, but dig it in as far in advance of planting as possible—early spring, or still better, the preceding fall. Work the ground at least eight, better twelve, and best eighteen inches deep. Add to the manure ground bone with a moderate amount of dried blood or tankage (see page 33). If stakes are to be used, put them in place before planting; they should be substantial, and at least five feet above the ground. The plants, if grown principally for big flowers for cutting, should be from three to four feet apart each way.

Dahlias may be bought as full-grown clumps, field-grown roots, pot-grown roots, "divisions," or "green plants," the latter being young plants from cuttings. Personally, I much prefer a good field-grown root to any of the others. There is no more advantage in overgrown, big dahlia tubers than in over-sized, but also over-aged, gladiolus bulbs (see page 145). Any of the others, however, will succeed with good care.

Plant Deep. Dormant roots, which must, of course, contain an "eye" to be any good, may be set out as soon as the soil begins to warm up—say about the middle of April or "corn-plantin'" time. Living plants should not be set out until later, when all danger of late frosts is past, or any time after that up to the end of June. Dig out generous-sized holes, and put extra manure (*if* well rotted) and bone flour at the *bottom* of each, mixing well with the soil or subsoil. If manure is not available, use peat or humus; then place the tuber on its side, with the eye near the stake. Put it five or six inches below the surface, but fill in only half the depth of soil at first. Plants should be treated similarly; be sure they are "hardened off" by exposure outside for several days and nights before setting them out; and if the soil is at all dry, give a thorough soaking in the *bottom* of the hole, when planting.

When the plants have made a few inches of growth, cut off all but the strongest shoot, and pinch that one back near the ground. If the plants are to be grown without "staking," it is essential to make them branch out almost at the ground level, so as to form a low-spreading "bush." A second pinching may be needed to accomplish this. Where stakes are to be used, keep the plants tied up as they grow (see page 126).

Cultivate. *Keep the soil cultivated*—this is the most essential thing in dahlia growing. Work the earth three or four inches deep at first; and then, as the buds form, not over two inches or so—just as in cultivating corn or potatoes. The object is to make them root as deeply as possible at first, and then, as the large roots nearer the surface develop, not to break them off. But keep the *surface* cultivated, especially after every rain. If dry, water thoroughly. Don't "do the daily sprinkle" that so many amateurs practice; it's worse than nothing.

Disbudding. To get the largest flowers on long stems, disbudding or removing some of the buds is necessary. This is essential in growing "exhibition" blooms. Proceed as follows: Leave the terminal or "end" bud on the main shoot or shoots, and pinch out the two side shoots or buds just below it. This will give a long stem for the terminal flower, and at the same time stimulate the growth of the two side shoots next farther down the stem. As these develop, leave the terminal bud on each of them, but pinch out the side buds just below them. And so on, as the plant keeps blooming. Near the end of the season, *all* the side shoots (which would not have time to develop flowers before frost) should be removed to throw the strength of the plant into those buds which can "make it."

Top-Dressing. With the tremendous growth made, the plants, especially in very dry weather, may become "bloomed out," as it is called, before the season is over. Watch your plant carefully, and at the first sign of this playing out, give a top-dressing or mulch with manure (see page 132). As soon as there is insufficient plant food, *or insufficient moisture,* to keep the plants growing vigorously, the *wood hardens,* and then it's good-by flowers! Prevent this condition if you can; but if you find it has taken place, prune the whole plant back severely; if fairly early in the season, say up to the end of July, *clear back to the ground.* If moisture is available, new growth will be made with astonishing rapidity, and the plant will usually flower freely. At any rate, nothing is gained by keeping the old plant, once it has ceased blooming.

Harvesting and Storing. The remarks made in Chapter XI (see page 130) apply to dahlia roots. In lifting them, care should be taken not to break or split the necks of the tubers, which are quite brittle. The biggest root, without at least one good sound eye, is absolutely worthless. Let the roots get thoroughly dried *off,* in some frost-proof place, but never dried *out.* They may be kept in open flats or on shelves in the cellar, but the safest and surest way is to cover them, or at least the most precious ones, with sand.

Raising Dahlias from Seed. This is so easy that any amateur who has had a little garden experience may readily accomplish it for his own amusement. It is extremely interesting work, and you get flowers the *first season* from spring-sown seeds. But remember that it is likely there will be only one seedling in thousands, sometimes in hundreds of thousands, which is really any improvement over existing varieties, of which, so far as the dahlia is concerned, there are already a very plentiful supply.

SOME EXCELLENT DAHLIAS

Cactus and Hybrid Cactus.

Ambassador, yellow-shaded amber and pink.
Attraction, silvery lavender.
Countess of Lonsdale, deep salmon.
Frances Lobdell, mallow pink, shaded lighter.
F. W. Fellowes, coral red.
George Walters, salmon, shaded pink.

Kalif, pure scarlet.
Mariposa, pure pink, shaded violet.
Mrs. W. E. Estes, pure white.
Mrs. Warnaar, white, shaded delicate pink.
Pierrot, amber, tipped white, distinct.
Siskiyou, mauve, largest of all.

Decorative.

Amun Ra, coppery orange.
Dr. Tevis, rose and old gold.
Fiet (Hortulanus Fiet), shrimp, shading to orange.
Insulinde, golden, shading to salmon.
Jersey's Beauty, the best rose pink.
Patrick O'Mara, coppery yellow.
Mrs. Carl Salbach, pinkish lavender.
Mrs. I. De Ver Warner, orchid mauve, extra fine.
Shudow's Lavender, silvery lavender shading to white.
The U. S. A., glistening orange, extra fine.

Show and Hybrid-Show (Ball-Shaped).

A. D. Livoni, soft pink.
Dorothy Peacock, shell pink.
Jean Kerr, pure white.
Yellow Duke, canary yellow.
Stradella, dark crimson.

Peony-flowered.

Avalanche, pure white.
Coppersmith, coppery bronze.
Geisha, red and gold tinted.
John Wanamaker, lavender pink.

Pompon.

Little Beauty, rosy pink.
Little Jewel, pink, shading lighter, extra fine.
Nerissa, mauve pink.
Sunbeam, crimson scarlet.

Colarette.
    Maurice Rivoire, dark red, white collar.

Single-flowered (Century).
    Eckford Century, pure white.
    Praxiteles, velvet purple, tipped white.
    Rose Pink (Rose Pink Century), clear rose.
    St. George, canary yellow.

Star.
    Crawley Star, crimson.

CHAPTER XV

TUBEROUS-ROOTED BEGONIAS

IF you read somewhere that Burbank, before he died, had wizarded into existence a family of plants that would bloom continuously from June until hard frost; that bore flowers of almost every conceivable shape, ranging in size from a small daisy to a giant mallow, six inches across; and in color from the purest glistening white through the most delicate tints and shades of pink, to intensively glowing crimsons and reds; and through every imaginable shade of salmon and orange to the purest yellows; that could be had in either upright or trailing form; that was free from insects and diseases; and that would grow and bloom as freely in the shade as in the sun—if, I say, you read of a plant with these attributes, you would immediately want to send across the continent in order to get some of them, regardless of price.

And yet this flower, known by every amateur on "the other side," but by comparatively few home gardeners in this country, is already in existence, and has been for years.

I do not hesitate to make the statement that the tuberous-rooted begonia is less well known to the American garden public than any other flower which has so many excellent points to recommend it.

Prices for this delightful flower are reasonable, splendid bulbs being obtainable at two to three dollars a dozen and up, according to size and type. Taking into consideration the fact that it costs several times as much to produce a begonia bulb as it does to produce a gladiolus bulb, and also that the begonia bulb may be kept year after year, the purchase of a supply of begonias constitutes one of the best garden values that you can possibly get.

If you try only one new bulb of the many mentioned in this book, let it be the tuberous-rooted begonia! The "miniatures" at the top show the crested, the single-frilled, and the double type of flowers. (*Below*) Massed planting of single type in a semi-shaded location.

When you buy dahlia bulbs, try at least a few of the smaller but more graceful types. (Left) "Collarette." (Right) A basket of singles, semi-doubles, and collarettes.

Culturally, there are few things easier to grow than tuberous begonias, when one plants the bulbs. They may be grown from seed, if one has a greenhouse, starting the plants in January or February, but the simplest method is to purchase the bulbs in early spring.

The dry bulbs may be started in the house or in a frame any time from February to the first of June, and set outside, after hardening off, any time after May 15th. Or the tubers may be planted directly outside after the first of May. For starting in advance, fill any ordinary seed flat with very light soil, say one part each of light loam and sand and two parts screened leafmold, commercial humus, or ground peat.

Place the bulbs close together, concave side up, with the surface of the bulb showing. Put in a warm, dark place, or cover with paper, and water very sparingly until growth starts.

As soon as the sprouts are an inch or so high, pot off, using the same soil, with a third of well-rotted manure, preferably cow manure, added. For bedding, the tubers may be started just in the flats in which the bulbs should be spaced three to four inches each way.

The beds where tuberous begonias are to go outside should be well prepared by forking in several inches of well-rotted manure and covering with leafmold, if the latter can be procured. If not, add a dressing of one to two inches of commercial humus or of peat after the bed is prepared, and mix this well into the *surface* soil. Cover the bulbs about one and a half inches deep.

Just after the started plants have been set out, or when the bulbs planted outside have made five or six inches' growth, a mulching of spent old manure, coconut fiber, or humus will be of great benefit. A thorough soaking once a week should be given during very dry weather.

The bulbs may be saved for use, year after year, getting bigger each year, by merely taking them up in the fall immediately after frost, keeping them in flats until the old stem parts readily from the tuber, and then storing them in dry soil or sawdust in a temperature of from 40 to 50 degrees.

HANGING BEGONIAS FOR PORCH BOXES

The two most marked divisions in type in the tuberous begonias are the bedding or upright growing, and the hanging or "basket" begonias (*begonia pendula*). The former are suited for planting wherever a wonderful show of color throughout the season may be wanted, particularly in locations so shady that most other flowers will not do their best there.

The hanging varieties are unsurpassed for making a wonderful display in vases, porch boxes, and window boxes, or for spreading down over a low terrace or the edge of a raised bed. Very often, under such circumstances, more or less shade is encountered by the gardener, and this makes the pendant varieties doubly desirable for this purpose. Either class does wonderfully as a summer-porch plant, and they will undoubtedly find great favor for use in "sun rooms." In the upright growing or bedding type there is a marvelous range to choose from, so far as the form of the flowers is concerned. I have picked out for exhibition purposes a collection of blooms, each one resembling some other flower—a rose, a mallow, a waterlily, a primula, a carnation, a gardenia, and a dozen others. So close was the duplication of form in each case that observers would often stand for many minutes and argue as to what these flowers could be; and whether they could possibly be artificial.

I know of no other flower in the entire range of our cultivated plants which lends itself to such an infinite variety of form. The tuberous-rooted begonia is among flowers what the mockingbird is among birds!

For the most satisfactory results in bedding, however, it is better to restrict the planting to a single type in a place, and generally to a single color. The mixed colors may be used, nevertheless, without fear of inharmonious results; for, in spite of the unparalleled range of colors that one may get, they all harmonize.

For beds to be viewed from a distance, the new large flowering singles, set in solid colors—orange, scarlet, yellow, pink, or white—are the most effective.

Along the base of a wall, in front of shrubbery, in shady nooks of the hardy perennial border—in any such location a bed of these singles will give the gardener a continuous show of color unequaled by any other flower.

Then there are the doubles, in varied forms in the mixed hybrids; the crested, the frilled, the fringed, and—one of the newest and most attractive of all—the frilled single, *crispa marginata*, which are quite distinct, even from any of the numerous old forms, in that the beautifully crimped petals have a delicate margin of scarlet or rose, in contrast to the yellow or buff colors of the petals themselves.

Any of these, separate or in mixture, make a wonderful treasure with which to fill any shady or semishaded nook.

In Europe, many named varieties of tuberous begonias are listed in the catalogues and prized highly by amateur gardeners. In this country, they are as yet to be found only on a few private estates. Still I venture to predict that this wonderful flower will yet come into its own in this country, and take American gardeners by storm!

CHAPTER XVI

OTHER SUMMER- AND AUTUMN-FLOWERING BULBS

ALTHOUGH space is somewhat limited to do full justice to all the remaining summer- and autumn-flowering bulbs, at least brief cultural directions for each will be given, so that the gardener who has space to try them may be safely started on the road to success.

These miscellaneous summer- and autumn-flowering bulbs fall into the three classes which we have already discussed (see page 125) as hardy, half-hardy, and tender; and the treatment which they should receive follows in general that which has been recommended for these three groups.

SOME ADDITIONAL HARDY LATE-FLOWERING BULBS

Summer-Hyacinths (*Hyacinthus candicans or galtonia*). The Summer-Hyacinth is also known as the White Cape Hyacinth and the Spire Lily. It is one of the finest of the midsummer-flowering bulbs, attaining a height of as much as five feet, with its stiff upright spikes carrying a score or more of large, pendant, pure white, bell-shaped flowers. The whole plant is extremely effective, particularly against a suitable background, such as green foliage or a colored wall. It flowers at the same time as the spring-planted gladiolus, and is very decorative when used with them or with montbretias. The bulbs, which are quite large, should be planted six inches deep, in a sunny position, and in thoroughly drained soil. They are most effective in groups of half a dozen or more, but are well worth while even when used singly. Large bulbs will produce a succession of spikes for two or three months, particularly if the old spikes are cut off as the flowers fade. Mulch thoroughly for the winter and give a top-dressing of fine manure and bone meal in the spring. In severe climates the bulbs should be taken up after the first frost, dried, and stored. While the summer-hyacinth is quite similar in appearance to a gigantic Dutch hyacinth, the two are not really related.

Daylily (Hemerocallis). These splendid flowers, which belong to the lily family, deserve a place in any garden. They will grow luxuriantly under a very varied range of soil and climatic conditions, from moist, shady situations to full exposure in the sun in rather dry soil. In the latter instance, they should be given plenty of water while making their early growth, and during their flowering period, which, with the several varieties, is from early May until late July. Varieties range in height from two to five feet; and include shades of color from light lemon yellow to very deep orange. While the individual flowers last but a day, they are produced so freely that the plants are constantly in bloom. Their decided fragrance adds to their desirability. The two varieties best known are flava, the Yellow Daylily, deep lemon in color and very fragrant, and fulva, the Tawny Daylily, dull orange, with darker shading. Both of these flower during June and July. Dr. Regal Daylily, with fragrant orange yellow flowers, blooms in May. Middendorfi, growing two feet tall, is the earliest flowering variety; and thunbergi, a rich bright yellow, four feet tall, is the latest. One of the lowest growing, and a little gem for the front of the perennial border, or a corner in the rockery, is dumortieri.

Funkia (Plantainlily). This is also sometimes called the "Daylily," which causes many beginners to confuse it with Hemerocallis; it would be well if this common name could be dropped. The plantainlily, like the daylily, is extremely easy to grow, and is fragrant. It blooms considerably later, from July to September, and the habit of the plant is entirely different, the best-known varieties having pure white lilylike flowers borne in clusters, several open at a time, and at right angles to the stem. The broad, tough foliage, variegated in some varieties, is of great decorative value throughout the season. *Subcordata grandiflora*, with immense pure-white flowers, blooming in August and September, about three feet high, is one of the best sorts. *Coerulea* has blue flowers in June; and *lanceolata* lilac flowers in September. *Variegata*, dwarf growing, with blue flowers, is an excellent plant for edging, and its variegated varieties are *aurea variegata* and *undulata media picta*, the former with golden and the latter with green and white variegated foliage.

Sternbergia (*Lily-of-the-field*). Sternbergias are also known as the Mount Etna lilies, and Autumn daffodils. It is rather difficult to understand how the last name ever got its vogue, as the flowers are not at all similar to a daffodil, but do quite closely resemble a giant yellow crocus, being by far the most showy of all the late-blooming fall bulbs. Flowers are frequently produced in November, the growth of the foliage following the succeeding spring. The plants grow six inches or so in height; sometimes, under good conditions, reaching twelve. They prefer leafmold and also a light, well-drained soil. Lime is objectionable. Plant in August or September, covering the bulbs three or four inches deep and planting about six inches apart. They should be put in a group, but also may be used singly in the late border. There is good reason to believe that Sternbergia is the "lily-of-the-field" of one of the parables, which was arrayed as Solomon in all his glory was not.

Of the several varieties, all bear yellow flowers: lutea is the best known; fishceriana blooms in April.

Incarvillea (*Hardy Gloxinia*). Incarvillea delavayi is a tuberous-rooted hardy perennial of comparatively recent introduction from northern China. Both the foliage and the flowers are exceptionally attractive, the former being a foot and a half or more in length and of a beautiful pale green. The gloxinialike flowers are produced in clusters on stems which attain a height of two feet, and are of deep rose with yellow throats. The plant is quite hardy if protected over winter with peat or coal ashes over the crown, and should be mulched each spring with thoroughly rotted manure, when the winter mulching is removed. In severe climates, the hardy gloxinia is easily grown with the protection of a shallow frame, or it may be planted each spring like tritomas (see page 123). Plant in late fall or early spring; it is also easily grown from spring-sown seed.

Ascelepias tuberosa (Butterflyweed or Orange Milk-weed), another tuberous-rooted plant, which is one of the most striking of all hardy perennials. If some plant explorer had discovered it in Africa or Tibet, it would prob-ably be one of the most popular of our garden flowers. Unfortunately, it labors under the double disadvantage of being a native American plant, and of having the word "weed" as part of its common name. Our foolish prejudice against anything which is termed a "weed" keeps us from enjoying in our gardens many beautiful things. We forget the fact that all our flowers are "weeds" as they grow naturally. The Butterflyweed, which is extremely hardy, will thrive on dry, well-drained banks in poor soil where many other flowers would do nothing at all. Its immense spreading umbels, ranging in color from lemon yellow to brilliant orange, are produced freely for two months or more, and make a display unsurpassed by any other hardy flower. The plants attain a height of from two to two-and-a-half feet. The tuberous roots may be set out in early fall or in the early spring. There is no cultivated variety, although the asclepia well deserves some attention at the hands of the hybridizers.

ADDITIONAL HALF-HARDY LATE-BLOOMING BULBS

Among the bulbs which may be left out over winter with protection in moderate climates, or in more severe sections, planted in spring and taken up in late autumn for winter storage, are the following, in addition to those already men-tioned:

Ixiolirion. The Ixiolirion is one of the few beautiful blue flowers of May. Growing about a foot in height, it has small lilylike flowers with narrow recurved petals, most distinct and charming in appearance. It should be given a sunny position, and have plenty of leafmold and some sand in the soil. Plant in September four inches deep, and protect with an extra thorough winter mulching or in a frame. It is one of the best blue spring flowers for cutting.

Watsonia (*Bulgelily*). Desirable not only because of their graceful form and beautiful colors, but also for their long-lasting qualities, are the Watsonias, another of the many cousins of the gladiolus from Africa. They are hardy, with a little protection, south of Washington, and do nicely in a frame much farther north; or they may be planted out in spring. In either case, plant the bulbs about three inches deep and six inches apart. They grow to a height of from two to three feet, and range in color from white, through pink and rose, to scarlet and purple. They prefer a position in full sun.

Alstroemeria (*Chilian Lily*). A very showy bulbous-rooted plant which merits much wider popularity than it has ever attained. The several varieties range in height from two to six feet, and the very striking lilylike flowers cover a wonderful range of shades of orange, scarlet, red, pink, and white, many of them being conspicuously striped or mottled. They are fairly hardy and will thrive in most sections outside if thoroughly mulched, and if given a well-drained, sheltered position such as in a raised bed against a wall. The tubers should be planted six inches deep, and about a foot apart, in October or early spring. They flower in July and August.

Kafirlily (*Schizostylis*). The Kafirlily, or Crimson-Flag, is still another relative of the gladiolus which, heretofore, has been limited to greenhouse culture, because the standard variety, *coccinia*, did not produce its beautiful crimson blossoms until November or December. Unlike the gladiolus, however, the Kafirlily continues to send up spikes of

flowers one after another for a considerable period. With
the advent of the newly introduced variety, Mrs. Hegarty,
which blooms early enough to be of value in the fall flower
garden, and which has flowers of a beautiful pure pink, the
Kafirlily becomes valuable for outdoors as well as for the
cool greenhouse. Set out in April or May and lift after the
foliage has been destroyed by frost, storing like gladiolus;
or plant in a frame in October.

THE TENDER SUMMER- AND AUTUMN-FLOWERING BULBS

Some of the most popular summer- and autumn-flowering
bulbs remain to be discussed. The majority of them are
of extremely easy culture, and, being of tall growth and
of imposing appearance, they should be taken advantage
of in planning the border, and particularly for planting
where they will show against evergreens, a hedge, or a house
wall, during the latter part of the season.

Cannas. Here is another fine thing which suffers unde-
servedly, merely because of the rut we so easily fall into
in using garden material. Years ago, when the canna was
planted for its ornamental, tropical-looking foliage, and the
insignificant spikes of bloom were entirely a secondly consideration, "Indian Shot," as it was then called, was used
almost entirely for bedding purposes. Many of the newer
varieties, particularly those developed by the late Leon
Wintzer of West Grove, Pennsylvania, who spent a considerable part of an energetic lifetime perfecting this flower,
are extremely beautiful. The "orchid-flowering" type has
blooms which, in some instances, are six or eight inches
across. No other class of tender bulb is so easily grown
and is so absolutely certain to produce satisfactory results;
and as they increase rapidly and are easily kept over winter, a single bulb of a new variety may quickly be developed into roots enough to make a very large and striking
clump, for use in the mixed border or against shrubbery.
Where a bed of solid color is desired from July to frost,
particularly if it is to be seen from a distance, no other

flower will make quite such a display as cannas. The roots may be planted directly in the soil early in May, or started in pots and set out the latter part of May after danger of frost is past. The bronze-leaved varieties particularly are extremely desirable for their foliage as well as for the flowers. A wide range of delicate shades, running from pure white through pink and rose to copper, orange, and brilliant red, is available. As the plants are gross feeders, the soil, in which the bulbs should be covered three or four inches deep, should be generously enriched with manure, which may be comparatively fresh, and with bone meal. Some of the best varieties are Eureka, pure white; City of Portland, light pink; Hungaria, deep salmon pink; Rosea Gigantea, deep rose; Wintzer's Colossal, bright scarlet; The President, deep glowing red; King Humbert, bronze leaves, with salmon-scarlet flowers marked deeper crimson, undoubtedly the most popular of all; Yellow King Humbert, yellow with orange scarlet blotches; Wyoming, one of the tallest, reaching six feet, with very dark bronzy foliage and fine orange flowers; Richard Wallace, canary yellow, extra fine; and Mme. Crozy, a striking French variety, with deep yellow flowers, bordered with red.

Tuberose. It is hard to understand why this really excellent summer-flowering bulb, with its permeating fragrance —always delicious out of doors in the garden, even though some people seem to think it a little overpowering in a room —should have fallen off, as it has, in its popularity. Possibly some day it will meet with a "revival," as have so many of the other flowers of "Grandmother's garden"; but those who grow things for their intrinsic value, rather than because they may happen to be "in style," need not wait for that day. As with the cannas, the bulbs may be started indoors and set out the latter part of May; or planted out, dormant, about the middle of May. The tall spikes, bearing a quantity of dainty white flowers, bloom from July on. The ground should be thoroughly enriched with manure, and plenty of water given during the growing season. Of the two varieties usually offered, Double Pearl, with double flowers quite thickly set along the spike, and Mexican Everblooming, a single pure white with blooms more loosely arranged and very free flowering, I personally prefer the latter. Both have the characteristic tuberose fragrance.

Tigridia (*Pavonia grandiflora*). The Tigerflower or Shellflower, which may be handled in the same way as the tuberose, is one of the most striking of the minor summer-blooming bulbs, bearing on stalks about two feet high large flowers with three broad outer petals and an inner cup spotted with yellow, the general effect being quite gorgeous and "tigerish." They are most effective when planted several in a clump. Plant about three inches deep and six inches apart, using plenty of old decayed manure. They require less water than most of the other summer-flowering bulbs.

Ismene calathina (Giant Ismene, or Peruvian Daffodil). If you can imagine a "cactus-flowered," pure white amaryllis of delicious fragrance, blooming continuously for a long period, you will get some conception of the Giant Ismene, or Peruvian Daffodil, one of the finest of our summer-blooming bulbs, and very easily cultivated; yet comparatively little known. Plant in fairly rich light soil, preferably in groups of half a dozen or so in late May or early June, covering three or four inches deep. Hold over winter in a fairly warm place, as for tuberous begonias. (See Chapter XV.) They multiply readily and an extra supply, which will soon accumulate, may be used for winter flowering, as they are extremely useful for this purpose.

Caladium. Of these tropical foliage-looking plants, there are two distinct types. The first is the "elephant eared" (caladium esculentum) which attains a height of eight or ten feet, with enormous light green leaves, often over two feet in width, unequaled for producing a tropical effect. The ground can hardly be made too rich, and it is well to use leafmold or peat as well as rotted manure. An abundance of water should be given as soon as growth is well begun, and continued throughout the season. When the leaves are blackened by frost, take up the bulbs, which are quite enormous affairs, dry thoroughly, and store for the winter where the temperature will not go below fifty degrees, as they are very tender. The Fancy-leaved caladiums, ordinarily handled as greenhouse plants, may be grown in the open by setting them out after the weather has become thoroughly warm, during the first week in June, in rich soil, where they will be sheltered from high winds. Plenty of leafmold and some sand are desirable. Cover the bulbs about an inch deep, or set out growing plants about June 15th. To get the full coloring of the beautifully striped and mottled foliage, they should be grown in semi-shade. Most of the bulbs of the Fancy-leaved caladiums are quite small. After growth starts, place them in pots but little larger than the bulbs. They should be repotted two or three times during the summer; "plunging" the pots level with the soil each time. Take the pots in when frost has killed the foliage. After being dried off, they may be stored in a warm place, preferably with a temperature of nearly sixty degrees, as they are even more tender than the type described above.

Agapanthus. The Blue African Lily, or Blue Lily of the Nile, while not a bulb, has fleshy bulbous roots and should be mentioned here in passing as one of the most striking of all plants for the summer garden. From its general appearance, it is often taken to be a bulb. Its long, narrow, lilylike foliage makes a clump from which grow up, sometimes twenty or more at a time, stems two and a half to three feet tall, surmounted by clusters of the bright blue lilylike flowers. It is easily suited outdoors during the summer, with plenty of soil enriched with manure, planted in a large pot or directly in the border. Liquid manure given occasionally during the flowering season, which lasts a long time, will increase the display. Late in the fall gradually withhold the water and dry the plants out, removing them before frost to a frost-proof room or a warm cellar for the winter. They always present a striking appearance in the garden or anywhere about the place.

Richardia (*Calla*). Here is another instance where custom strangles opportunity. People are so accustomed to thinking of the calla lily only as the large, white, waxy, artificial-looking white calla (*richardia aethiopica*), long familiar as a florist flower for funerals, or as an old-fashioned house plant, not suitable for growing out of doors, that it is extremely difficult to get them to realize that there are other callas, some of which are excellent for summer-bedding plants; for certain situations, quite ideal. They may be either planted directly out of doors when danger of frost is passed, or started in pots and transferred to the open when the weather has become really warm. Plenty of humus or peat and decayed manure will give more luxuriant growth, although the bulbs will grow very satisfactorily in ordinary garden soil and under the same conditions as cannas. Callas require an abundance of moisture, and are both easily grown and particularly effective when used near water, as when planted near the edge of the water garden, or along the banks of small streams or ponds. The roots should be taken up and dried off at the first sign of frost, as they are easily injured. In planting, the roots should be placed so that the neck of the bulb comes just above the surface. The varieties suitable for outdoor planting are the golden yellow (*richardia elliottiana*), Godfrey's Everblooming White, and the Spotted White Calla (*albomaculata*).

Oxalis. Unlike other bulbs mentioned in this section, the oxalis are dwarf growing or trailing little plants. They produce an almost unbelievable abundance of small buttercuplike flowers which, with the shamrocklike leaves, make a very pretty effect. They are especially fine for hanging baskets, the edges of window boxes, and for the edges or borders of small beds. They may also be brought inside for winter blooming. The standard sort, known as the

Bermuda buttercup, has flowers of a pure buttercup yellow. A newer strain of more compact growth, with flowers held well above the foliage, is the "Grand Duchess," which may be had in separate shades such as pink, lavender, and white. Deppei is especially good for border planting. Cover about two inches deep outside, or start in pots or pans, covering one inch. When the foliage begins to turn yellow, the plants have reached their rest period. Dry them out and let them remain dormant for a couple of months; new bulbs form readily in the pot.

Vallota (Scarboro-lily) is usually grown as a window-garden plant, where it requires little attention except an occasional repotting, when it has become absolutely pot-bound.

Sprekelia formosissima (Jacobaean-Lily), formerly classed as an Amaryllis, is somewhat similar to that flower in foliage and in general appearance, but is incomparably more graceful in form. The large flowers are dark scarlet and extremely handsome, either for growing indoors, where it will succeed in a cool temperature, and needs repotting only once in three or four years, or when grown in the garden and planted out in May and taken up in the fall after the leaves turn yellow, and kept *with the dried tops on,* over winter.

Amorphophallus Rivieri. Of the two common names for this plant, "Devilstongue" and "Snake Palm," the first refers to the gigantic spathe or tongue of the single calla-like blossom, which is produced before any sign of a leaf; and the second to the tropical-looking palmlike foliage, borne on a green and brown mottled stem, after the flower disappears. The worthless if not objectionable flower is merely an interesting "freak," one of the few flowers to make you wonder if either Darwin or the fundamentalists are right in their theories on Evolution! Nevertheless, the foliage itself is so absolutely different from that of any other summer bulb or perennial that it may well be employed where a tropical note is wanted. The plant is striking by itself but even better when associated with other things. Give a rich soil and an abundance of water during growth. Keep in a warm place, as for tuberous begonias, over winter.

VINES FROM BULBS

Every garden should have its vines, and while there are many excellent hardy ones, there are also some which grow from bulbs which have advantages possessed by none of the others. One or two particularly are equaled by nothing else where quick growth is wanted for shade, or for covering a trellis or some unsightly object such as a wall or the side of a building. A number of them are extremely pretty in their combination of foliage and flowers.

Tuberous-Rooted Wisteria (*Apios tuberosa*). In habit of growth, in foliage, and in its pendant clusters of flowers, this rapid growing, hardy vine bears a striking resemblance to the wisteria, except that it reaches a height of only about ten or twelve feet. The flowers, which are a deep brownish purple, and are freely produced, have a marked and pleasing fragrance. The apios is hardy and will come up again each spring. A better effect is obtained where two or three bulbs are planted together. They may be set out at any time during spring or early summer, covering the bulbs about two inches deep.

Mignonette Vine (*Boussingaultia baselloides*). Another fragrant and very rapid climber, with large, thick, heart-shaped leaves, which makes a very pleasant shade during midsummer and flowers in late summer and autumn, bearing in profusion long spikes of small white flowers. It attains a height of from fifteen to twenty feet, and will succeed in rather light, dry soil, in full sun. It is not quite so hardy as the preceding, but may be left out over winter if the roots are mulched with manure or coal ashes. The mulch should be removed early in the spring. The bulbs should be planted about four inches deep.

Cinnamon-Vine (*Dioscorea batatas*). This is much the

tallest growing of the bulbous vines, attaining a height, under good conditions, of fully forty feet. The heart-shaped bright green leaves are of very peculiar glossy texture. The small white flowers have a peculiar cinnamon-like fragrance, which gives the plant its common name. It is quite hardy. The soil should be thoroughly enriched, and the roots, which resemble somewhat a long, thin, sweet potato, should be planted in a perpendicular position with the top or eye two to three inches below the surface.

Abobra. A very pretty little trellis plant, attaining a height of about six feet, and growing well in light, rich soil. It is not quite hardy and the bulbs, after being taken up, should be stored in sand or sawdust, as with tuberous begonias, and set out again about the middle of May. The flowers are inconspicuous, but they are followed by bright scarlet globular fruits which give it a most distinct appearance.

CHAPTER XVII

IRISES AND PEONIES

THE irises discussed in this chapter are the perennial, herbaceous, or hardy garden irises, entirely distinct from the bulbous iris already described on page 113.

Irises and peonies are not bulbs. On the other hand, they are quite different from the ordinary "hardy perennials," being sold generally as dormant roots, for planting in the fall. The large fleshy roots are, like bulbs, of the "storehouse" type, serving to carry over the year, for the next season's new growth, an immediately available food supply. As with the bulbs also, their success the following year depends directly upon the growth made *after the flowering period.*

There are, therefore, practical reasons why irises and peonies should be given a place in this book, though they are not, even under the layman's license for a rather loose interpretation of botanical terms, to be classed as "bulbs."

As irises will remain several years after planting, and peonies indefinitely, unless one wishes to increase the stock of plants of certain varieties, the ground should be prepared for a long lease. Peonies prefer a soil rather on the heavy side, but I have seen them do excellently in light, almost sandy loam, where plenty of humus had been added. Irises in their several types vary somewhat in their soil preferences; all, however, appreciate a deep, rich soil. Well-rotted cow manure, if it is to be had, is excellent for both; and with this bone meal and wood ashes may be added to the soil; which should, of course, be well drained. Chemical fertilizers and stimulants, such as nitrate of soda, it is best to avoid, as with most bulbs (see page 32). Both irises and peonies require a season or two to become thoroughly established, before reaching full flowering development.

FOUR MONTHS OF THE RAINBOW FLOWER

The iris, emblem of the goddess of the rainbow, is still thought by many to be one of the choice flowers of the few; though, in fact, there is no plant better adapted to be every man's flower.

Not only is it perfectly hardy, but the original cost of the roots is so little that any one can afford them. The best of the standard varieties, and many of the new, may be had at from twenty to fifty cents each. Even the finest new things, including some of the wonderful "pink" irises, cost but a fraction of what you have to pay for some other new flowers, and they will increase rapidly in your garden under ordinary care.

The wonder and the glory of the iris, so far as the iridescent beauty of its coloring and its delicacy of form and texture are concerned, are matters of common information. But there is still much misinformation current in regard to the growing of this most desirable flower, even among gardeners who are no longer amateurs.

There is a common belief, for instance, that the iris requires a wet, or at least a very moist, situation. A further belief is that, although it is a flower of wondrous beauty and range of color, it has but a comparatively short flowering season.

Both of these impressions are absolutely wrong.

The iris will thrive in a wider range of soil conditions than most of the other hardy flowers. Its season of bloom, by using judgment in selecting types and varieties, may easily be extended over a period of many weeks without a single break; in fact, it may be enjoyed from the latter part of April until well into July, in an unbroken succession of gorgeous bloom.

And few flowers are so well adapted to so many different

uses: for the mixed hardy border, especially with and to follow the "Dutch" bulbs; for long, curving solid beds, against shrubbery; for the rock garden; for naturalizing by streams or ponds;—there is a type of iris ideal for each of these purposes.

Some of the irises, including the German section, have underground root stocks or rhizomes—long, irregular, fleshy roots which should be covered *not over* one or two inches deep, and, if parts of the roots protrude above the soil, where the sun can "cook" them a bit, so much the better. But be sure to pack the soil down *solidly* about the roots. The German iris and most of the dwarf irises like a situation in full sun, and rather light soil, on the dry side. Plenty of lime in the soil is also desirable; in fact, it is a good plan to give a light application each fall, or each spring, after pulling the dead leaves off the roots, over the soil where they are growing.

Other irises have fibrous roots, more like ordinary perennial plants: these include the Japanese (*kaempferi*), and the sibirica and orientalis species. Plant in deep, rich soil, where moisture is available, but where the water level is well below the crowns of the plants—a stream or pond bank is the ideal situation; they will thrive, however, in any ordinary border, if generously watered at the roots during the growing season. It is well to mulch new plantings the first winter, to prevent frost from loosing or "heaving" the roots.

THE FIRST IRISES TO BLOOM

The first of all to bloom are the dwarf irises, Iris pumila and pumila hybrids, sometimes called Alpin or Crimean iris. These grow but eight to twelve or fifteen inches tall, but they are little gems. Spreading with great rapidity and being very hardy, they are most desirable as border plants for "Dutch" bulbs, tulips, and narcissus, which are in bloom at the same time.

They are also one of the most attractive of all early

flowers for the rock garden; in fact, they lend themselves to so many uses that you will find ample employment for your extra stock as it increases.

The earliest of the type to bloom is Atroviolacea, violet mauve. Then follow Caerulea, sky blue; Citrea, yellow; Schneekuppe, white; and Cyanea, a rich purple. These five will give you a good range of color; but if you want to start a collection, you can get a dozen different varieties for three dollars.

Following close on the heels of the little Pumilas, beginning to bloom, in fact, before the latest of the Pumilas are through, come the varieties of the newest class of irises, the "intermediate." This section, which is the result of crosses between I. Pumila and the "German" iris (*germanica*) fills in the gap that formerly existed here.

The intermediates are half dwarf in growth, with flowers from twelve to twenty-four inches tall. They are also very hardy and vigorous growing, and very free flowering, coming in mostly during early May to mid-May. Of the intermediates, though there are now quite a number of fine varieties, it will serve to mention five which have been well tested and proved.

These are Walhalla, with upper petals of lavender and falls, or lower petals, of deep wine red—a most striking combination; Etta, cream and yellow, and very sweet scented; Helge, citron yellow and pearl; Ingeborg, very large pure white; and Blue Boy, clear blue with still darker blue falls.

The next class to bloom is the most extensive of all; the German irises or "Liberty" irises, as you will now find them listed in some catalogues.

AN EMBARRASSMENT OF RICHES

The earliest of the German irises will begin to open before the intermediates are through. Among the best of the earliest blooming of these are Florentina, a very old variety, white with slight lavender shadings; Kochi, a very striking deep claret; Plumeri, deep coppery red; and Germanica, a very free-flowering deep purple.

Following these comes the great range of the medium-flowering German irises, the tall bearded sorts. In this group there are so many to select from that I shall attempt to mention only a few of the most outstanding, say a dozen of those which the beginner can bank on as being thrifty growers and free bloomers.

In selecting this list, prices have been kept in mind. Most of them can be purchased for less than a dollar each, although many of the very finest irises of this class are included. It is possible to get a dozen good standard varieties for two or three dollars, but it will prove well worth while to invest a little more and have the finest.

The ten I would suggest follow: Dalila, pale, almost white petals, with deep purple falls; Flavescens, a beautiful artistic pale yellow; Iris King, dark brown with a contrasting border; Lohengrin, deep mauve, and an exceptionally vigorous grower; Maori King, golden yellow and deep crimson, dwarf growing; Minnehaha, very large creamy white flowers with maroon veining, and very fragrant; Montezuma, deep yellow standards, with lighter falls, both dotted with brown; Mrs. Alan Gray, lilac, very distinct; Quaker Lady, most unique, the upright petals being dull lavender with yellow shadings, and the falls clear blue and old gold; Sherwin-Wright, a clear bright golden yellow of most vigorous growth, probably the best pure yellow yet attained.

Following these, and extending the long season of the German, or tall bearded irises, still further, are the latest flowering varieties, such as Black Knight, sometimes called Black Prince, a deep purple with black purple falls, a most striking variety; Cytherea, dark lavender and blue; Boismilon, bronze and lilac white; and Pacquita, a light claret.

LOVELY PINK IRISES

It is perhaps an unreasonable thing, but it is nevertheless

a fact that the one color which may be wanting in any flower is always the one which the enthusiastic collectors and the breeders set their hearts upon as being the great desideratum, the gem without price.

Just so we have had the centuries-long hunt for the blue rose, though why any one should wish to possess a blue rose, except as a curiosity, is more than I can imagine.

In irises, the search has been for a really pink flower, and the search has been both more reasonable and more successful. Within the comparatively recent past a number of pink varieties have been developed, and some of these are now within reach of any amateur, having come down to a dollar or less in price.

The pink irises are not at all just freaks; they are very beautiful and deserve a place in any considerable collection. Perhaps the finest so far developed is Wild Rose; another is Troost. Less expensive are Edouard Michel, a tall, splendid real rosy red; Caprice, reddish purple; Rose Unique, violet rose; Queen of May, rosy lavender; Wyomissing, soft rose with deep rose falls; Her Majesty, rosy pink, veined crimson; and Isoline, a lilac pink with darker rose falls.

Beautiful as are the pinks and the other splendid varieties available among the Germanicas described, if I were restricted to one single variety for all purposes, it would be Pallida Dalmatica. This is often listed in catalogues among the Germanicas, but is really a distinct type. When ordering, try to be certain that you are getting the true Pallida Dalmatica, Princess Beatrice, which has extremely large flowers of most beautiful form, light lavender in color, which tones down to an indescribable silvery blue at the base of the petals; also it is deliciously fragrant.

In habit of growth, the plant is unusually vigorous, with exceptionally fine, heavy foliage, and growing to a height of from three to four feet. It blooms over a long period and produces its wonderful flowers with the greatest generosity, being equally fine for cutting and for mass effects in the

Iris are most beautiful when associated with water, but it is by no means necessary to have a moist situation to grow them. They will thrive in any ordinary garden soil.

Both of the flowers above are peonies. You are probably familiar with the type at the right. When you buy plants include at least a few of the Japanese and the singles.

garden. The comparatively new Lord of June, blue and rich purple, rivals Pallida in great size and beauty of form, and makes a grand companion for it.

I have spoken of German irises because that is the designation still given them in the great majority of catalogues and by the trade in general; but the Iris Society of America has tried to encourage a new system of classification which makes one group of the bearded irises and another group of the beardless varieties, which have several characteristics which distinguish them from the bearded class.

The Japanese irises, which in many respects are the most glorious of the entire family, are the latest to bloom; but coming in with the late Germanica varieties, and linking them up with the Japanese varieties, are the earlier-blooming members of the beardless class—the Siberian and the Oriental varieties, most of which have medium-sized flowers on long, slender stems and are particularly desirable for cutting.

The list of varieties of this type is more limited. Sibirica, with purplish blue flowers; Sibirica Alba, white with light lilac veining; and Orientalis Snow Queen and Blue King will make a very good selection here. The newer Siberian hybrid, Perry Blue, with a large, clear blue flower, is extra fine.

THE GORGEOUS JAPANESE IRIS

These varieties will bring us, in flowering time, to the last and the most gorgeous of all, the "imperial" Japanese iris— and the adjective is well deserved. Coming on after the types last mentioned, it winds up the iris season with a blaze of splendor extending far into July.

Here the selection of varieties becomes largely a matter of taste in colors. There are many to choose from, but the seven following will give a good range of colors: Alba Plena, pure white; Amethyst, delicate lavender; Gold Bound, white with yellow center; Painted Lady, white flushed with bright pink; Pyramid, light blue, veined white;

Vesta, ash gray with purple veining, and F. S. Ware, dark garnet.

The Japanese and Siberian iris will thrive in a more moist situation, such as the edge of a pond, than suits the German and other similar types; in fact, if planted in a dry location, they should be given an abundance of water during dry weather to produce their best.

But if you want iris in a really wet, marshy location, use Pseudacorus, the European yellow-flag, and our own native blue-flag or water-flag, which is catalogued as iris versi-color. And for exceptionally dry locations, such as the rockery or for edging a border, use the little "crested" iris, I. cristata.

PEONIES, THE LIFETIME FLOWER

Peonies have been termed "at once the most beautiful and the hardiest of all perennial flowers." Many flower lovers will agree with the first part of that description, and certainly there is no question concerning their wonderful hardiness.

There comes to my mind the picture of my first "discovery" of this glorious flower—a row of plants along the edge of what was formerly the garden of a place which had stood vacant for several years.

Suddenly I came upon their gorgeous display, in the solitude of that grass- and weed-grown garden. Though still in my early teens, I was a flower enthusiast, and had grown many kinds myself, in addition to working around the perennials and shrubs in our home grounds.

But the peony was new to me, and I stood scarcely able to believe the evidence of my eyes that there could be flowers so beautiful, of such great size and so lavishly borne.

But my admiration turned, I remember very distinctly, to a sort of blind envy that these flowers should have produced such an unmatchable wealth of beauty when they had received absolutely no care or attention for years, while many of my own flowers fared but indifferently, despite all the trouble I took with them.

One of the great advantages of the peony as a flower is illustrated by this incident—it will live longer with no attention, almost utter neglect, than any other worth-while hardy perennial, often continuing to bloom year after year even when sod-bound and abandoned.

Instances are numerous where plants which have remained in the same spot for thirty to forty years still give their annual beauty show as generously as ever, despite a lack of care.

Peonies, when properly utilized in the landscape planting, will serve a double purpose; that of making the greatest flower "show" of the year during their blossoming season; and also of adding to the general planting effect during the balance of the season, with their really decorative foliage. Against a background of peonies, either before or after blooming, other flowers show off to great advantage. On large places, peonies are extremely effective in long rows, especially along a curved drive, or around the edge of the shrubbery border; but on the smaller place, where they must be given a position at the back of the mixed perennial border, they should be used somewhat sparingly, lest they overbalance everything else. Do *not* spot them around the lawn in single clumps, as one so frequently sees them.

Because they are slow to propagate, and take up a good deal of space, peony roots offered for sale vary considerably in price and in size. In buying, do not consider price alone, for a two-or-three-eye young root is worth much more than a "division" from an old clump. The roots should be set from three to five feet apart, in a row or a "bed" of peonies; but are better planted at intervals of from five to eight feet when used in the hardy border, so that other plants may be used between them.

In planting, cover the roots *not more* than two to three inches deep. Mulch the first season or two with light straw or hay, but not thereafter: the peony is a cold-climate flower. Deep planting and heavy winter mulching are two of the most general causes of peonies failing to bloom. Plenty of moisture during the growing season, and an annual dressing of shredded manure and bone meal worked into the surface of the soil early in the spring, will help keep the plants vigorous and the blooms large.

THE PRESENT-DAY PEONIES

The matter of selecting varieties, which is important for any flower, is doubly so for peonies, because when you buy them you are buying for a lifetime.

Beautiful as were the old-fashioned peonies—the "pineys" of grandmother's garden—they had three serious handicaps: the range of color was very limited; the blooming season was short; and, despite their beauty—well, they were never asked into the house with the other flowers. Even their best friends would not tell them why, but it is doubtful if even Listerine would have deodorized those old-fashioned peonies.

It was many years after my first introduction to the peony that I "discovered" it again, and this time with a surprise even greater than on the first occasion. Of course, I had kept up a sort of speaking acquaintance with them in the meantime, and knew that some handsome new varieties had been introduced. But I didn't dream of the development they had undergone.

This second discovery of mine occurred when the peony garden came into bloom on a large place of which I had charge at the time. The nucleus of this garden was a wonderful collection of Japanese peonies which had been imported directly from Japan. This collection was supplemented by many of the newer French, English, Dutch, and American varieties.

But it was the "Japs" which were the greatest revelation to me.

The most striking thing this garden demonstrated was that all the handicaps of the old-time peonies that I had known had been overcome. First, most of the newer varieties are fragrant, many of them deliciously so.

Second, the range of colors has been increased immensely, and, though there are no yellows or blues, there are whites with enough sulphur at the center to give a decided yellow effect, and wonderful shades of lilac, mauve, and purple. It is in its great range of pinks, from the most delicate flush of dawn to the warmest deep satin, that the peony is unrivaled in color.

And third, but by no means least, the flowering period has been so extended that, with a careful selection of varieties, it is now possible to have blooms continuously over a period of six weeks or more.

THE PEONY SOCIETY "RATINGS"

The American Peony Society has made a radical departure in providing help to the uninitiated. In 1919 and again in 1921 the Peony Society conducted a symposium in which all the leading peony authorities were submitted a list of varieties—over a thousand in the second instance—and asked to judge each variety according to a standard scale of points. Each variety was given a rating accordingly.

Le Cygne, with 99, attained the highest rating. Next came Therese with 98, and Solange with 97. But only twenty-two out of the thousand plus thus scrutinized came off with a rating of 90 or higher. Four of these—Festiva Maxima, Mons. Jules Elie, Milton Hill, and Baroness Schroeder—were introduced from thirty-five to seventy-five years ago.

These ratings are given in the catalogue of some of the peony specialists and form a very reliable and unprejudiced guide to the intending purchaser.

Recommending specific varieties is something of a venture where there are so many to select from, and where prices, which is usually a consideration, vary so much. But as the beginner usually wants advice on just this point, I am submitting the following suggestions; presenting them in such a way that a long period of bloom may be assured, with a generous assortment of colors.

The figures in parenthesis, after each variety, show the American Peony Society's rating. Practically all of these varieties, with the exception of Officinalis rubra, are fragrant, and many vie with the rose in this respect. Under each color I am listing two groups, the first being the moderate priced varieties which may be bought at from 50 or 75 cents to $2 each. The second contains the newer or rarer sorts, which cost $5 to $15 each.

Here are my recommendations, the several varieties under each color blooming, approximately, in the order named.

SOME GOOD PEONIES, OLD AND NEW

White.—Among the whites are Duchesse de Nemours (81); Mme. de Verneville (79); Festiva Maxima (93), the most popular peony; Baroness Schroeder (90), delicately flushed white, especially good for cutting; Couronne d'Or (81), one of the latest and especially fragrant.

Three of the newer whites are particularly good. They are Le Cygne (99), "the world's most perfect peony," a distinct type with incurving petals and golden stamens showing through; Kelway Glorious (98), glistening white, with rose splashes on its outer petals and very fragrant; and Elizabeth Barrett Browning, "the finest American peony."

Light Pink.—In the light pinks there are Umbellata Rosea (74), especially good for landscape planting; Eugénie Verdier (86); Milton Hill (90), lilac rose; and Grandiflora (86), silvery pink.

Among the newer light pinks are several top-notchers such as Lady Alexandra Duff (91), a delicate flesh pink, extremely fragrant; Therese (98), violet rose pink; Tourangelle (94), soft rose with salmon shading; Solange (97), very distinct and light pink with salmon center.

Deep Pink.—In the deeper pinks and dark pinks there is a very long list, including Edulis Superba (76), brilliant pink; Mons. Jules Elie (92), one of the finest of all the pinks; Reine Hortense (87), white and hydrangea pink with crimson splashes; Eugénie Verdier (83), Albert Crousse (86), and Claire Dubois (87), violet rose.

There are not so many really striking new varieties among the darker pinks, the best, perhaps, being Walter Faxon (93), a wonderful clear bright rose, deeper at the heart; La France (90), really a light pink, but with crimson splashes which give it a darker effect, and Sarah Bernhardt (90), a very fine apple blossom pink, fragrant and deserving a place in any collection.

Reds.—In the newer introductions are some very excellent reds, including Richard Carvel (88), very deep red; Mons. Martin Cahuzac (88), the darkest of all reds; Karl Rosenfield (88), the best "all-round red peony"; and Mary Brand (87), Brand's best Red.

Yellow.—In the so-called "yellows" are Laura Dessert (88), creamy white with bright canary center; Primevère, sulphur yellow, and Golden Dawn.

THE GLORIOUS "JAPS"

By all means, when you are ordering, include at least a few of the singles, semi-doubles, and "Japs." These really should have a separate rating in a class by themselves, but so far, they have never been handled that way.

Some of the finest are Albiflore (The Bride) (84); Snowflake, pure white; Pride of Langport (89), a delicate peach blossom pink; Alpha and Omega, a very early anemone type, deep rose with a golden center; Bridesmaid (83), white with a pink tinge and golden stamens, resembling a great waterlily; Darkness; Dawn; Departing Sun; Golden Nugget, a deep orange yellow, distinct from all other peonies; King of England (84), a rich ruby with center of pure yellow; Snow Wheel, like a gigantic white daisy; Marie Jacquin, sometimes called Waterlily, a semi-double white with a rose tinge and yellow stamens; Lady Helen Vincent, and Yeso, white with a straw-colored center and occasional crimson edgings.

FOR THE SMALL GARDEN

For grounds of limited area, where the ordinary varieties of peonies would be rather too much of a good thing, there are a couple of dwarf-growing varieties and half a dozen

PEONY FLOWER TYPES

Rose

Crown

Semi Double

Single

Bomb

Japanese

of very moderate growth which may "fit in" better: Pierre Reignoux, an early light rose, and Claude Cellee, a late creamy white, two of the smallest growing peonies, and Alexandre Dumas, violet-rose, fairly early; followed by Marcelle Dessert, cream white, flecked; Germaine Bigot, pale rose; L'Eclatante, brighter rose, and Mme. Jules Elie, rose and cream white, all mid-season; with Edmond About, pale pink, coming a bit later.

CHAPTER XVIII

BULBS FOR WINTER BLOOM

GREAT as is the pleasure which the flowers of the summer garden give us, there is a certain thrill about those which bloom during the long bleak months of winter which the summer visitors can never possess. Nor can any number of cut flowers, no matter how beautiful they may be, ever take the place of a living, growing, flowering plant.

In many homes, however, the winter garden is merely an unrealized possibility; but it need not be. Where, for any reason, it may not seem possible to take care of the ordinary house plants which may be grown in pots, there is no reason at all why some bulbs should not be grown. There are several sorts for which the indoor culture is as simple as anything which can be imagined. It is necessary only to procure the bulbs, place them in pebbles and water or moist fiber, keep them in the living room until the flowers develop, and then throw them out. This is possible, because the flower, completely developed, is already lying in wait within the bulb, requiring merely moisture and warmth to bring it forth.

The real lover of flowers, however, will hardly be contented with such a program for the winter garden in the home, even though it may be much better than nothing at all, for the city apartment. He—or she—will want a number of those beautiful flowers, which may so easily be had from bulbs, in constant succession from the time that the first snows destroy the remnants of the outside garden, until long after the first snowdrops or crocuses are again pushing through the sodden soil of early spring. Once you have had your living room or sun parlor made bright through the darksome days of midwinter by a few pans of hyacinths, tulips, daffodils, crocuses, oxalis, freesias, anemones, or any other of the score or more of bulbs which may be grown with the greatest ease under ordinary living-room conditions, you will never again want to go through a winter without their cheery companionship. And the majority of them may either be kept for the garden, after flowering in the house, or used year after year for winter bloom.

There are two advantages which bulbs possess as flowers for the winter garden which make them preëminently suited for this purpose. The first is that the results are as absolutely certain as anything in the world of growing things can be; and the second is that practically all the work in connection with growing them can be done *at one time*. Preparing bulbs for winter flowering is something like canning vegetables or fruits for winter—they will remain in a dormant or "canned" condition as long as you wish and may be brought in to the house to flower, as wanted.

No matter how simple or how elaborate a winter garden you may wish, then, you will find in the various bulbs available for the purpose material to meet your every requirement. Whether it be for a single bowl, for a table or a plant stand, of some particular shade to match the color scheme of your interior decorations; a window-sill garden where at least a taste of spring or summer may be maintained throughout the winter months; or a more extensive collection to make bright for week after week the sun parlor or the small greenhouse, you will find the various types of bulbs offered in the fall bulb catalogue waiting to respond, as though by magic, to make your winter garden dream come true.

THE THREE METHODS OF GROWING

In talking to garden clubs, and in answering the inquiries in various magazines, I have been frequently surprised at the confusion which seems to exist concerning the grow-

GROWING BULBS INDOORS

Forcing in water

Forcing in fibre

Growing in pot

FORCING BULBS IN FIBRE

Cover to tips of bulbs

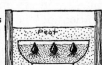

Place in dark to make roots

Bring into cool temperature

Higher temperature full sunlight

FORCING IN SOIL

Bulbs in bulb pan

Bringing into heat

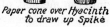

Cross section of pot

Burying out of doors for root growth

Paper cone over Hyacinth to draw up Spike

ing of bulbs indoors for winter bloom. Much of this is undoubtedly due to the careless use of the word "forcing" by many writers on this subject, using it indiscriminately in regard to the growing of any or all bulbs, by any or all methods, so long as they are flowered in a pot or in a bulb pan. So I shall endeavor to make clear at the outset the several different methods of growing bulbs for indoor bloom; and then will describe each in detail, making it unnecessary to repeat instructions in connection with each of the bulbs recommended for indoor culture.

A bulb may properly be said to be "forced" when it is grown well out of its normal season for flowering. Hyacinths and some of the daffodils, for instance, are usually "forced" to bloom by Christmas, or the first week in January. The same bulbs, or Darwin tulips, so treated that they will be in flower a few weeks before they would naturally out of doors in the open, are not really "forced." Secondly, the term "forcing" does not imply, as so many beginners are apt to assume, that the plants are grown in a very high temperature. This interpretation of the word is often responsible for failure. The majority of bulbs should be grown very gradually, in rather moderate temperature; and, as a general rule, the more nearly conditions may be made to parallel those which the bulbs would have in growing naturally, the more successful the "forcing" will be. Bulbs which have been grown in pots for winter bloom, such as tuberous-rooted begonias, freesias, and oxalis, are not "forced" at all. They are merely grown indoors instead of in the open garden.

And now we will turn to the different methods by which the bulbs may be handled. There are three. Some bulbs are best suited to one method; some to another; and some may be handled in different ways, as the grower may prefer.

First: Forcing in Fiber, Pebbles, or Water. This is the simplest method of all and the least trouble. It has the advantages of convenience and cleanliness, and the disadvantages of producing less perfect results, and of causing the bulbs to so exhaust themselves that they are practically worthless for further use. The Chinese Sacred-Lily, "paper white" narcissus, and most of the other daffodils and narcissi, may be satisfactorily forced by this method, as may also hyacinths, crocuses, and many other bulbs.

Second: Forcing in Soil with Preliminary Root Growth. With this system the bulbs are given some substantial material in which to make roots, placed in pots, bulb pans, or boxes, and given the opportunity to develop a substantial root system before being brought into light and heat. While this means more work than the method mentioned above, it is well worth the difference in time required; and the bulbs, if carefully handled and not grown in too high a temperature, may be saved and planted out in the garden, where, after a season's recuperation, they will again bloom satisfactorily. All of the bulbs mentioned, and the great majority of the hardy and half-hardy spring-flowering bulbs, and many of the summer-flowering bulbs, can be most satisfactorily handled in this way.

Third: Growing in Pots. With this method, the bulbs are given sufficient substantially enriched soil in which to make normal growth and development, instead of relying, as with both systems described above, upon the food supplies stored within the bulb itself. Repotting may be necessary once each year, or only once in two to four years. Bulbs which can be grown by this method, include those which retain their foliage throughout the year, such as vallotas (Scarborough-lily) and crinums; the majority of the tender and autumn-flowering bulbs; and many of the half-hardy ones, which have already been described (see Chapter IX).

The beginner who gets well fixed in mind the differences between these three methods of culture, and the essential details of each, will be well on the way to success with the growing of whatever bulbs may be desired for winter beauty. Let us look for a moment at the details of each system, before taking up the individual flowers.

FIRST METHOD: GROWING IN PEBBLES, FIBER, OR WATER

By this system, advantage is taken of the fact that the bulb itself contains sufficient food to produce a satisfactory flower without an additional food supply being taken up by the roots. The root system, it is true, must be developed before the flowers are produced, but the function of the roots in this case is chiefly to supply the necessary moisture to the bulb. This is true whether it is grown in pure water alone, in pebbles, or in fiber. The purpose of the pebbles is merely to support the bulbs and to hold them in position; and where fiber is used it answers much the same end. Formerly, special containers known as hyacinth glasses, made with a cup-shaped neck that would hold the bulb in position while allowing the roots to grow down into the water, were largely used. They held only single bulbs, and as they were rather unsightly and awkward in shape themselves, the general effect, although perhaps preferable to no flower at all, was anything but artistic. They have been largely replaced by shallow bulb bowls and fiber. Where water is used it is very important to let it be clean and pure. By far the best is rain water. But whether rain water, spring water, or city water is used, it is a good plan to put a few pieces of charcoal into it, as these help to keep it clean and sweet. The bulbs should be so placed that the water does not quite touch them; the growing roots will reach it, but if the water touches the bulb itself, slime or decay will develop.

If pebbles are to be employed, ordinary small ones will do; but clean smooth white or colored ones, evenly graded, are neater in appearance and the bulbs may be pushed down into them and held firmly in position. As the roots develop and spread out through the pebbles, they will give firm support to the flowers.

Ordinary Dutch peat, coconut fiber, or humus may be used as mediums in which to grow bulbs. The very best material for this purpose is the specially prepared "bulb fiber" sold by seed houses and bulb dealers. This contains

some plant food and gritty material, in addition to the fiber
or peat, and will give ideal results. Even with the fiber,
however, it is best to add some charcoal, broken up into
small pieces, in the bottom of whatever receptacle is being
used for the bulbs; particularly so if it is a glazed jardinière or a bowl without a drainage hole. A water-tight
container may be employed where peat or fiber is used;
but great care must be exercised to see that the bulbs are
not kept *over wet*. In using fiber, peat, or humus, get the
material thoroughly moist before attempting to plant the
bulbs, by sprinkling it and mixing it with the fingers, or a
trowel. It should be moistened to the point where, when
squeezed in the hand, the water will drip from it. In planting, place in the bowls half an inch or so of broken charcoal, and then a layer of fiber a half inch to an inch deep,
according to the size of the bulbs and the receptacle being
used. Press the fiber down firmly, but not hard, and then
place the bulbs in position, putting them from a half to a
full diameter apart. The points of the bulbs should come
slightly below the rim of the bowl. Then surround the
bulbs with fiber, pressing it gently into place, until the
bowl is filled to within half an inch or so of the top. It is
all right if the tips of the bulbs are exposed, but the shoul-
ders should be covered.

After planting, add water gradually, until the fiber has
absorbed all it will take up. Let the bowl stand for a half
hour or more, and then, with one hand over the surface to
hold the contents in position, tilt up on one edge, to let any
surplus moisture drain out. (This, of course, is necessary
only when there is no drainage hole in the container.)

Getting a Strong Root System. Whether bulbs be grown
in water, in pebbles, or in fiber, the most important single
point in their culture is to obtain a substantial root development *before top growth begins*. This is merely following
Nature's lead; for when a bulb is planted in the garden, it
has weeks or months to develop a root system, before any
top growth is made. In the garden, of course, the roots

continue growing long after the surface of the ground may be frozen.

Bulbs placed in water, therefore, should be put away in a dark closet where the temperature is as cool as possible— without danger of freezing, of course—and kept there for several weeks. (Some of them will flower if kept in the light and started into immediate growth; but the results will not be nearly so good as when they are allowed to make roots first.) Here they should be left until the roots are at least two or three inches in length, and if they can be left longer without the tops beginning to make growth, so much the better. Remove them from the closet and place them where they will get plenty of light, but not strong midday sunlight, and where the temperature is quite cool, say from forty to fifty degrees. When the tops have become entirely green, they may be transferred to a window or to full sunlight, and given a somewhat higher temperature. When some of the water has been lost through evaporation, and by having been taken up by the roots of the growing plant, it should be replaced, keeping it at about the original level.

Bulbs planted in pebbles should be treated in the same way as when grown in water, care being taken to water often enough to keep the level almost up to the surface of the pebbles.

Bulbs which are planted in fiber may also be put in a closet or in a cellar to develop roots, but it is far better to put them out of doors where they can be completely buried, and be brought in as needed. The advantages of doing this, instead of merely placing them in a closet or cellar, are several. In the first place, they can all be planted at *one* time, instead of making several different plantings in succession, as will be necessary, to obtain a succession of blooms, by either of the methods described above. In the second place, the conditions under which the roots are produced will much more closely approximate the natural growth of the bulbs out of doors, resulting in a maximum development of the root system, with a minimum growth of tops. And in the third place, the weight of the covering material over them will hold them in position, instead of allowing them to be forced up by the growth of roots, as sometimes happens when they are merely kept in the dark without any covering over them. Where it is not convenient to provide as many bowls or jardinières as might be required to plant a quantity of bulbs to store them in this way, they may be planted in bulb pans, which are merely very broad, shallow flowerpots fitting into the containers in which one may wish to have them flower in the house.

Preliminary Root Development. After planting, the first object is to develop root growth while holding the top growth in check. If no space outdoors is available, place the bowls, pans, or pots in the cellar or in a cool, well-ventilated closet away from the light; have them as completely in the dark as possible; the longer they can be kept here without top growth starting, the better. When they are two or three inches high and the fiber is fairly well filled with roots, remove them to a cool room, and keep out of direct sunlight until the tops, which will be somewhat white and "drawn," get green and more vigorous growth. Water them very moderately at first, but keep the fiber evenly saturated. Care is required in this respect, as it may *look* moist even when fairly well dried out. If too much is added at any time, the surplus may be drained from bowls, pans, or pots by tilting them up on edge as already described.

As the buds begin to develop, bring the plants into full light, preferably where they will receive direct sunlight at least part of the day, and where the temperature is higher, but be sure that they get plenty of fresh air.

After the plants come into bloom, the flowers will last much longer if they can be kept in a somewhat cooler temperature, particularly during the night.

While a closet or cellar will serve as a place in which to

develop the roots, if no outside space is available, it is much better to bury the containers outside as described later on, under the next method of forcing. Even in the cellar it is of advantage to cover the containers with three or four inches of peat or coconut fiber duing the storage period.

SECOND METHOD: FORCING OR GROWING IN SOIL

If one lives in an apartment or in a house with no garden, the growing of bulbs in water or in fiber, as already suggested, affords a great deal of pleasure. But where a little outdoor space is available, and there is a shed or cellar in which it will be convenient to handle soil and to fill the pots, bulb pans, or boxes in which the bulbs are to be placed, the real gardener will not be content with any method except that which is really best—and that is, to force or grow them in soil, thereby getting the best possible root growth, out of doors, before allowing the bulbs to flower.

As containers for the bulbs, ordinary pots, bulb pans— which are shallow pots—and bowls may be used for flowers to be brought into the house. Wooden boxes or "flats," four or five inches deep and a foot or so in width, and two to three feet in length, may be used for growing an extra supply for cut flowers, if one is so fortunate as to possess a heated frame, a small greenhouse, or even a sunny corner in the cellar or in a workroom, where they may be brought into flower. Very beautiful early spring effects are often obtained by planting bulbs in window boxes, burying them for the winter as described below, and bringing them out in the spring when all danger of frost is past. These bulbs will have finished flowering by the time it is safe to put out the ordinary window-box plants.

Soil for Forcing. Many "formulas" for special soil for bulbs have been used in literature on the subject, including among the ingredients "hop manure," "silver sand," and manure from the mushroom bed, or the melon frame. These, like many other suggestions from European garden literature, mean nothing to the average American home owner. All you need to get perfect results is *a light, rich soil which will drain perfectly,* no matter what it is made up of. For many years I have used the following simple method of preparing my soil for bulbs: To an average garden loam, I add an equal amount of commercial humus, or peat, or, if I happen to have them both on hand, the two mixed together. To this I add sufficient sand (of any kind) so that the mixture is somewhat gritty in texture, and will crumble freely even when quite moist. While stirring these things together, I add fine bone meal or bone flour at the rate of a five-inch potful to about a bushel of soil. That is all there is to it. If *very old,* thoroughly rotted manure, such as you would get from a last spring's hotbed, is on hand, that may well be added, but it is not at all necessary. If either humus or peat are not available, hardwood leafmold rubbed through a coarse screen may be used in their place. The soil, after being mixed, should be gradually moistened, and, if necessary, turned once or twice with a spade or trowel, so that, when ready to use, it will be quite damp, but not sticky or muddy. *This is much better than to attempt to water it after the bulbs are planted.*

Earthenware pots or bulb pans should, if possible, be old ones. If dirty on the outside, they may readily be cleaned by scrubbing with sand and water. If new ones *must* be used it is quite important to give them two or three soakings in a tub of water, at intervals of a day or so, at least half a day at a time. The reason for this is that brand-new pots will absorb a considerable amount of water from the soil which they contain. Any one who has ever potted up a batch of small plants or cuttings in new and old pots cannot fail to have noticed the great difference between the two in this respect. So, if new pots are used, it is very important to pack wet peat or sphagnum moss in between them in the rooting bed so that they can absorb moisture from this source rather than from the soil in which the bulbs are planted.

Planting the Bulbs. Bulbs in pots, as well as out of doors, should have the soil thoroughly well drained. For this reason, and also to prevent the soil from working out through the drainage hole, a bit of some coarse absorbent drainage material, such as sphagnum moss or very coarse leafmold, should be placed in the bottom. Bulb pans that are more than four inches in diameter should be properly "crocked"; that is, have the drainage hole covered with a few small overlapping pieces of broken pot or small flat stones. On top of this, place say a half-inch layer of coarse leafmold or peat, to keep the soil from working down through. Where boxes or flats are used, there will be a hole or drainage holes in the bottom which should be covered with a layer of an inch or so of coarse leafmold or sphagnum moss.

We are now ready for the actual planting of the bulbs. Almost without exception, they are much more pleasing in their general appearance if placed several together in a pot or bulb pan, rather than singly. With most sorts of bulbs, five may be placed in an ordinary five-inch pot, or in a six-inch "azalea pot," which is not quite so deep. To accommodate more bulbs or larger bulbs, regular bulb pans are the most satisfactory to use. Of small bulbs, such as crocuses, grape-hyacinths, snowdrops, or freesias, a half dozen to a dozen will go into a six-inch pot or pan. Fill in the prepared soil to a depth which will bring the tips of the bulbs, when placed upon it, a half inch or so below the rim. Make it fairly firm by striking the bottom of the pot two or three times against the bench. Then place the bulbs, and fill in the soil about them until the soil is level with the tips of the bulbs. Label each pot as the work progresses. They are then ready to be transferred to the rooting bed outside.

Burying Bulbs Out of Doors to Develop Root Growth.

So far as the development of the roots is concerned, the simplest method of burying would be merely to dig a hole or trench in some well-drained place, and cover the bulbs in with four or five inches of soil; but convenience is also to be considered. Where a very considerable number of containers have been prepared, and where it is planned to "bring them in" at intervals during fall and winter, this matter of being able to get at them quickly and handily is very important. For this reason it is usually recommended that the containers be covered with coal ashes. But if these are placed around and immediately over the bulbs, it is rather difficult to clean them from the soil when the latter are taken off, and also to get the outer surface of the bowls themselves perfectly clean and bright. My own preference is to fill in and around the containers, and to cover them about half an inch above the pots with peat, which is made thoroughly moist after being put in place; then put on four or five inches of coal ashes over this. A dollar's worth of peat will cover a considerable number of bowls and pots, and is, of course, just as good as ever for soil improvement after it has served this purpose. Where peat is not available, leafmold may be used. In addition to being cleaner and more convenient in taking the bulbs out, the peat has also the extra advantage of holding a greater reserve supply of moisture.

If a well-drained, empty frame is available for burying the bulbs, no better place need be sought. If not, they can be put in a trench about ten inches deep, with a two-inch layer of cinders in the bottom, to insure perfect drainage, or in a narrow bed made for the purpose against the shady side of a wall. This bed need only be a foot to two feet in width, and may either be made directly on the surface, or dug out a few inches deep, the outer edge being formed by a board held in position by small, neat stakes. A bed so located will be protected from the sun when the bulbs are buried in the fall, and will usually be convenient to get at any time during the winter. Details of these various methods of burying are shown in the accompanying cross section line drawings. (See page 197.)

A small but important detail which is often overlooked in most of the articles and books on this subject, and which I mention last in these directions for burying the bulbs, in the hope that it will be the more firmly impressed upon the mind of the reader, is this: *label each pot as you plant it.* For this purpose, procure some ten- or twelve-inch painted labels, where you buy your bulbs. They cost about a cent apiece, and may be used a number of times. A label of this size will be long enough to come up through the covering over the pots or pans so you can see just where each item is when you want to bring it in.

Bringing in From the Rooting Bed. How long can the bulbs be left before they can be brought in?

That is a question which cannot be answered in terms of so many days or weeks, as it depends both upon the kind of bulb, or even upon the individual variety, and also upon how favorable the weather conditions have been. Some of those which are quicker to root, such as Paper Whites, and the other cluster-flowered narcissi (see page 69); Roman hyacinths (see page 80); extra early tulips, and crocuses may develop a suitable root system and be starting top growth within four weeks; but as a general rule, it is best to give even these six weeks, and still better, except for the few which one may wish to have in flower by Christmas, eight weeks. Where one is in a hurry, a sample pot or pan may be examined at the end of four weeks. Darwin tulips and other things which will not respond favorably to "forcing" do best if not brought in until late January or February.

Starting Growth Indoors. When the root systems of the earliest bulbs have sufficiently developed, the first pots or pans may be taken out of the rooting bed and brought indoors to begin top growth. It is just at this point that a mistake is often made by the beginner which will spoil the results of all the preliminary work that has been done.

It is not difficult to have beauty from bulbs indoors during the winter. (*Upper left*) Shows an ordinary flat with drainage material and soil ready for planting. (*Upper right*) Bulbs in position ready for covering. (*Lower left*) Tulips ready to bring indoors after rooting outside. Flat at left contains American-grown bulbs; the one at right, imported bulbs, same variety, planted at the same time. (*Lower right*) Hyacinths ready to "bring in" —note root development at bottom of glass container.

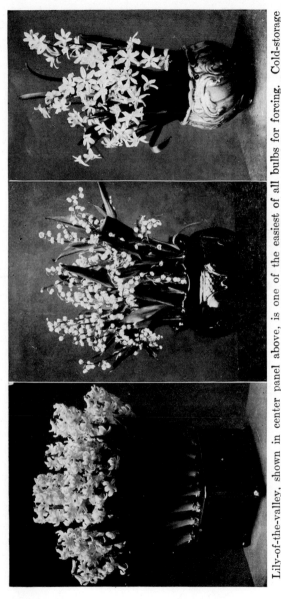

Lily-of-the-valley, shown in center panel above, is one of the easiest of all bulbs for forcing. Cold-storage pips planted at intervals of two or three weeks will yield a constant succession of blooms from Thanksgiving to Easter. The attractive bulb pan at the left contains single hyacinths, but the picture conveys no idea of their fragrance and color. At the right is a jardinière of chionodoxas, as charming indoors as they are outside.

Do *not* place the bulbs from the rooting bed directly in full sunlight and in a high temperature. To do so will force the tops into growth so quickly that the bulbs will "come blind." Place them, rather, in a subdued light in a north window or behind a shade or screen, where the temperature will average only from 40 to 50 degrees. At first, water only gradually, increasing the amount as the growth begins to develop. They should be kept under these conditions until after the flower stalk has begun to shoot up and the bulbs are formed. Then they can be placed in full sunlight and given a temperature of from 50 to 60 degrees. Take care that the soil is kept evenly moist. To let the soil dry out, and then to overwater, may result in imperfect flowers or in "blind" growth. At this stage, additional plant food in the form of a top-dressing or liquid manure (see page 130) may be given. Keep well ventilated to make sure that plenty of fresh air is supplied at all times. Remember that the bulbs cannot get out for a daily walk as you do! To be shut up continuously in a super-heated atmosphere with all the moisture drawn out of it by "modern" heating is as undesirable for plants as it is for humans. It is often noticed that bulbs as well as other house plants do better in the kitchen than in the other rooms of the house. The simple explanation of this is that there is more moisture in the atmosphere. It is an excellent plan to keep some large flat vessel, or one of the pans which are now made especially for attaching to radiators, and can be bought at small cost, near the bulbs and filled with water at all times.

After the buds begin to open, they will keep in perfect condition much longer if they can again be put in moderate light, or be somewhat shaded from direct sunshine in the window where they are growing, and given an abundance of fresh air and a lower temperature. This may easily be accomplished by giving them a little more ventilation at night, avoiding, of course, any risk of actual freezing, and also a direct draft of cold air upon the plants.

If the bulbs, after they have flowered, can be placed in the cellar or anywhere where they will get some light and will not freeze, the foliage will go on growing for some time, thus leaving the bulbs, when they do dry off, in much better condition for planting outside in the garden than if they are taken out of the pots or pans immediately after flowering. They can be planted out of doors any time during the spring, and will start growth themselves in the early autumn.

THIRD METHOD: GROWING TENDER BULBS IN POTS OR TUBS

The system described above is, as has already been mentioned, adapted to hardy and half-hardy bulbs that ordinarily bloom in spring or early summer. For all the more tropical bulbs, such as callas, amaryllis, gloxinias, tuberous begonias, and the like, a different system is needed, and these must be handled as follows.

Indoor Culture of Tender Bulbs. To grow such bulbs as cannot be planted outdoors to the best advantage, a greenhouse or a conservatory is, of course, necessary. However, there are a number of them which do excellently, with a moderate amount of care, in the sun parlor, a sunny bay window, or even in a sunny window in the ordinary living room.

There is a great deal more variation in the cultural requirements of these tender bulbs than is the case with the hardy and half-hardy ones. Nevertheless, there are many points in the culture of the hardy and the tender sorts which are similar. Among these are good drainage; the preparation of the pots or pans for planting; the gradual increase of temperature and water as growth develops; and a somewhat cooler temperature after the flowers open; together with not exposing to direct rays of sunshine through glass excepting during the short days of December, January, and February.

One of the chief points of difference in their cultural requirements is that they do not require a preliminary rooting period at a very low temperature; although it is best to start growth gradually, after they are potted up, at a much lower temperature than they will require later on, and to give only a moderate amount of water at this time. In this, of course, we are but duplicating the conditions under which they grow naturally.

In preparing the soil for this class of bulbs, it is much more advisable to use rotten manure in the mixture. A good soil is made up of one-third each of garden soil, old rotted manure, and humus or peat; with sand and bone meal added as already described.

When their flowering period is over, the plants should be kept in vigorous growth for some time, and dried off gradually only when the foliage shows signs of beginning to "ripen" by loosing its normal green color. During this period the amount of water given should gradually be decreased. A very few which are evergreen in habit should be kept growing throughout the year, but even these have their "rest periods," during which growth is practically at a standstill. The others should be removed, as their foliage dies, and left in a warm cellar, or placed under benches in a greenhouse, where they may be allowed to dry out. Some of them do best when repotted each year; and others may be kept in the same pots, and merely started into growth again by giving water gradually as the proper season arrives. Further details of culture are given under the paragraph headings which follow, describing the special requirements of the individual sorts, or of groups which require similar treatment.

HARDY BULBS FOR FORCING

Hyacinths. These are among the easiest and the most satisfactory of all bulbs to force for winter beauty. All sizes of bulbs (see page 80) will flower satisfactorily. The largest are used for exhibition purposes, but the smaller are quite as beautiful. For extra early flowers get the especially "prepared" bulbs which may easily be had in flower by Christmas. Liquid manuring during growth is especially helpful. If the flower stalks seem inclined not to grow up as they should, a cone of stiff paper open at the top, inverted over the pot (page 97) will help to "draw" them up; but this will seldom be necessary if they are given time to make good roots, and kept cool during early growth. They may be grown in water, fiber, or soil (Methods One and Two above), but best results are obtained when they can remain in the rooting bed out of doors for from two to three months.

Among the many good Dutch varieties for winter bloom are La Grandesse, pure white; Lady Derby, pink; Roi des Belges, red; Orangeboven, deep apricot; Enchantress, pale blue; Grand Maitre, porcelain blue; Ivanhoe, dark blue. (For others see page 84.) The Dutch "Miniatures" are the earliest of this type to flower. The "Roman" and "Italian" hyacinths are still earlier.

Daffodils and Narcissi. All the types and most of the varieties may be grown easily indoors, or in a frame or cool greenhouse. Most sorts will flower satisfactorily under Method One, but forcing in soil (Method Two) is better. For the species, Method Three may be used, keeping the bulbs in the same pots or pans for two or three years, until they overcrowd.

The "Chinese Sacred-Lily" (*narcissus orientalis*) and the polyanthus type, such as "Paper White" grandiflora, Grand Monarque, white with a primrose cup, and Grand Soleil d'Or, rich yellow, are "tender" varieties, and the easiest and quickest to flower. Of the "Dutch," or hardy sorts, Golden Spur, pure yellow, is one of the best and earliest; and King Alfred, yellow, extra tall and fine; Empress, white and yellow; and Mme. de Graaf, all white, are among the best for forcing. The cluster-flowered daffodils (Poetaz type) are also easily grown indoors, and are extremely graceful and pretty. Most of the other types may be forced readily except the Poets and the species, but these may be easily grown for early spring flowering. (For varieties suggested see page 73.)

Tulips. All of the Earlies, single and double, force readily in fiber or in soil, and may be had in bloom by the first of the year. The May-flowering type, Darwins, Breeders, and other late sorts, with few exceptions, should be given considerably more time.

American-grown bulbs will flower ten days to three weeks ahead of the imported ones. I tested some thousands of each three years in succession, in a number of varieties, and the results proved this most conclusively. The species also grow excellently in pots or in pans, and are most dainty and beautiful. Good varieties of tulips for growing indoors in a cool greenhouse or a frame are as follows: Early; White Hawk and Pelican, pure white; Rose Luisante, rose pink; Proserpine, carmine, *fragrant;* Hobbema (Le Reve), rose and buff; Pink Beauty, brilliant pink; Brilliant Star, scarlet; Keizerskroon, scarlet-edged yellow; Fred Moore, orange, extra fine, and *fragrant;* De Wet, flaming orange, also *fragrant* (try these two and get a new thrill!); Rising Sun, golden yellow; Goldfinch, pure yellow.

Of the Cottage class, Picotee (Maidens Blush), white, edged deep rose; Yellow Picotee, yellow-edged deep rose; Inglescombe Pink; Vitellina, very pale yellow, *fragrant;* Mrs. Moon, pure yellow, late, *fragrant;* are all excellent.

Of the Darwins, two in particular break the general rule and will respond to quite early forcing; they are William Pitt, very dark scarlet with purplish bloom, and William Copland (Sweet Lavender), a beautiful bright lavender and very *fragrant.* Others for fairly early bloom are Clara Butt, salmon pink; Le Notre, pink; Baronne de la Tonnaye, bright rose with lighter margin; Bartigon, fiery crimson; Isis, crimson scarlet; Farncombe Sanders, rose scarlet; Wally Moes, light lilac; Rev. H. Ewbank, heliotrope; and Philippe de Commines, dark purple. Some of the best Breeders for forcing are St. James, old rose and bronze; Samson, violet and bronze; Feu Ardent, fiery red; Bronze

Queen (Clio), buff and bronze; Jaune d'Oeuf (Sunrise), orange red; and Dom Pedro, very rich mahogany.

Crocuses. These may be grown in pebbles, in fiber, or in soil, but must be kept cool at all times, as they will not respond to "forcing" in any high temperature. They naturally bloom so early, however—within eight to ten weeks from potting—that this is no great disadvantage. The autumn-flowering sorts can hardly be kept from flowering: a few bulbs in moist sand or pebbles, placed in a sunny window, will soon be in bloom even without prerooting. All sorts are best planted quite close together, say six to eight in a five-inch pot, or a dozen or more in a small pan. Good varieties for winter flowering are Kathleen Parlow, pure white; Maximilian, porcelain blue; Mme. Mina, violet, striped, early; Julia Culp, purple, late; Large Yellow, yellow; and Pallas, white, striped light purple, with orange anthers, most attractive.

Minor Spring Bulbs. Chionodoxas, galanthus ("Snowdrops"), Grape-Hyacinths (muscari), Scillas, especially the tender sorts, such as *peruviana,* and Leucojums (see page 92), are quite easily grown, if not given too much heat. Follow the suggestions given for crocuses.

Bulbocodium vernum is one of the earliest to flower; given a sunny place in the window, after rooting, its cheery, rosy flowers will greet you even before the crocuses.

Ornithogalum, give the same treatment accorded hyacinths.

Lily-of-the-Valley (Convallaria). This most exquisite flower is forced by the hundreds of thousands by commercial florists, but is too seldom found in the amateur's winter garden. While florists often use a temperature of from 80 to 90 degrees in forcing "valley pips," obtaining flowers in less than three weeks, the amateur should be in no hurry with them. They may be grown in either sand, fiber, or soil. "Cold-storage forcing pips," entirely distinct from field clumps for planting outdoors (see page 101), are obtainable at any season of the year; they are usually imported,

and sold as "German," "Berlin," or "Hamburg" Valley
Pips, although they are now produced, to some extent, in
America. These cold-storage pips are ready for immediate
growth. Lily-of-the-Valley, unlike the Dutch bulbs, *does
not require any preliminary rooting period.* It may be given
a fairly warm temperature, from 50 to 60 degrees, immediately after potting; but it should be *placed in the dark*
for from ten days to two weeks, until the foliage is two
to three inches high; otherwise the flower stalks are likely
to sprout up ahead of the leaves, and it is the combination
of the two which gives the plant its peculiar dainty charm.
Then remove to full light. As the roots are quite long,
standard pots or azalea pots are better than bulb pans or
bowls for valley pips. The roots may be trimmed somewhat
to fit the container. While fiber alone may be employed,
I like to use sand around the lower two-thirds of the
roots, as this holds them more firmly, covering the surface
with bulb fiber or peat. The buds or points of the pips
should be left nearly an inch *above* the surface. Keep cool,
and give plenty of ventilation as soon as the flower buds
open, and each lot will last for several weeks.

Fritillaria. While these may be grown in pots (Method
Three above), and kept without repotting for several years,
they are more adapted to the greenhouse than to the house,
especially as their characteristic musty odor is more notice-
able when they are confined. The lower-growing varieties
(see page 95) are best for pot culture.

Liliums. As in garden culture, so in pot culture (Method
Three, page 133), lilies require special treatment in several
respects. First of all, additional peat and sand—or better
still, *old*, soft-coal ashes—should be added to the potting
soil already described; and as a rule, only one bulb should
be placed in a six-, seven-, or eight-inch pot, according to
the size of the bulb. Stem-rooting varieties (see page 139),
should be placed near the *bottom* of the pot, first covering
the crocking with an inch or two of prepared soil, and an
inch layer of sand, soft-coal ashes, or sphagnum moss.

Then cover the bulb only slightly above its top. Base-rooting kinds should be placed at the top of the pot.

It is important to have the bulbs sound and plump *before* potting them. When received they may be soft and flabby, if not actually withered, from loss of moisture during shipment. Place them at once in a deep flat or box, in a cool place, and cover them with moist, not *wet*, peat or moss. Spray this covering moderately every few days until careful examination, from time to time, shows that they have again become plump and crisp. Then they will be ready for potting, taking care not to break any roots which may have started.

After potting, plunge the pots level to the rim in ashes, preferably in a shaded frame. If no frame is available, cover each pot with an inverted pot one size smaller, and place in the rooting bed (see page 197). As freezing weather approaches, fill the frame with leaves or hay, or cover the inverted pots with ashes. When the root system has developed, and top growth starts, bring into moderate temperature. As the stems of the bulbs which were planted at the bottoms of the pots develop, gradually fill in with prepared soil to within half an inch of the top. As growth progresses, top dress or water with liquid manure, which may be continued, every two to four weeks, until the buds begin to open. As the last flowers begin to fade, reduce the frequency of watering, until, as the foliage dies, the soil is almost dry. Then store in a cellar, or under a greenhouse bench, where the soil will not get bone dry. In August or September, repot in fresh soil, but disturb the roots and the soil adhering to them as little as possible. While lilies will sometimes succeed without following out all these details, they are so beautiful that the slight extra care which assures success is well worth while.

Most of the varieties recommended for outdoor culture may be grown in pots. (Those marked S should be planted at the bottom of the pot.) These include candidum; auratum(S); regale(S); speciosum(S); testaceum;

elegans(S); japonicum (*krameri*) (S); chalcedonicum; henryi(S); the new Sulphur-Gale hybrids(S) and many others. The tender lilies—harrisi, usually available in August, longiflorum formosum, obtainable in September, and longiflorum giganteum, arriving about a month later—are particularly recommended to the beginner, as they will have made considerable growth before freezing weather; the same is true of candidum and of regale, which, being American grown, may be obtained early.

Iris. It is to be regretted that the bulbous irises, the "poor man's orchids" of the open garden, are not suitable for house culture. In the cool greenhouse, or in an unheated frame, however, they may be grown to perfection. Light, rich, well-drained soil; planting three to four inches deep, and four to five inches apart, in rows twelve to fifteen inches apart; mulching thoroughly as the ground freezes, with hay or leaves; and removing same as growth starts in the spring, are the simple requirements for frame culture. If the sash can be supported *above* the frames, as the growth reaches the glass, the flowers will be kept in perfect condition. For the greenhouse, plant the bulbs two inches deep in pots, pans, or flats; plunge to the rim in cinders in a frame; mulch before danger of freezing; cover the frames, and bring in as wanted after the first of the year. The above applies to the Spanish, English, and Dutch types (see page 114). Reticulata, tingitana, and filifolia will respond to gentle forcing, even when started directly indoors, and may be had in bloom much earlier.

HALF-HARDY BULBS FOR WINTER BLOOM

Being halfway between the hardy and the tender bulbs, some of the half-hardies will require treatment similar to the former class, and some like the latter.

Cyclamen. This excellent winter-flowering plant is at once one of the most beautiful and most satisfactory of all bulbs for house culture, or for the conservatory or cool greenhouse. Usually they are bought as growing plants, in bud or in flower. The blooming plants offered by florists around Christmas time are seedlings, some fifteen months old. If they are kept in fairly steady temperature, not too high or dry, and watered evenly, they will bloom, even in the house, for three months or so. After the last blooms fade, water more moderately, *but do not cease watering,* as is done with most other bulbs. In April or early May the plants may be put out of doors, plunged to the rim in peat, leafmold, or moss in a frame or a sheltered spot, where they will get early morning or late afternoon sunlight, but be shaded during the middle of the day; or under a lath sash. Keep the soil barely moist, but *do not let it get entirely dry,* until late August or early September; then repot in fresh soil, being careful not to injure any young roots. Merely press the corm into the soil, leaving more than half of it above the surface. If growth is vigorous, and extra fine plants are wanted, shift to larger pots in October, pinch out the first flower buds, and occasionally water with weak liquid manure, or top-dress lightly. (Raising plants from seed is described in Chapter XXI.)

Anemones and Ranunculus. These wonderfully bright little flowers (see page 115), while better adapted to a cool greenhouse than to the average living room, may, nevertheless, be grown with care in conservatory or sun parlor or in a cool, well-ventilated sunny window, where the temperature will run from 45 to 50 degrees. They may be handled by either Method Two or Method Three. In the first instance, leave the pots or pans in the rooting bed, preferably in a frame, until February or March. In the second, keep the pots or pans very cool and only moderately moist until the roots are well developed. Succession plantings may be made up to February, keeping the extra roots in sand or peat to prevent drying out. As the roots should be covered two to three inches deep, azalea pots are better than bulb pans for these flowers. After flowering, the bulbs may be planted outside in the spring. Fresh bulbs should be used each year.

Freesias. Those who are familiar with this extremely pretty and very fragrant flower only in its older forms, will find a revelation in the new colored varieties. Like anemones and ranunculus, freesias require a cool temperature; they may readily be grown in a sunny window as well as in the greenhouse *if* the following method of handling is followed, and may be had in flower continuously from early in the year until Decoration Day. Plant the bulbs one inch deep, a dozen or so to a six-inch pan. The soil is best mixed with humus rather than with peat or leafmold; or plain, light garden loam will do. Plunge to the rim in cinders, outdoors, in a sheltered, sunny nook; or, better, in a frame. Do *not* cover the pots. Water moderately until the tops are an inch to two inches high; then increase. They will now be ready to take in. A succession of bloom may be obtained either by making succession plantings, at intervals of three or four weeks, from late August to mid-October; or by planting all at one time, and holding back some of the pans in a cold but frost-proof frame; or in a box or pit with a northern exposure. Under greenhouse culture, for cut flowers, they are grown in flats or directly in benches, planted two inches deep and two inches apart, in rows four to six inches apart. As the buds show, moderate extra feeding may be given. Water plentifully, and keep *well ventilated*. After flowering, dry off only gradually to allow the natural growth to be completed. When the foliage yellows, put in a frost-proof, sunny place to ripen up; after ten days to two weeks here, the bulbs may be taken out and stored until the following July. Since the commercial culture of freesia bulbs, which are largely used by florists for cut flowers, has been perfected in California, many new varieties have been developed there, especially by Rudolph Fischer. Among these are Purity, pure white, and its improved form, splendens; Yellow Prince, light yellow; California, golden yellow; General Pershing, a peculiar violet pink, which I have had produce stems well over two feet; June Michelson, deep rose pink with yellow throat; Katherine Watkins, an extraordinary charming salmon buff.

Oxalis. A charming little plant (see page 177), ideal for house culture, especially in a small pan for a shelf or bracket, or in a hanging basket, as they are semi-trailing in growth. Use four-inch pots for single bulbs; or better, put three or four in an eight-inch pan or hanging basket, covering at least an inch deep, and place immediately where it is to flower, as near the glass as is possible, as the blooms will be produced in a few weeks' time and will continue throughout the season. Water only sufficiently to keep the soil fairly moist. After the leaves die down, let the pots dry thoroughly in a warm place. In July or August, repot the new bulbs, which will be found to have developed at the ends of long, stringlike roots.

Brodiaea and Brevoortia. These fine, long-lasting gay flowers (see page 120) are easily grown in a cool greenhouse. Pot in August or September, putting plenty of sand around the bulbs, and covering about two inches deep. Root outside (Method Two) and then bring in and give full sunlight, preferably near the glass. Very moderate watering will be required. Dry thoroughly to ripen, and either store in pots, or repot immediately.

Alstroemeria (*Chilian Lily*). Give same treatment as above, except that bulbs will need repotting only every second or third year.

Babiana. Pot in October or early November, two inches deep; bring in from rooting bed or cellar, when top growth has just started, to cool greenhouse. Water freely during early growth and after flowering, and ripen off in full sun, and store in pots until following September.

Calochortus (Butterfly Tulip). These remarkably brilliantly colored flowers (see page 121) are ideal for the cool greenhouse. Pot in September or October, root outside (Method Two) and bring into cool temperature, with liberal watering. Except the "Globe" varieties, all should have full sun while growing. Dry thoroughly in full sun after foliage dies, and store in pots.

Crinums. Lilylike flowers with very narrow curving petals, and handsome, broad-pointed foliage. Some require cool and some warm greenhouse temperature; and the same culture as amaryllis (page 223). They may be grown outside in a sheltered position, south of Washington; or in a well-protected frame farther north, and are most imposing in effect.

Crocosmia. These beautiful orange-colored crocuslike flowers may be given the same treatment as brodiaeas.

Ixias and Sparaxis. The ixias (see page 119) are delightful as winter flowers, and easily grown inside or in a frame for early spring blooms. Pot in September or October, and give the same treatment as bulbous iris (page 113).

Pancratium and *Hymenocallis.* The "Sea Daffodil" and the "Spanish Lily," while interesting for the greenhouse collection, have no particular appeal to the amateur. Pot in March, like amaryllis bulbs (page 223), give temperature of from 65 to 75 degrees, and plenty of water; and 50 degrees, with almost dry soil, during winter; carry over in same pots.

Zephyranthes (Fairy Lily). While they may be grown outdoors under favorable conditions (see page 122), these charming flowers are excellent for the house or greenhouse. Planted half a dozen bulbs in a six-inch pot or pan in the fall, covered one inch deep, and grown in a moderate temperature, they will produce their dainty flowers freely for many weeks.

TENDER BULBS FOR INDOOR BLOOM

Most of these, unlike the Dutch bulbs and other hardy bulbs, give a long succession of flowers instead of a single comparatively short-lived crop. Many of them can be grown for several years without repotting, and several of them are among the most satisfactory of plants for the living room or sun parlor. For details of their culture, refer to Method Three (page 210).

Begonias. While both the fibrous and the tuberous-rooted begonias are quite ideal as house and greenhouse plants, it is with the latter, of course, that we are here concerned. Many types are splendid for summer bedding outdoors (see Chapter XV). All of these may be grown indoors; but in addition to these there are more fragile varieties, and many marvelously and delicately beautiful named sorts, which are better grown inside where the flowers may reach perfection without the chance of damage by wind or rain. It is greatly to be regretted that these named varieties, so well known abroad, are not more generally available here. The tubers should be started any time from February to April. They may be first placed quite close together, in a flat or bulb pan, containing only moist peat, humus, or screened leafmold, packing the material around them so that the bulbs, *concave side up*, are level with the surface. Place under a greenhouse bench, or in any other warm, shady place. When the new sprouts start, place singly in three- or four-inch standard pots. The rotting compost should be of light loam or humus, in equal parts, with finely screened rotted manure, and sand, added, to make a fairly rich and very friable soil. In potting, be careful not to break the fine roots which will have started. Grow in a fairly cool temperature, from 50 to 60 degrees, protected from bright midday sunshine; and repot *as soon as the roots are through the soil.* Shift to five- or six-inch pots, or six- to seven-inch azalea pots, using more manure and less humus in the soil, and adding bone meal, with a little tankage or dried blood, if desired. Keep the tubers well to the surface of the soil, which should be below the rim of the pot, as generous watering will be required. Pinch out the buds until the plants are strongly established; and then a wonderful display of flowers may be enjoyed for several months. Many varieties will require light staking, or wire supports to show the flowers to the best advantage. As the last flowers fade, decrease watering gradually and stop it entirely as the stems yellow and fall off. Then dry the bulbs in the pots for a couple of weeks; after which they may be removed, and stored in sawdust or dry soil, in a moderately warm cellar, about 50 degrees, until time for starting again. The bulbs may be used for many years. (For starting from seed, see Chapter XXI.)

Amaryllis (*hippeastrum*). This old-time favorite has enjoyed a revived popularity with the advent of the splendid new hybrids now available. Any one who has ever seen the annual show of these gorgeous flowers staged at the greenhouses of the Department of Agriculture at Washington, D. C., as it has been my pleasure to do a number of times, cannot but admit a certain degree of admiration for them, despite any previous prejudice against their somewhat stiff, formal, and bulky habit of growth. There are few bulbs which will give the beginner more for his money than the amaryllis. Pot the bulbs when they are secured, which may be any time desired from January to spring, in soil containing a third rotted manure and bone meal, preferably both fine and very coarse. Put the bulbs, which are very large, in pots one to two inches more in diameter, and cover only to the shoulder of the bulb, leaving the neck protruding. Pack the soil firmly. Give very little water until growth starts. A temperature of from 50 to 60 degrees is ample. The flower spikes, often three to a bulb, will develop quickly, and each bears several of the immense lilylike flowers. The colors, which are very vivid, include particularly vermilion, crimson, scarlet, and ox-blood red, as well as pinks and whites, and blotches and stripes on white. The plants are gross feeders, and will thrive with considerable liquid manuring or top-dressing. After blooming, it takes the foliage a considerable length of time to complete its growth, and the plants should be well cared for to provide for next year's flowers. Dry off gradually and store in pots. Repotting each season will give good

results, but is by no means necessary. The first amaryllis
I ever owned flowered year after year for many seasons in
the remains of a graniteware double boiler, with a few nail
holes punched in the bottom for drainage. The new American hybrids are sold in mixture.

Gloxinias. While usually grown in a greenhouse, with a
moist atmosphere and from 60 to 70 degrees temperature,
gloxinias may readily be handled in an ordinary living room
or sun parlor, with a temperature often going ten degrees
cooler. The large bellflower-shaped blossoms, ranging in
color through white, pink, crimson, scarlet, mauve, and
vinous purple with various shadings, are borne above a
crown of large plushlike, deeply veined leaves which are
very ornamental. Start the bulbs in the same way as
tuberous begonias, and give the same general culture, except
that the soil should contain, if anything, more sand; and
care should be taken, in watering, to *keep the foliage dry.*

Gesneria. It is strange that these beautiful flowers,
natives of Mexico and South America, and much more
graceful in habit and more beautiful in foliage than gloxinias, which they resemble in many respects, have never
become more popular in this country. The brilliant, tubular flowers of yellow, orange, or scarlet are produced on
long spikes, from which they stand out on slim stems, rising
well above the richly metallic-colored, velvety leaves. The
several varieties bloom in succession, and as the bulbs may
readily be started at intervals of a month, in March, April,
May, and June, a constant supply of flowers may be had
from July through the following spring. Their cultural
requirements are the same as those of gloxinias and tuberous begonias, except that the dormant bulbs may better
be left in the pots until wanted for starting again.

Caladiums. The fancy-leaved caladiums are among the
most impressive of all foliage plants, and unsurpassed for
color effects in the conservatory or sun room, on the veranda
or in a sheltered nook outside. Start the tubers, preferably

with "bottom heat," in a greenhouse or over a radiator. Half bury them in small pots of moist peat or humus, placing the pots in a forcing frame or a flat, surrounded with peat. Water very sparingly, preferably with a syringe, until growth starts. Repot, before the roots crowd, into slightly larger pots, using a very light, rich soil (such as for begonias), and shift once, or even twice more, to get fine plants. A moist atmosphere is one of the chief requirements, and they should have, if possible, at least 60 degrees of temperature. As the leaves fade out and yellow in the fall, dry off; and store the pots for the winter in a thoroughly dry place, with a temperature of at least 50, and better 60, degrees.

Achimenes. These semi-tropical, very pretty little trailing plants, with tubular flowers, so flared open at the ends as to give somewhat the effect of pansies growing on a small bush, are charming in a hothouse or warm conservatory. Culturally, their requirements are much the same as for gesnerias, above.

Eucharis (Amazonlily). This tropical flower, with fragrant, waxy, pure white flowers somewhat the shape of a daffodil, borne in clusters on stems fifteen to twenty-four inches tall, above callalike leaves, is one of the most beautiful of tender bulbs, but hardly for the amateur to attempt, unless he or she possesses a greenhouse with a very warm section, and is willing to take some pains with its culture. The soil should be made up of equal parts of loam sod, leafmold, or peat, and cow manure and sand together, composted at least six months in advance. Pot very firmly, leaving the necks above soil, and putting four to six bulbs in an eight- or ten-inch azalea pot. Start growth in a forcing frame, with the pots plunged in peat, with a temperature of at least 65 degrees, and water very moderately at first. March or April is the most convenient time for starting the plants, but this may be done at any time of the year, if the proper temperature can be maintained. As growth develops, give 75 degrees, plenty of sunshine, and abundant moisture. As the flowers cease, cut down the water; but as the plants remain evergreen, give just enough to keep the foliage in condition until time for repotting.

Lycoris (Golden Lily). A very pretty Chinese bulb similar to the amaryllis, and requiring the same treatment.

Nerines (Guernsey-Lily). Miniature, lilylike flowers growing one to two feet high, and of various fine colors, including pink, rose, red, salmon, scarlet, and orange. Easily grown in a conservatory or cool greenhouse, or even in a sunny window. Pot firmly, in the fall, as soon as received, covering only the lower half of the bulbs, which are most effective when put three in a five-inch, or five in a seven-inch pot or pan. Give the same treatment as for cyclamens, plunging the pots outdoors during the summer; leave in the same pots for several years, replacing the surface soil annually.

Sprekelia (Jacobaean-Lily). This very attractive flower (see page 178) may be handled in the same way as amaryllis, which it closely resembles; or it may be grown in pebbles or fiber like hyacinths.

Vallota (Scarboro-Lily). An evergreen plant of easy culture, unfortunately now quite "out of fashion" though well worth growing. Treat much the same as amaryllis, potting newly purchased bulbs, when received, usually during early spring, covering about half the bulb. The foliage, which makes little growth until after the flowers are produced in July to September, should be kept growing vigorously for a considerable time thereafter, being allowed to "rest" but *not* to get dried out, during late winter and early spring. Repotting, which will be required only once in several years, as they flower better when the roots are crowded, is best done in May or June. There are several varieties, orange, brick-red, white, crimson, and vermilion being among the shades of color.

Gladiolus. Both commercially, and in private houses, the

gladiolus is being more and more grown as a winter cut flower. Not only the early-flowering strains, such as Colvillei, nanus, and the new Heraut, which are earlier than either, but also specially prepared or early-ripened bulbs of the standard large-flowered and primulinus strains are now available for this purpose. In the greenhouse, they are best planted in solid beds or deep benches, covering the bulbs three inches or so deep, spaced four to six inches, in rows a foot to a foot and a half apart, according to the vigor of the variety. The smaller, earlier-flowering sorts do well in pots, three or five in a five- or six-inch pot. Pot any time from October to February, using early ripened or "retarded" bulbs for the early planting, and taking care to secure strong, *young* bulbs (see page 145). Do not attempt to force in high temperature, but grow slowly, surface feeding moderately as the flower spikes begin to shoot. Deep flats will answer for flowers for cutting, where a bench is not available. If the foliage is kept growing after the flowers are removed, until it dies naturally, the bulbs may be stored and kept for next season's use, being ready for planting earlier than field-grown bulbs. Good varieties for indoor growing are Colvillei, The Bride, white; nanus, Peach Blossom, delicate pink; Blushing Bride, white with crimson spots; Sapho, soft lilac; and primulinus, Maidens Blush, soft rose; Souvenir, pure yellow; Alice Tiplady, brilliant orange salmon, deservedly the most popular of all; and Salmon Beauty, very deep orange salmon with lighter throat, which at many exhibitions has been considered the finest of all "prims." Some of the extra early large-flowered sorts are Mary Pickford, white; Halley and Prince of Wales, both coral pink, and the new and most satisfactory of all, Early Sunrise.

Tigridias and Watsonias. While usually grown out of doors, these two attractive flowers, the one from Mexico and the other from Africa, may easily be grown in pots indoors, or for early summer bloom in the sun parlor, by potting early in the spring when the bulbs are received, and given the same culture as for gladiolus in pots.

Many of the other summer-flowering bulbs, such as cannas and galtonias, may readily be flowered in the greenhouse, if desired, but offer no particular advantage for that purpose.

CHAPTER XIX

FLOWERS FOR CUTTING, AND HOW TO HANDLE THEM

While part of the purpose of every good garden is to extend the house to the outdoors, by supplying an attractive outdoor living room, it should also serve the important end of making it possible to bring the outdoors into the house.

This is one of the wonderful things which cut flowers can accomplish. Vases and bowls filled with them for the living room, the dining-room table, and even for the bed-rooms, particularly the guest room, not only double the enjoyment which is to be had from a good garden, but possess an actual practical value in increasing general good spirits and good health. Concerning the truth of this last point, your psychologist can give a deep scientific explanation; but any one who has ever had a bit of experience in a hospital, either as a "paying guest" or a visitor, will need no proof further than personal observation.

But the joy of having an abundance of flowers for cutting is not limited to one's own use. There are few pleasures which the garden yields—or which are to be obtained from any other source, for that matter—which exceed the real "kick" that there is to be had from presenting some friend with beautiful blossoms from your own garden, of your own growing. It is then that the florists' slogan, "Say It With Flowers!" achieves its real significance, and the blooms become truly articulate!

The growing of flowers in the garden as part of the garden picture, and the growing of flowers for cutting, while they have many points in common, are, as a matter of fact, two very different things. In the former case, they are a means to an end—the creation of a beautiful landscape picture, and the beauty of the individual blossoms is, or should be, a secondary consideration. In growing flowers for cutting, however, the blossoms themselves are the end which we are seeking to attain. With many perennials, some flowers may be "stolen" for the house or for giving away, without greatly damaging the picture. But with most bulbs, this cannot be done. And, therefore, with bulbs it is doubly desirable that a separate planting should be made specifically for furnishing an abundance of cut flowers for the house.

This, fortunately, is a very easy matter with most of the spring-blooming flowers, such as tulips and daffodils; and with the summer-flowering things, such as dahlias, gladiolus, and the others.

YEAR-AROUND FLOWERS FOR CUTTING

With a little planning, it is an easy matter to have an abundant supply of flowers for cutting from the first warm days of March straight through spring, summer, autumn, and most of the winter, until early spring again returns.

For Early Spring. While many of the bulbs described in Chapters V to IX bloom very early when planted outdoors, in the ordinary way, the majority of them may be had still earlier, and in perfect condition for cutting, by planting them in an ordinary coldframe, such as is used for starting vegetable plants. A frame of this kind can be very easily made out of secondhand or scrap lumber, and as bulbs for cutting can be planted very close together, a space as small as six by six feet will give a surprising number of blooms. It is well to provide some means of increasing the height of the frame used for this purpose by putting on extra boards, when the flowers have grown tall enough to be in danger of touching the glass. A method of adding side pieces in this way is shown in the accompanying cut. The cleats slip down over the top board of the frame, and hold the additional boards securely in place. Many of the lower-growing things, such as hyacinths, grape-hyacinths, and early tulips, will have sufficient headroom in an ordinary frame. Late tulips, tall daffodils, and iris need more room which must be provided either by planting them in an extra deep frame, or by putting on the side boards described above.

For Spring and Early Summer, bulbs may be planted in the usual way in the open. These include late tulips, Cottage or May Flowering, Darwins, and so forth; daffodils;

GROWING HALF-HARDY BULBS IN FRAME

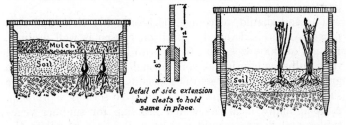

Detail of side extension and cleats to hold same in place.

and bulbous irises, and will supply flowers until the peonies, hardy irises, and other early summer flowers are ready.

For Midsummer, there are the Japanese irises, the early "glads," tuberoses, and summer-hyacinths; to mention but four of the many which may be grown for this purpose.

In midsummer comes the wonderful range of gladiolus of different types and varieties, making possible a long and constant succession, and also the early hardy lilies.

For Autumn, there are the late-flowering "glads," montbretias, the later hardy lilies; the infinite variety of form and color available in the different types of dahlias; winding up with the gorgeous display of tritomas, which last until hard, killing frost out of doors, and make one of the most effective of all cut flowers for the house.

Winter rooms may be made gay with freesias, "paper whites," tulips, and daffodils, and other flowers easily grown in pans or in flats for cutting, particularly if one has a heated frame or a small greenhouse.

The flowers mentioned above are, of course, but a few of the many available for the different seasons of the year, but even these will give lasting beauty indoors, with very few breaks from one end of the year to the other.

FLOWERS THAT ARE WANTED PARTICULARLY FOR CUTTING

The flowers that are wanted especially for cutting need not be planted in the flower garden. In fact it is not only easier but also better to grow them in separate beds which are made for the purpose, or in a section of the vegetable garden.

The soil should, of course, be thoroughly rich; and care must be exercised that the position chosen is well drained. If part of the vegetable garden is to be used, keep in mind that bulbs remain in the soil through the winter, while the great majority of vegetables occupy it only during the summer season, when drainage is not so serious a problem. A good many locations which are fine for summer vegetables and flowers would not be well suited at all to the growing of bulbs or bulbous-rooted plants occupying the soil during the winter months. In planting bulbs for cut flowers, they are best placed in straight, narrow rows, which can be easily cultivated and cared for, rather than in groups or colonies, as when planting in the flower garden. The bulbs may be set almost close enough to touch, and the rows spaced a foot to two feet apart, according to the size of the plants. The latter distance is far enough for gladiolus, if they are to be cultivated by hand. Dahlias will, of course, require three to four feet. Plant the same depth as recommended for garden planting. It is a good plan, however, to throw a ridge of soil four inches high or more over each row of bulbs, working this down with the rake or wheel hoe, early in the spring before the bulbs come through the ground; or, in the case of summer bulbs, ten days or so after planting. By this method, the first crop

The one great secret in getting artistic effects with flowers is not to crowd them too close together. Above are shown three different types of tulips—grown, arranged, and photographed by the author.

Flowers for cutting may be grown, as are the gladiolus above, in single rows in the vegetable garden. The narcissus flowers at the right give a good idea of the Japanese method of flower arrangement.

of weeds will be destroyed with no hand work, and the bulbs will have a moist, mellow surface to come up through.

Watering, mulching, feeding, and other details of culture are the same as when the bulbs are grown in the flower garden.

The growing of bulbs in flats or pans for cutting, during the winter, has already been described (see preceding chapter).

THE TREATMENT OF FLOWERS FOR CUTTING

Practically all flowers from bulbs should be taken just as the buds first open. The most important exception to this general rule is Darwin and other late tulips, which should be allowed to open three or four times before they are cut. They do not attain their full size until they have opened several days in succession. The flowers close again at night, and each day increase in size. Even these, however, should be cut while the buds are closed in the morning. Flowers which grow on spikes, such as gladiolus, should be cut when the first two or three buds are beginning to open.

The length of time in which flowers will keep in good condition after cutting depends very largely upon how they are treated. Unless they are needed immediately, after being cut, they should be placed where it is dark and cool, or cold. In cold water in a cool cellar—with pieces of ice in the water, if convenient—is a good place for them. After being kept so for from eight to twelve hours, they will last much longer than if taken directly into the living room when first cut. To make them last as long as possible, the water should be changed daily, and a half inch to an inch of the stems cut off each day. If they can be put in a cold place overnight, so much the better. A strong breeze is one of the worst things, as this greatly increases evaporation; and while this produces the effect of coolness, so far as humans are concerned, it will make flowers "go down" more quickly than a very high temperature.

It is often recommended that a tablet or two of aspirin in the water in which cut flowers are placed will keep them fresh. Experiments have proved conclusively that flowers treated with aspirin will not last as long as those kept in plain water. If you happen to have a friend who says she has obtained beneficial results from using the aspirin treatment, just ask her to take a lot of flowers, divide them into two parts, and keep them under exactly the same conditions, treating one half with aspirin, and putting the others in plain water.

Flowers for shipping should be kept cold for a number of hours, and then wrapped in *waxed* tissue paper, which holds the moist air around the blooms and greatly retards evaporation. Moist sphagnum moss, or ordinary soft tissue paper, wrapped around the base of the stems, may be used; but it is injurious rather than otherwise with most flowers to sprinkle the flowers themselves copiously with water before wrapping them up. Many flowers will become badly spotted in transit if so treated.

THE ARRANGEMENT OF CUT FLOWERS

Space will not permit any lengthy discussion of this interesting question in these pages, but it may be worth while, in passing, to call attention to the fact that a great deal of the pleasure to be derived from them depends upon taste and skill in this direction. There are many excellent gardeners who do not realize at all that there is such a thing as an "Art" of flower arrangement, and who get the minimum rather than the maximum in the way of effect with their cut flowers merely by crowding them into vases or bowls in solid masses instead of giving any thought to this important detail.

In Japan, the arrangement of flowers is taught as an art, just as is painting or music. And there are certain elementary rules which should be followed if an artistic display is to be obtained, even though we may never take the subject up with the same thoroughness as the Japanese.

The most common error in arranging flowers is overcrowding. The second, perhaps, is the habit of attempting to use flowers with the uniform length of stem. A third is the absence, or the too little use, of foliage. By employing some light and airy plant, such as babysbreath (*gypsophila*), asparagus—the foliage of the ordinary vegetable variety is extremely beautiful when used with other flowers —or some of the ornamental grasses, the beauty of the flowers will be greatly enhanced. The illustrations facing pages 232 and 233 will give at least a hint of the method of artistic arrangement. To those who would follow this interesting subject further, I would recommend Professor White's book on "The Arrangement of Cut Flowers," which is most interesting as well as instructive.

The several simple but effective mechanical devices, now available, will be found to be a tremendous help in the artistic arrangement of flowers. One of the simplest of these is merely a heavy base containing a quantity of upright, flexible wires, and looking not unlike an immense pincushion well filled with large pins. This may be placed in any jar or bowl, and will prove to be such a tremendous help that any one who has once used one will not again be without it.

As a parting word on this topic, I would caution against the altogether too common practice of using entirely too many flowers for one container. If there are no other bowls, jars, or vases to take care of the surplus, one could often give away a half to two-thirds of the flowers which are ordinarily crammed into a single container, and when create a much more pleasing flower picture with the remainder than would have been possible with the entire lot!

FLOWERS PARTICULARLY GOOD FOR CUTTING

Among the wealth of flowers from bulbs, there are, of course, numerous kinds which are more desirable for cutting than others. Those which will last the longest, which have particularly pleasing colors, and which most readily lend themselves to artistic arrangement, are naturally to be preferred to those which will not "stand up" long after being removed from the plant; or which are so stiff and formal that it is almost impossible to do anything with them, in vases or bowls. In the following list, the kinds which are suggested are among the most pleasing of those which may be grown particularly for flowers for cutting. While there are, of course, scores of others which will serve the same purpose, the beginner will be on the safe road in making his selections from the list below.

SUGGESTIONS FOR FLOWERS FOR CUTTING

Hardy.

Most of these may be grown either outside or indoors. The dates mentioned are for the usual flowering period out of doors. For further information concerning varieties, refer to the bulbs themselves. (This applies also to the half-hardy and tender groups below.)

Tulips, *April–June.*
Daffodils, *April–May.*
Hyacinths, *April-May.*
Lily-of-the-Valley, *April–May.*
Scilias, *March–May.*
Brodiaea, *May–June.*
Calochortus, *June–July.*
Iris (Hardy), *May–July.*
Spirea, *June–August.*
Hemerocallis, *May–July.*
Tritoma, *June–October.*

(The "minor bulbs"—see page 92—while not ideal for cut flowers, are, nevertheless, very welcome in early spring, and excellent if properly arranged in shallow bowls or small vases. The same is true of the crocuses.)

Hardy Lilies.

No flowers are more beautiful for cutting than the hardy

lilies, and practically any of the varieties mentioned in Chapter XIII may well be used for this purpose, depending upon whether one has a sufficiently large stock to grow some just for cutting. Half a dozen sorts which may well be bought for the purpose are candidum; any of the speciosums, but especially magnificum; auratum; regale; browni, canadense, and tigrinum.

Half-Hardy.

Iris (bulbous), *March–May.*
Anemones, *April–May.*
Ranunculus, *May–June.*
Ixias, *May–June.*
Sparaxis, *May.*
Watsonias, *May.*
Milla, *August.*
Montbretias, *August–October.*
Schizostylis, *September–November.*

Tender.

Gladiolus, *June–October.*
Dahlias, *July–October.*
Begonias (tuberous), *June–September.*
Tuberose, *July–August.*
Galtonia (*Hyacinthus candicans*), *July–August.*
Ismene, *August–September.*
Freesias, *Winter (indoors).*
Callas, *Winter or summer.*
Nerines, *Winter (indoors).*
Eucharis, *Winter or summer.*

CHAPTER XX

THE PROPAGATION OF BULBS

BULBS may be propagated or increased in many different ways. The commercial propagation of bulbs, which were formerly almost altogether imported from foreign sources, has, during the last ten to fifteen years, increased rapidly in this country, and has now assumed the proportions of a very important industry. This has been given fresh impetus as a result of the various government quarantines prohibiting the importation of bulbs from foreign countries. Daffodils are the latest important class to come under the ban; and for the future, American gardeners must look to home production for this valuable class of plant. It is not our intention to touch upon commercial production in these pages, however, further than to say that, on the whole, it is proving successful; with gladiolus, dahlias, freesias, and many other things formerly imported, it has, of course, been completely so. And the development of new varieties, better suited to American conditions than those formerly available, has invariably accompanied the commercial growing of the bulbs in this country.

Bulb propagation, as it interests the amateur, is, however, what we are here concerned with. Let it be said at the outset that, while home propagation is possible, it is not likely to prove profitable. It offers a tremendously interesting field for those who wish to take this up, as a hobby, but the gardener who is interested solely in growing good bulbs will probably do better, for the most part, to rely upon the ordinary commercial sources. There are, however, a number of things of which almost any gardener will wish to maintain if not to increase his stock; and therefore some information concerning the fundamentals of successful propagation will be of practical use to him, or to her.

EQUIPMENT FOR HOME PROPAGATION—THE HOME NURSERY

Propagating bulbs is not nearly so simple as buying bulbs, putting them into the garden, and getting good flowers from them. It is well that this be understood at the outset. The gardener who intends to grow some bulbs of his own should provide suitable equipment for this work.

Such equipment will consist, first of all, of a small plot of ground, thoroughly well drained, well enriched, and well protected, so that the things planted in it will be safe from molestation. Such a plot need not be large. A goodly number of bulbs may be raised on a few square yards of soil. If it can be protected on the north and west side with a board fence, three or four feet high, so much the better. It will be advisable to incorporate plenty of peat or humus with this soil. And, if it is at all heavy, mix in it sufficient sand to make it very friable.

In this miniature "nursery," it will be possible to grow many of the hardy bulbs without any additional protection. A substantial, tight coldframe will, however, be found to be a tremendous help, particularly if the attempt is to be made to grow anything from seed. A frame of this kind can be used not only in winter and spring, but also in summer when it can be covered with lath sash, or plant-protecting cloth, instead of the ordinary glass sash. In the winter you can put into it small bulbs and some of the semi-hardy things which would not be safe in the open.

If a small greenhouse is available, that will of course greatly increase the possibility for successful work with the numerous things which may reasonably be attempted.

METHODS OF PROPAGATING

While most garden plants are readily propagated with entire convenience from seed, or from divisions of the crowns or roots of the plants, this is not true of most bulbs.

While they can be grown from seed, it usually takes several years to bring them up to flowering size. The methods which may be employed for propagating bulbs include the growing from new baby bulbs, or "offsets," which are exactly like the old bulbs but smaller; from bulblets, cormels, or bulbils, which might be called "seed bulbs," although they are quite different from seeds; the scales of bulbs, such as lilies; from seed; from actual divisions or pieces of the parent bulb; and from cuttings, pieces of the stems, or leaves, of the bulbs.

Offsets. Most of the real bulbs (see Chapter III) such as daffodils and tulips, propagate naturally by dividing up into smaller bulbs. In the case of the daffodil, these form part of the parent bulb, gradually separating from it as they grow, and, in the case of tulips, being produced as a crop or culture of entirely new bulbs, some of them very small, that take the place of the old bulb, which disappears entirely. The large bulbs from which the small ones are produced are called the "mother bulbs."

At harvesting, the offsets, sometimes called also "splits" or "spoons," at times cling quite closely to the parent bulbs. After they are dried and cured, however, such of these as are ready to be taken off will separate readily and should be carefully saved and planted by themselves in rows in the nursery. They may be put quite close together, as it will take them a year or two to develop to full-sized, flowering bulbs.

Cormels or Bulblets. Cormels or bulblets, also sometimes called "spawn," are produced by corms of the gladiolus type. There may be but a few, or considerable quantities of them, adhering to each of the old corms at the time of harvesting. In saving valuable new varieties, it is important to take them up before they have become absolutely dry in the soil, and the bulblets are still rather firmly attached to the old corm. The bulblets may be kept over during the winter in sand or soil, in a cool, dry place, and planted out the first thing in the spring, rather thickly like garden

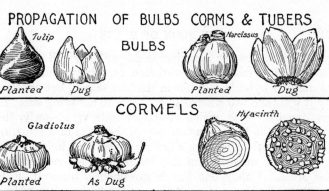

PROPAGATION OF BULBS CORMS & TUBERS

BULBS

Tulip — *Planted* — *Dug*
Narcissus — *Planted* — *Dug*

CORMELS

Gladiolus — *Planted* — *As Dug*
Hyacinth

SCALES AND BULBELS

Bulbel Tulip — Lily Bulb — Scales — New plants started

Daffodil insects and diseases (see Page 253).

Narcissus Fly

Larva

Pupa

A B C D

I II III IV

(*Upper left*) Hot-water bulb bath apparatus. (*Upper right*) A, Stem inoculated with eelworm after removal of flower; B, Injured leaves inoculated with eelworm; C, Uninjured leaves inoculated with eelworm; D, Control. (*Lower left*) Eelworm—magnification 148 times. (*Lower right*) I, Section of bulb from Pot A; II, Section of bulb from Pot D; III, Section of bulb from Pot B; IV, Section of bulb from Pot C.

peas, in drills two or three inches deep. They will come up, looking like grass. Some varieties, especially some of the primulinus hybrids, will bloom the first season, but ordinarily it will take two seasons to get them to flowering size. In growing hyacinths, which produce offsets very slowly, the bottom of the bulb is cut deeply in the form of a cross, or scooped out so as to form a hollow space, thus inducing the formation of quantities of tiny bulbs along the cut edges of the scale. Unless one has a greenhouse, however, it is hardly advisable to attempt this, as the bulbs, after cutting and being dusted with sulphur, must be kept in a very moist atmosphere, as in a propagating frame, or in an enclosed space under a greenhouse bench, for several weeks for the tiny bulbs to form. They are planted out thickly in rows, but it requires from three to five years to bring them to blooming size.

Bulbels. Bulbels are small above-ground bulbs which sometimes grow in the axils of the leaves of certain of the lilies, such as the tiger lily, and are found occasionally on tulips. These may be planted in soil such as is used for seed, and kept in the frame where they will make small plants the succeeding year.

Scales. The large fleshy leaves of some of the lilies may be utilized for propagation. Pull off carefully the outside scales from the base of the plant, and either place these in a tray or flat where they may be handled in the same way as hyacinths, or, where no greenhouse is available, covering them two inches deep in a mixture of sand, and peat or leafmold, in flats or directly in a frame, where the temperature should be kept warm and moist. A small plant will form at the end of each scale, and these may be transferred to the soil in late autumn, to go through the winter in a frame, or protected outside. If a greenhouse or heated frame is not available, the scales should be planted as early as possible. The bulbs from which they are to be removed should be taken up while they are still in flower, or immediately after flowering. The beautiful white

Madonna Lily, of which one can never have too many, is very easily propagated from scales; and, as it is one of the first to flower, the scales may be planted while the temperature is naturally still warm.

Propagation from Seed. Any one who expects to do hybridizing or crossing, should, of course, become familiarized with this method of propagating. As with anything else, it takes practice to make perfect, but a number of bulbs are easily propagated from seed, and even the beginner may reasonably expect satisfactory results. The beautiful Regal lily is one of the bulbs readily grown from seed. This can be obtained from most seedsman. If the same is sown in a frame early in the spring in well-prepared soil, it will produce good-sized little bulbs by the end of the first season. The bulbs shown in the accompanying illustration were grown from seed which were not planted until early May, but they were kept well irrigated during dry weather. The seeds should be sown in rows, six to nine inches apart and covered a half inch or so deep. Most of the hardy bulbs may be sown directly in a frame, planting the seed as soon as it is gathered from the plant, and keeping it somewhat shaded until germination, which is prompt in the case of some things, and will take weeks or even months for others. Grape-hyacinths grow from seed very readily, as do many of the others. Tulips and narcissus may be attempted, if one has the patience to wait several years for the first flowers, after one has attained a little skill with the easier things. The half-hardy bulbs, including such things as anemones, ranunculus, and the bulbous irises, are readily grown from seed, as are also the hardier of the tender bulbs, such as gladiolus, dahlias, and cannas. The seed of the latter, which is extremely hard, should be soaked in hot water for twenty-four or forty-eight hours, previous to planting, and the shell cut through with a file or sharp knife.

Growing the tenderer bulbs, such as tuberous begonias and gloxinias, from seed is a more difficult matter. For this purpose, a greenhouse is essential, unless one is content merely to start the plants the first year and to carry the small bulbs over winter to bloom the following season. The seed of tuberous begonias particularly is exceedingly fine, being like red pepper, and the little seedlings must be handled with great care. The soil in which to sow the fine seed should be made up of leafmold, peat, or humus and sand, a mixture of one-half each, and powdered charcoal may well be added. Plant in well-drained small pots, seed flats, or bulb pans, and gently but evenly press down, particularly in the corners. When the soil is prepared, soak the container in water until it absorbs all the moisture it will hold from the bottom, leaving the surface undisturbed. After this has drained off, scatter the seed, which should be mixed with several times its bulk of dry sand, to facilitate even sowing, over the surface, and very gently press it in. No covering should be given unless a thin layer or two of sphagnum moss which can be removed after the seedlings begin to show. A temperature of from 65 to 75 degrees is desirable for starting seed, and if a tight place, such as a propagating frame, can be used, it will be much easier to keep the atmosphere sufficiently moist. By far the best system of watering small seedlings of this kind which I have ever used is a greenhouse irrigation nozzle inserted in a three-quarter inch galvanized iron cap, which can be screwed on to the end of a short piece of three-quarter inch pipe, the other end of which should be fitted to a hose coupling. With this simple devise, you have an absolutely fine, mistlike spray under complete control, which is bound to be superior to the finest rose on a watering can, and with which it is possible to thoroughly saturate soil without getting it muddy or disturbing the finest seed or seedlings in the slightest degree. This can be used equally well for all kinds of small seeds, either in or out of doors. The greenhouse irrigation nozzle may be obtained from any of the irrigation companies, and any plumber or pipe fitter can make up the other parts in a few minutes. The irrigator which I now use is made completely of brass. It was made by one of the irrigation manufacturing companies, who modeled it after a homemade contrivance which I had been using. It has, I think, since been placed on the market. I have described this watering device in some detail, as failure with fine seedlings is very frequently due to injury from heavy watering, or failure to keep the soil moist enough, through fear of doing them injury.

As soon as the little seedlings are big enough to be handled at all, they should be transferred to other flats, spaced from two to three inches apart each way, or transferred to small pots. In the case of begonias, they should, of course, be kept slightly shaded from the midday sun. From then on, their culture is the same as with other growing plants, and as already described for the individual kinds of bulbs in the preceding chapters.

Division of Bulbs. Many corms and tubers, such as gladiolus, tuberous begonias, and dahlias, may be propagated by cutting old bulbs, which have more than one eye or bud, into two or more parts. The cut surfaces should be dusted with sulphur and the pieces handled as individual bulbs. (See illustration.)

INCREASING TUBERS AND CORMS BY CUTTINGS

These may be grown from cuttings of the young growing shoots, as with dahlias or with tuberous begonias; or leaf cuttings, such as are used for increasing individual specimens of gloxinias or tuberous-rooted begonias (and also with other fleshy-leaved begonias).

Dahlia cuttings are secured by starting the dormant tubers into growth in a bench in the greenhouse, or in a flat, and allowing them to grow until the fresh shoots are a half a foot or so high; they should not be forced under too high a temperature, as the wood for the cuttings should be as firm as possible. The cutting should be taken just below the joint. If cut between joints, they will

PROPAGATION OF BULBS CORMS & TUBERS

SEEDS

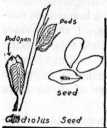

Pod Open
Pods
seed
Gladiolus Seed

Compost

Gladiolus seed planted

seed
Filed
Notched

Canna seed

seeding

CUTTINGS

Dahlia started

Cutting

Rooting Cuttings

Pot grown plant

Leaf Cutting

Begonia

DIVISION

Old Clump

Same Divided

grow satisfactorily, but the plant will not form bulbs for next year's growth. Several sets of cuttings may be taken off before time to set the plants out of doors, but the tuber will be weakened if too many are taken, if it is wanted for planting outside. The cuttings should be inserted in white sand or peat, kept in a moist atmosphere, and started as soon as roots form, and should be shifted to larger pots before being set in the open. Where the object is merely to obtain bulbs, the plants may be left in the pots and the latter plunged in a frame outside. These pot-grown roots, while not so large as field-grown ones, will give perfectly satisfactory plants for another year.

Tuberous begonia cuttings should be made from the soft branches of wood that is old enough to be fairly firm, and cuttings should be taken with a "heel," including a small portion of the main stem upon which the side shoot was growing, as otherwise the new plant will not form a tuber.

Leaf cuttings are made in two ways: full grown, or old but not withered leaves, should be used, but these may be cut away so that the top of the leaf and the lower portion of the vein or midrib is left, so that this can be inserted in the sand or peat in the same way as an ordinary cutting; or the entire leaf may be used, by making transverse cuts across the largest rib at a number of places, and then laying the leaf firmly down right side up on the sand or pot, holding it in position with a few small pebbles or, better, by staples made of florist's wire (hairpins will do, if you still can find a place to buy them) to hold the leaf securely in position and firmly against the sand or peat. In either case, the cutting should be kept in a warm temperature, and where the air is thoroughly moist. An outside frame will answer the purpose, but a propagating box in a greenhouse is, of course, better. New bulbs will form at the bottom of the main rib, or at the intersection, where the ribs of the leaf have been cut, and as these attain some size, they may be carefully taken off and potted up in the soil specially recommended for growing begonias (see Chapter XX).

In growing both seedlings and cuttings, "damping off" and other fungous diseases constitute the greatest element of risk. These can now be largely controlled by either Semesan or Uspulon, two new materials for disinfecting soils and for general sanitation in plant propagation of all kinds.

While the limited space available has made it necessary to treat the subject of plant propagation in a very brief way, I trust that this information will be enough to give the beginner a practical idea of what is necessary to start with this tremendously interesting work. Even if you cannot do things on a large scale, you can at least have a lot of fun in maintaining your stocks of various bulbs, and even at trying your hand at hybridizing some of the simplest things, such as gladiolus and dahlias, for your own pleasure and amusement. This work will give you an added and new interest in bulb growing.

CHAPTER XXI

INSECTS AND DISEASES

As I have already remarked, bulbs, as a class, will give the home gardener very little trouble in the way of insects and diseases. Such as there are, are very much more likely to be of concern to the commercial grower than to the amateur, for the reason that most of the insects which attack the bulbs are not widely spread, as are those which appear upon vegetables and many flowers; and diseased stock is usually discovered and destroyed before the bulbs are passed on to the retailer.

If, then, good garden sanitation is practiced, and the plants are kept in vigorous growth, there will usually be little in the way of plant enemies to cause the bulb gardener any anxiety. Keeping the plants in vigorous growth may, in times of protracted drouth, mean watering or mulching or both. The subject of irrigation has been treated elsewhere (see page 34), and is mentioned here only to emphasize the importance of keeping the plants robust and healthy, and to that extent more capable of resisting the attacks of insects or diseases. With bulbs, as with other plants, these are more likely to prove serious if growth has been checked, due to dry weather, under-nourishment, lack of cultivation, or the growth of weeds which not only rob them of plant food and moisture but also cut off the air circulation, which also makes a condition entirely favorable to the attack of any plant enemies which may be within reach.

Despite all care, not all plants are always immune, however, and the most important of the insects and diseases which are likely to be encountered are described briefly in the paragraphs following. More detailed information can of course be obtained from the literature concerning commercial production.

Ants. These busy little creatures are usually blamed for troubles which they do not cause. Sometimes they may be the signal of trouble rather than the cause of it, as when they are running up and down plants, the lower sides of the leaves of which may be becoming infested with aphids or green plant lice. They are likely to cause more damage, when they become very numerous in the soil, by honeycombing the earth around the roots of the plants or under bulbs.

While there are several special ant exterminators on the market, I have never found anything more effective than carbon disulphide, which will effectively destroy them in the soil. This is a liquid which forms a heavier-than-air gas upon coming in contact with the air. Make holes with a pointed stick or the end of a hoe handle a foot apart and three inches deep, and pour a tablespoonful of the liquid in each, covering the holes immediately.

Aphids. The aphids or green plant lice make no exception of bulbs in the general list of plants, which they attack. The foliage of most bulbous plants, however, is such that the aphids can be got at readily with the spray or dust. It is necessary to watch carefully and be ready to get after them the very minute they put in an appearance.

Aphids, which are sucking insects and therefore immune to "poisons," are easily controlled with a nicotine spray such as Black Leaf 40, *if used in time.* In a greenhouse, they may be completely got rid of either with fumigation or by tobacco or cyanide.

Borers. There are several of these pernicious pests which attack bulbous plants; the most likely to be encountered being the dahlia borer and the iris borer. The former works inside of the stalk, causing the foliage to wilt, particularly on hot days. The affected part may be cut off and burned, or it is sometimes possible to kill the borer with a piece of wire, without destroying the stalk. The iris borer is much smaller, but can usually be located by the bleeding or weeping of the plant at the hole where entrance has been made, and shows a wet stain on the foliage, usually well down toward the base. The leaves may be cut off and burned, or the grubs may be killed where they are by grasping the leaf firmly between thumb and finger and drawing them upward. This crude but effective treatment may be used in a garden where there are not too many plants.

Cutworm. These familiar pests attack the tender shoots of some bulbs, particularly the dahlias, in the same way that they do other garden flowers and vegetables. They are soft-bodied, grayish, or brownish worms which keep out of sight during the day and work at night, cutting off the young plants a little above the surface of the soil.

They may be caught by placing pieces of shingle or flat stones near the plants, and usually may be found where a plant has been cut, in the soil adjacent, early the following morning. There are several effective "cutworm foods" now on the market, or a homemade poison bait may be made by mixing together one half pound of arsenate of lead or Paris Green, 25 pounds of bran, middlings, or coarse flour; and then add sufficient water to make a moist but not wet mash. A half pint or so of brown sugar or molasses may be added to this mixture. Scatter it in small quantities, a tablespoonful or so in a place, late in the afternoon, when the worms are likely to appear.

Grubs. The two most likely to be encountered are the large, dirty white soil grub, an inch and a half in length, which is the larva of the June beetle, and the "leather jacket" grub, which is somewhat similar with a dark-colored exceptionally tough skin, which is the larva of the crane fly or giant mosquito.

The grubs are most likely to be troublesome in damp ground.

As large grubs and worms cannot easily be killed in the

ground, the best way of getting rid of them is to take up the infected plant, kill the grub, and carefully replant, keeping shaded for some time until new growth is established. The wire worms are especially fond of freshly cut pieces of root crops, such as carrots or beets, and these may be buried a few inches below the surface with a small stick or garden label near each, where they can be readily located, taken up every three or four days, and the worms destroyed.

Thrip. These inconspicuous, very minute, but very active little bugs are not particular, but like the green aphis cause quick and serious injury by sucking the plant juices, with the result that the foliage turns a yellowish, unhealthy color.

Indoors they can be controlled by fumigation, but outdoors it is difficult to do anything with them, except to watch carefully for their appearance, and immediately remove the affected foliage. Lemon oil, kerosene emulsion, and a number of the standard tobacco extract remedies will help in their control, but are not as effective as they are against the aphis.

Mites. There are several different bulb mites which attack tuberous begonias and other bulbs. They cannot be seen with the naked eye, but under a glass appear as tiny yellowish white or pinkish, smooth-bodied active insects. On most plants they will cause the foliage to turn yellow or reddish brown, or make reddish-looking patches on the bulbs or roots.

The infected bulbs should be carefully taken up with the soil surrounding them, and burned. In valuable varieties, the bulbs may be washed off before planting with one ounce of sulphide of potassium diluted in three gallons of water. Dormant bulbs may be treated with bisulphide of carbon: put in a perfectly air-tight container, and pour in the liquid at the rate of a teaspoonful to a box or pan of a bushel capacity.

Mealy Bug. This bug which is more likely to attack in

the greenhouse than out of doors is easily controlled by spraying with Black Leaf 40, or by painting the individual insects with a little alcohol and a small brush.

Narcissus Fly. These are two, known as the greater and the lesser narcissus fly, and are the most serious insect pests troubling daffodils, but are not likely to appear in private gardens. The grubs of the larger fly (*Merodon equestris*) are large white reddish maggots which attain a length of a full half inch. They are quite easily detected, at planting time, by carefully examining the bulbs, as any bulb containing a grub—there is usually only one present—is quite likely to be very soft and light in weight. Again, when the bulbs are first coming up in the spring, any containing a grub will show a very weak growth, usually throwing only one or two leaves. Any doubtful-looking bulb should be taken up and examined at once. Mature insects look and act much like a small bee. They appear when the plants are full grown, about the time the flowers are fully developed, and lay their eggs where the plants enter the soil.

The lesser or small narcissus fly appears in the bulbs in the form of a small maggot, not unlike the onion maggot, usually a dozen or more in each bulb. The parent fly, which appears in May or early June, is less than a half inch in length, and has two light transparent wings. They seem much less likely to attack strong, vigorously growing plants.

In commercial places, both of these maggots are controlled by what is known as "hot-water" treatment, which consists in soaking the planting stock of bulbs for two and a half to three hours in water maintained at a steady temperature of 110 degrees Fahrenheit. This treatment is being rigidly enforced by the Department of Agriculture and organized bulb growers themselves, and it is quite reasonable to hope that American-grown daffodils will be quite free from these two pests. The home gardener, unless he has the equipment to maintain water at this temperature, and a thoroughly reliable thermometer, will hardly be able to so treat his bulbs, in case of infestation, so the only remedy is to take up any bulb which appears to be infested and burn it. An English firm has recently developed a small sterilizing equipment suitable for the amateur's use.

Red Spider. This pernicious insect is not likely to prove troublesome out of doors, but often it appears in the greenhouse. Syringing with cold water is an old remedy and seems to be as effective as any. There are several insecticides which are effective, if the ground around the plants can be kept moist, such as lemon oil and "O. K." plant spray.

Wireworm. These long, slim brownish, or reddish and exceedingly tough-skinned worms are the larvæ of the common "snap beetle" and in sufficient quantities are often quite destructive. They are familiar to most gardeners, attacking potatoes, corn, and other seeds and roots planted in the soil. They are best controlled by trapping (see grubs above).

White Fly. This minute white-winged little pest, like the red spider, is much more apt to be troublesome under glass than in the open. Fumigating indoors, or nicotine spraying outside, being sure to spray the under sides of the leaves, will generally keep it under control.

BULB DISEASES

While there are a number of diseases, they are for the most part "secondary" troubles and appear only after the bulbs have been injured from some other cause or weakened in growth due to unfavorable conditions.

The eelworms or nematode (*Tylenchus devastatrix*) is usually described as a disease, although the cause of it is a microscopic organism which breeds and works in both the bulbs and the tissues of the leaves. In the former it causes discolored brown rings and streaks, and in the latter irregular, light-colored raised stripes or markings and a stunted growth, and also stunted flowers. These characteristics are most likely to be noticed as warm weather begins in the spring, later than the results of frost injury, which causes an irregular and distorted growth. The hot-water treatment already described above is effective for eelworms as well as for the narcissus fly. The home gardener is not likely to be troubled as this particular form of nematode is not native to the United States; any suspicious-looking bulb, however, should be carefully examined, and if any doubt exists, taken up and burned, or, if one wishes to be sure for the future, sent to the Department of Agriculture at Washington for identification.

Fire is a disease attacking tulips which is called Botrytis. Its characteristic is a yellowing of the foliage, as though it had been burned or scorched by fire. It seems to be more likely to appear where the bulbs are left in the ground from year to year, than where they are lifted annually, and is seldom found in thoroughly clean and cultivated soil, and where there is plenty of ventilation. Leaves which look suspicious should be cut off and burned, and the flowers picked before the petals fall.

Mildew, Mold, and Rot. There are a number of forms of mildew, mold, and rot attacking the different bulbs, but, as already stated, they usually appear only when the bulbs are weakened from some other cause, or when they are exposed to too much heat or moisture—the same conditions which induce mold in stored grain or vegetables, or, for that matter, in the kitchen pantry.

All infected bulbs should be destroyed, but exposure to bright sunshine, good ventilation, and dusting with sulphur will usually cure them.

Where mold or rot appears on the growing plants, they should be thoroughly sprayed with bordeaux mixture or some form of sulphur.

Where the bulbs themselves are affected, control may be obtained by soaking them for two hours in bichloride of mercury dissolved in hot water, at the rate of one ounce to six gallons. The mixture should be made, of course, in a wooden or glazed earthenware container and not a metal one.

The recent development of organic mercury compounds like Semesan and Uspulon have made the treatment of many of the molds, rots, and mildews, such as the Black Rot on hyacinths, grape-hyacinths, and scillas, and others affecting lily bulbs, more simple and certain than in the past. Gladiolus bulbs affected with Scab or Neck Rot, may be treated with one of these preparations, soaked for two hours in a solution of corrosive sublimate, 2 ounces to 15 gallons of water, or formaldehyde, ½ pint to 15 gallons of water, before planting.

It should also be remembered that the use of manure in connection with bulbs, with either the Dutch bulbs or the hardy lilies, seems to favor the development of the various rots, molds, mildews, and rusts which attack them, especially when it is used on the surface of the soil. This is an additional reason for using coconut fiber, humus, or peat where mulching is required.

INDEX

A

Abobra, 180

Achimenes, culture of, 225

Acid soil, for lilies, 137; for bulbs, 33

Aconite, 92

African corn lily, 119

African lily, 176

Agapanthus, 176

Allium, 102

Alstroemeria, 172; growing indoors, 220

Amaryllis, culture of, 223

Amazon lily, 225

American Peony Society, 191

Amorphophallus, 178

Anemones, 115; growing indoors, 218; types and varieties, 117

Annuals, for use with bulbs, 42, 48; planted with bulbs, 17

Ants, control of, 249

Aphids, control of, 249

Apios, 179

Arrangement of cut flowers, 234

Ascelepias tuberosa, 171

Ashes, coal, for growing lilies, 136; use of, 31

Asparagus, 235

Aspirin, for cut flowers, 234

Asphodel, giant, 122

Astilbes, 106

Autumn-flowering bulbs, 125; culture of, 127

Autumn-flowering crocus, 89

B

Babiana, 120; growing indoors, 220

Baby's breath, for use with cut flowers, 235

Bamboo cane, 126

Barri daffodils, 67

"Base" of bulbs, 25

Bedding, bulbs suitable for, 17; tuberous begonias for, 167

Begonias, culture indoors, 222; from seed, 243; hanging, 166; tuberous-rooted, culture of, 164

Bermuda buttercup, 178

Bizarre tulips, 52

Black leaf forty, 253

Black rot, 255; of hyacinths, 255

Bleedinghearts, 105

Bloodroot, 108

Blue African lily, 176

Blue lily of the Nile, 176

Blue milla, 120

Bluebells, 92, 99; Virginia, 108

Bone flour, 33

Bone meal, 33

Borers, control of, 249

Botrytis, disease of tulips, 254

Boussingaultia, 179

Breeder tulips, 51

Brevoortia, 120 (see Brodiaea); growing indoors, 220

Brodiaea, 120; growing indoors, 220; varieties of, 120

Bulbils, 240, 242

Bulblets, 240; definition of, 25

Bulb fibre, 200

Bulb gardens, 17; making of, 26

Bulbocodium, 93; growing indoors, 214

Bulbous irises, 113; types and varieties of, 114

Bulbous plants, for spring flowering, 100-101

257